The Laity Fix

An Inclusive Approach to Church Growth

LYNDA R. BYRD

ISBN 978-1-64299-031-7 (paperback)
ISBN 978-1-64299-032-4 (digital)

Christian Faith Publishing, Inc.
832 Park Avenue
Meadville, PA 16335
www.christianfaithpublishing.com

All scripture is taken from the New Revised Standard Version (NRSV) translation.

Printed in the United States of America

DEDICATION

To my daughter, Jolanda, for her inspiration through
unwavering support; challenging me to always walk
the walk, especially through rough terrain.

CONTENTS

I will never leave you or forsake you... the Lord is my helper
Hebrews 13:5b

Now there are varieties of gifts, but the same Spirit
1 Corinthians 12:4

Now when they saw the boldness of John and Peter... they were amazed
Acts 4:13

The whole group of those who believed were of one heart and soul
Acts 4:32

And what does the Lord require of you, but to do justice, and to love kindness, and to walk humbly with your God
Micah 6:8

ACKNOWLEDGMENTS

The genesis of this book goes back as far as my childhood, watching church members engage and disengage with ongoing ministries and changes. It would be impossible to list all who have contributed to this effort, but a sincere attempt is warranted.

Clergy persons, serving as pastors and in a variety of administrative positions have shared wisdom, experiences, and challenges that not only deepened my faith, but encouraged me to explore possibilities for growth and contribution beyond any extent that a nascent Christian could imagine. Rev. John W. Heyward, Jr. insisted that I attend a general agency event on Stewardship. That event redirected and changed my life. Other clergy have accompanied me on my faith journey in countless ways, offering clarity, raising questions, agreeing and disagreeing, and always supportive: Rev. Terrence K. Hayes, Rev. Ann Helmke, Rev. J. Jeffrey Irwin, Rev. J. David Trawick, Rev. Robert Harmon, and Rev. Joseph Ghunney.

Rev. Herbert Mather introduced me to the possibility that lay persons can make vast contributions to the growth and sustenance of the church, and generously gave me ingress to do so. Herb taught me that stewardship is what I do, after I say I believe. A truth that has stood the test of time.

Lay colleagues and friends have accompanied me into and out of stages of discovery; encouraging me to always take the next step. Diane Johnson, my friend of more than thirty years, always listens and insists that I should do more. Deborah Bass gave me unexpected opportunities to work at the highest levels of our denomination, and became a friend and spiritual companion. Jerald McKie and I worked side by side, traveling together and seeing the church in the most amazing ways, forging a sisterhood along the way. Likewise, Linda Bales Todd and I share a unique journey of faith and have experienced memorable epiphanies.

As the message of *The Laity Fix* became a more compelling need to communicate, friends have read and reread the manuscript, offering insights that expanded and enriched the narrative. Dr. Charles Donaldson, Kathleen Zeltmann, Jane Brice Briddell, and Connie Garza each offered thoughts that propelled deeper perspectives. Caryn Wideman gave me invaluable editing tips. Dr. Cynthia Bond Hopson encouraged me to push the writing of this book beyond a dream.

I would be remiss were I not to recognize those who are now a part of the great cloud of witnesses, whose belief in me and unfailing encouragement were constant incentives: my sister, Beverly Brown, Dr. William 'Bill' Carter, and Bishop Rhymes H. Moncure, Jr. And of course, Mother and Daddy, who were my first teachers and role models. I watched them stay the course in times of joy and disappointment within the church, never faltering in their commitment or allowing their faith to be compromised.

These persons and so many others have left indelible imprints of faith, encouragement, hope, and love. Please know how grateful I am.

FOREWORD

Without a doubt, the American church faces complexities and complications unknown to earlier generations of churchgoers and church leaders. Between growing secularism and increased competition for the attention of an increasingly disinterested American society, the local church can no longer simply wait for people to come looking for a "church home". Spend any time among church leaders and one hears the constant concerns regarding attracting younger church goers and the reality of impending losses of those from the WWII generation.

The world has changed! What do we do now? *The Laity Fix* challenges us to put first things first and to remember who we are, reclaim our mission and stay true to the core principles of the Gospel. Lynda Byrd reminds us that the church belongs to the laity and at our core, the laity are the most important resource the church has ever possessed.

Keeping a strict accounting of our financial resources, Church Treasurers and Accountants provide a full accounting of every cent received, spent, and invested. We know who gave and where those dollars were used. What might happen if the church kept a strict accounting of our most prized resource, the laity, as carefully as we watch over financial resources? Lynda Byrd's *The Laity Fix* offers tools and strategy designed to help both identify and deploy the very resources and gifts of those who inhabit our local churches.

The treasure of the church lies within its members, those who claim the name of Jesus Christ. The word, "laity" actually comes from the Greek term, laos, meaning "people of God", which underscores God's original plan for the church. Jesus deployed leaders to make disciples who would in turn make disciples. The church has always grown through the impact of the laity. Time and again the church has been renewed through lay movements, the early church grew through the witness of not only the apostles but through the witness of laity. Scripture notes that "all except the apostles were scattered throughout the countryside of Judea and Samaria…and those who were scattered went from place to place, proclaiming the word." (Acts 8: 1-4). The church grew through the witness of the laity, "the people of God."

Stories of church history remind us of the impact of laity in raising up the church, whether remembering the impact of the Reformation or the Wesleyan Revival, the American Great Awakenings or more recent movements of the nineteenth or twentieth centuries, laity always lead. The renewal of the church has always brought together an amazing linkage of lay and clergy under the movement of the Holy Spirit.

In the words of Apostle Paul to one of his congregations, he acknowledged that Christ has given leadership gifts to the church so that leaders might "equip the saints (the laity) for the work of ministry, for building up the body of Christ" (Ephesians 4: 12, NRSV). The "work of ministry" is the responsibility of the whole congregation. And in fact, Paul notes in his letter to the Corinthian Church that the church has all the "gifts" needed to accomplish the calling and mission of Christ. "4 For as in one body we have many members, and not all the members have the same function, 5 so we, who are many, are one body in Christ, and individually we are members one of another." (Romans 12: 4-6a, NRSV).

Lynda brings a lifetime of experience in both Corporate America as well as years working within the institutional church, and offers unique insight toward a prescription for church health. She writes as one who understands the necessity of charting clear direction for developing a healthy organization and of the importance of investing in leadership. Speaking forcefully and plainly she offers tools and recommendations that congregations of any size can put to work. Lynda loves God and loves God's church and from the vantage of her experience calls out to the laity, "it's our time to bring our gifts to renew, rebuild, and restore our congregations."

Where is the treasure of the church? The story is told of Lawrence, a deacon responsible for keeping and distributing money to the poor in Rome near 250 A.D. The Roman Emperor at the time sought to gain the church's treasure and under penalty of death demanded that Lawrence hand over the church's treasure in three days. At the end of those days, Lawrence stood before the Emperor and pointed to a vast crowd of the poor, destitute, and members of the church and declared, "This is the church's treasure".

While serving as a District Superintendent in The United Methodist Church, I had the difficult assignment of either closing a small congregation or seeking a different alternative. With no more than twelve in worship attendance, an aging congregation, and nearly depleted finances, finding a pastor to lead the congregation was simply impossible given the lack of resources. Most disheartening was the reality that this small town lay within a growing corridor of expansion. People were moving into the area and the future of the small town never looked brighter. What to do was this leader's question. Approaching a larger church in a nearby town we set in motion a plan for merger, live streaming Sunday sermons via a computer link, and leaving the fate of the local church in the hands of the laity. Months passed as we hoped that this plan would help hold the church together until better days emerged. Checking in on the congregation one Sunday, I couldn't hold my excitement as nearly forty worshippers showed up. Asking what in the world had changed in that short time, one of the leaders pointed to Mary Lou, an elderly widow who generally sat quietly near the back of the congregation. "Mary Lou happened," he replied. "When the fate of the church fell into the hands of the laity she began going door to door, inviting friends and neighbors to join us. And this is the result!"

Admittedly, our world has grown evermore complex and evermore distant from the years when the church was welcomed in the public square. Our world has changed but the need for what the church brings is as great as ever. We need healthy congregations, filled with committed and well trained laity, committed to the mission of Jesus Christ. How can the church gain the attention of a disinterested culture? I believe Lynda Byrd's calling to get back to basics, restore the ministry of the laity to its central place in the congregation, and to focus on building healthy congregations is the antidote the 21st century church requires.

I hope that you will read and absorb *The Laity Fix* over and over again and that your local church will put into operation the recommendations found here. I believe that any congregation can grow healthier and if we follow Jesus' mission, even the most unlikely setting can continue to reach new generations for Christ. Lynda is right! The church belongs to the laity and as the people of God take up the challenge of leading, praying, serving, planning, and loving in Christ's name the church can grow. Your church can come alive. Thank you Lynda for leading us.

Rev. Guy C Ames, III

LAITY — consists of all members who are not members of the clergy.

Laity — plural - Noun

Pronounced - Lei-i-ti

Laity
The body of religious worshipers, as distinguished from the clergy.

Laity — the ordinary people who are involved with a church, but do not hold official religious positions.

INTRODUCTION

One man was there who had been ill for thirty-eight years. When Jesus saw him lying there and knew that he had been there a long time, he said to him, "Do you want to be made well?"
—John 5:5–6

This scripture is intriguing. It addresses the natural state of inertia. Even when we believe we are busily getting a job done, avoiding procrastination or finding long-sought solutions, a tendency may remain to not move beyond certain places of comfort or familiarity. "Do you want to be made well?" is a question for many of today's congregations. Of course, to raise the question, one must first come to the realization that an unhealthy condition exists. The premise for *The Laity Fix* rests on the certainty that in an alarming percentage of congregations, a condition exists that is in need of being made well.

What is this condition? Protestant churches are especially vulnerable to the ebb and flow of shrinking congregations. Christian bookstores are stocked with new concepts and tried processes to stimulate growth, deepen spiritual commitment, and solve social challenges all for the sake of growing membership. Congregations make constant changes to worship structures, preaching methods, music choices, logos, resource materials, and every imaginable aspect of the worship experience. These changes are initiated to get people excited. The changes seek to reach new communities and respond to demographic shifts.

The unhealthy condition that seemingly permeates congregations arises from overwhelming brokenness in society: broken families, broken relationships, broken communications, broken commitments, broken hope, and—alas—broken faith. In the last two decades, the Protestant Church in North America has undergone more reconstructive changes than in most of its previous history. Untold energy is being expended describing what congregations need to do to be relevant. *The Laity Fix* evolves from the presumption that congregations want to be made well. Just as the man lay by the pool of Bethzatha for thirty-eight years waiting for someone to help him into the water (John 5:5–7, NRSV), so too is the church languishing on the precipice of relevance, waiting for some neatly packaged quick fix to assuage, if not heal, the brokenness.

"Do you want to be made well?" is a direct question. It has either a yes or no answer. Answering this question does not require research. It does not require a meeting. It does not require the election of officers. It does not require funding. It does not require a leadership appointment or removal. "Yes, I want to be made well" is the resounding response at the heart of the church. But who's posing the question? Does the question delve deep enough into the condition? And what does "being made well" look and feel like?

Congregational structures are as varied as the plethora of changes the human mind can fathom. Some congregational structures are relatively constant; they have leadership: clergy and laity. Congregations have members that constitute every category of human existence: young, old, wealthy, poor, white, black, brown, red, yellow, gay, straight, educated, uneducated, rural, urban, introverted, extroverted, mentally challenged, and countless other living conditions. Congregations are populated with successful business men and women, physically and mentally challenged children and adults, high school athletes, Eagle Scouts, scholars, cheerleaders, soccer moms, single dads and moms, autistic children, youth, and adults. In effect, congregational structures can be vastly varied in composition. Nonetheless, whatever the composition, the core component of every congregation is laity.

The church holds a relationship with its members like no other organized entity. The church is where birth, marriage, and life are celebrated. The church baptizes our children, prays for us in times of strife, illness, joy, and the multitude of stages that chronicle our lives. The church is where we see and participate in miracles through its care and commitment to its members. The church is where we come to offer our services and receive the blessings of service from others. The church counsels us through our grief and stands with us at the gravesite. The church visits us when we are hospitalized, incarcerated, or homebound. No other chosen relationship has the potential for such prominence in our lives or can accompany us through every portal of our existence.

If the church is all these things, why is its relevance diminishing in current society? While no other relationship compares with the church when it is fully operative and connected with its members, it remains in a continuous struggle to position itself as valued and relevant. Perhaps this struggle is an outgrowth of the church's failure to do all the things that it alone has the power, position, and presence to accomplish. And if it is failing, how can the failure be fixed?

While effectively addressing this challenge is certainly a team effort, laity can best shoulder the greater share of its accomplishment. If there is the slightest belief that a congregation can flourish without laity, this book will have no value. The purpose of this book is anchored in the supposition of laity's value in establishing and maintaining flourishing congregations. If it is accepted that laity is necessary for any congregation, healthy or needing to be made well, you will find use in the pages that follow. You will accomplish even greater benefit if you have personally questioned if you want to be made well; and in posing the question, you are honestly considering the answer.

You will note that the question is not "do you want your congregation to be made well?" The question is, *Do you want to be made well?* A congregation is in need of healing only as much as its members are in need of healing—individually and collectively. *The Laity Fix* is about you and me and every person who considers herself or himself to be a member of a family of faith.

Having participated in a variety of facilitative roles over more than thirty years in various configurations of districts, conferences, programs, and training events with laity and clergy across different denominations, I find some truisms to be evident. Recognizing the value of every person is critical. As perpetual as the need is for a tangible fix, the resolution is a combination of complexity and simplicity.

Communication between clergy and laity with genuine collaborative efforts is invaluable and tantamount to success and lasting change.

Some years ago, I heard a story about a little girl being placated by her father in an effort to entertain her while minimizing attentiveness on his part. Seeking to find something to keep her busy as he read the paper, he pulled out a page of the newspaper that had a large image of the world on one side. He tore the page into small pieces and asked his daughter to put the world back together, knowing this would keep her occupied for some time. In just a few minutes, she brought the paper back with the world perfectly reconstructed. Shocked, her father asked her how she could have possibly put the world back together so quickly? The little girl replied, "There was a man on the other side. When the man was put together, the world was put together." I invite you to take this image into the pages that follow.

CHAPTER ONE

The Long Haul

*I will never leave you or forsake you. So
we can say with confidence, "The Lord
is my helper; I will not be afraid."*
—Hebrews 13:5b-6

Growth takes time. At birth, weight and length are measurements that are taken, shared, and repeated. As the child grows, measurements continue to be monitored. Family homes have door frames marked with little etchings denoting the height of children across years. We compare academic achievement from one period to the next. Progress is compared from one child to the next: which child walked first, talked first, or read first. Measurements and milestones are important, signaling growth and progress. Throughout the life cycle, progression is a desired and expected part of the experience. The extent of progression shapes our acceptance and our assessment of our self-worth.

Integral to the human experience are relationships. Not just to humans, relationships are integral to all animal life. The need to belong is as old as recorded history. Relational stability might well have been the impetus in the Genesis story of Adam's acceptance of the off-limits piece of fruit from Eve, as well as Eve's offer of the fruit to Adam (Genesis 3:12). We are relational and we want to, need to, belong. The church offers an opportunity for belonging like no other human structure, with the family as the only possible exception. Christian tradition tells us that acceptance in church comes with a profession

The church offers an opportunity for belonging like no other human structure, with the family as the only possible exception.

of belief in Jesus Christ. Denominations may differ in how the membership invitation is extended, but the basic requirement is an acknowledgement of belief in Jesus Christ as the Son of God and the desire to follow Christ's teachings.

Membership in the church does not require that we know the teachings of Jesus Christ; only that we desire to learn and follow them. To an alarming extent, follow-up is limited to assess understanding of and commitment to Christ's teachings. Memberships with other organizations, however, have far more stringent requirements. Entry into preschool requires specific medical immunizations, proof of legal status or citizenship, a mailing address, guardian and emergency contacts, and other requirements. As our secular memberships increase, further validations are required. Employment, marriage, parenting, and social and political affiliations are among the more common relational memberships. Each of these relationships requires much more than an expression of belief or a one-time declaration of a desire to belong.

> To an alarming extent, follow-up is limited to assess understanding of and commitment to Christ's teachings.

The extent to which we go to acquire these secular memberships is astounding. Fraternities are too frequently cited for excessive hazing—an unofficial prerequisite for membership. Bodies are marked with tattoos and brandings signaling membership in specific groups or preference for certain relationships. The presence or absence of wedding bands can indicate marital status. We exhibit tangible, visible displays to represent our membership or our relationship with another or groups. There seems to be no line too broad to cross when identifying what is important to our belonging and to our relationships.

> The church simply requires an acknowledgment of belief in Jesus Christ. Perhaps the requirement for membership should be more.

The church simply requires an acknowledgment of belief in Jesus Christ. Perhaps the requirement for membership should be more. It is a well-known adage that we value less what requires less of us. We pay membership fees to belong. In our valued relationships we invest time and money; the greater the value, the greater the investment. The Old Testament prophet, Micah, suggests that in our faith journey more than an acknowledgment of belief is required: "And what does the Lord require of you but to do justice, and to love kindness, and to walk humbly with your God?" (Micah 6:8). Church membership today can be just too easy to attain with no tangible expectations and accountability. Ease of entry leads to ease of exit.

The disciples, Peter, John, James, Philip, and—later—Paul and Timothy did not have an easy go of establishing the church. Persecution and death were the ultimate payments made by most of the early church starters. It is hardly expected that such extreme sacrifices might be made today. And yet even today, in some areas of the world, Christians have been beheaded as infidels by religious zealots that abhor followers of Jesus Christ. While devoted Christians are punished with the ultimate sacrifice on foreign soil, at home, the value of being a Christian, active in a faith community, can be relegated to a preference for contemporary music or contrasting colors to accent the chancel area paraments.

> While devoted Christians are punished with the ultimate sacrifice on foreign soil, at home, the value of being a Christian, active in a faith community, can be relegated to a preference for contemporary music or contrasting colors to accent chancel area paraments.

Growing up in the Baptist Church, I remember the fear and trepidation in my congregation associated with becoming a member. When the decision to join the church was made, much thought was given to what would be said. It was not an accepted practice to just walk down and appear at the time of the invitation to Christian discipleship. It was necessary to publicly give a reason for why you were coming forth and how your life would be different as a result of that decision. At the age of eleven, I made that long, frightening walk. I stood before the congregation declaring my desire to have Jesus as the center of my life helping me to make all decisions from that day forward. Admittedly, the more accurate reason was my wish to sing in the children's choir. My decision to become a member had been brought about by a rule in that congregation that participation in some of the regular worship activities required church membership. Church membership should certainly demand more than access to activities.

In many congregations, no public declaration is required. New members are discovered when photos are displayed on the wall. Where nametags are common place, the change from a written nametag to a preprinted one can denote the transition from visitor to member status. The idea of coming forth to express one's desire to become a member of a family of faith is an obsolete expectation dispensed with to make membership easier and more inviting. Rarely is a sermon text taken from Jesus's admonition that we acknowledge him before others so that he acknowledges us before God (Matt 10:32-33).

Over the years, church affiliation rules have been interesting to observe. Some denominations disallow participation in the sacrament of communion unless one is a member of that denomination. Some denominations disallow active participation in church events unless membership is held with that denomination, more specifically with a particular congregation within the denomination. Other congregations place no restrictions and from every perspective quite literally embrace the invitation, "Come, let everyone who hears… Come" (Rev. 22:17). As diverse and numerous as they are, none of the church affiliation requirements fosters the sense of belonging, relationship, and commitment that characterize sorority, fraternity, civic, political, or employment affiliation.

Membership in no other group or relationship delivers the irrefutable commitment that Christ offers to "never leave you or forsake you." Becoming a part of a Christian faith community ushers its members into this sacred relationship. Laity has the unique privilege of choosing a congregation and entering into a relational status through membership. The

> Laity has the unique privilege of choosing a congregation and entering into a relational status through membership.

current shrinking membership numbers in North America's churches question the seriousness of commitment that is associated with membership. Perhaps it is this diminished value in membership that moves so many through what has become perpetually revolving doors, in and out of congregations. Regrettably, the ease with which church membership is entered and exited devalues the importance of nurturing a fundamental step toward a Christ-centered life.

What does the church require?

No probationary period is required. No time is set aside while interest is assessed and potential members learn about the culture, the expectations of membership, and become immersed in the understanding and practice of what the Lord requires. Is this a good match? Does the prospective member know what the Lord requires and the commitment needed for fulfilling the requirements?

Spiritual assessment inventories are a popular activity in many congregations. These tools of inventory serve to identify what the individual has to offer. Might it be even more relevant for prospective members to discover what the congregation has to offer and what mutual benefits might be realized through the sharing of gifts? The absence of definitive membership requirements is in no way beneficial to the congregation or to the prospective member.

Might it be more relevant for prospective members to discover what the congregation has to offer and what mutual benefits might be realized through the sharing of gifts?

While membership in Protestant churches in North America is shrinking, church membership in other parts of the world is experiencing significant growth. Particularly within countries in Africa, the swell of Christianity is taking on movement proportions. In the lives and communities of growing churches and new Christians, the role of the church is central. Membership expectations to be followers of Jesus Christ are consistently communicated and embraced. Perhaps the most compelling characteristic of these congregations is the sense of belonging.

What *should* the church require?

A getting-acquainted period can help membership candidates develop relationships. Laity must be the catalyst for such approaches. Members have greater relationships with other members than with the pastor, priest, rabbi, imam, or other spiritual leader. Clerical positions are often itinerant with an expectation of movement at some point. In today's highly transient culture, church members will likely move between congregations over time as well. The relationships established between church members, however, are substantially different than relationships between clergy and church members. The probability of relational longevity across time and distance is more likely in member-to-member relationships.

John Wesley, the father of the Methodist movement, instituted a basic concept of the Class Leader. This concept involved membership cells which permitted each member to be a part of a smaller group. Regular small group meetings helped members to be in touch with their spiritual selves. Teachings and discussions on repentance, justification, faith, love, forgiveness, redemption, stewardship, sin, pride, and sanctification were common topics. Expectations of the Christian faith were enumerated and persons were nurtured and supported within their small groups. Such potential for spiritual intimacy is seldom espoused in today's congregations.

Certainly, there are small group configurations in many congregations. Members join groups for a variety of reasons, and quite often strong relationships are forged. Foundational teachings of Christian tenets are generally relegated primarily to clergy. The expectation of lay persons can become derailed by seeking to qualify our spiritual growth with how well it aligns with what others say and do; a cautionary possibility in small group settings. Such alignments may compromise the need to take personal responsibility and accountability that mirror the time-tested mandates of the Gospel.

To an alarming extent, congregations can become disrupted when leadership changes are controversial. The goals of the building fund might run aground when the wishes of a faction within the congregation find fault or displeasure with the building plans. At a broader level, when renowned theologians fall from grace, tens of thousands of his or her followers find that circumstance to be just cause to redirect or abandon their personal faith commitment.

From a Wesleyan perspective, the emphasis was to keep it simple while addressing some of the more profound and decisive characteristics of Christian faith. When congregations are limited in channels for developing spiritual growth, likewise are members susceptible to limited direction when challenges arise. The faith community serves an important supportive role, but the ultimate health of one's soul is a personal responsibility.

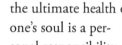

> The faith community serves an important supportive role, but the ultimate health of one's soul is a personal responsibility.

Jesus Christ had an astounding aptitude for simplicity. While biblical parables may lend themselves to multiple interpretations, all human behavior throughout history can be much more simply ordered. The Old Testament gave the Ten Commandments:

1) You shall have no other gods before me.
2) You shall not make for yourself an idol.
3) You shall not make wrongful use of the name of the Lord your God.
4) Remember the Sabbath day, and keep it holy.
5) Honor your father and your mother, so that your days may be long in the land that the Lord your God is giving you.
6) You shall not murder.
7) You shall not commit adultery.

8) You shall not steal.
9) You shall not bear false witness against your neighbor.
10) You shall not covet your neighbor's house; you shall not covet you neighbor's wife… or anything that belongs to your neighbor. (Exod 20:3–17)

Centuries later, Jesus offered an abbreviated version, condensing the Ten Commandments to two:

> The first is love the Lord your God with all your heart, and with all your soul, and with all your mind, and with all your strength. The second is you shall love your neighbor as yourself. And Jesus concluded that "there is no commandment greater than these" (Mark 12: 28–31).

As simple as these two commandments are, in practice, they can be daunting. As is suggested in learning any new behavior, baby steps can be the best beginning. Making the church relevant can be accomplished in the midst of what may seem to be constantly changing realities. These two commandments are the time-tested framework for guiding the growth of both individual and corporate relational and spiritual growth.

With Whom Do You Worship?

The first step for the established congregation is to begin developing relationships with its membership. This does not suggest delving into the personal recesses of members' lives. It does involve creating venues where relationships can flourish. Individual Facebook content often provides much more information than most congregations know about its members. The willingness to open oneself up to a broad audience, as demonstrated through the plethora of social outlets, suggests a basic need for relational participation. Social networking is commonplace in today's culture. Continuous advent of social networking mediums abound, with myriad outcomes ranging from inconsequential to wonderful to catastrophic. Might structured spiritual interaction provide venues for growing deeper faith? Likewise, such venues can provide more saving grace in response to the conditions and challenges all too often faced by individuals at all of life's stages. Amazing opportunities are resident within our congregations to find new relationships of encouragement and to nurture those that may be taken for granted.

Children and Youth Networks

What are issues facing the children and youth in the community? Laity knows and is involved at every level of the community's structure. The escalation of bullying has gained prominence across far too many communities. Bullying seems to transcend economic, social, racial, and ethnic compositions.

Amazing opportunities are resident within our congregations to find new relationships of encouragement and to nurture those that may be taken for granted.

Imagine the healing possibilities that children and youth might discover in the sanctity of the congregation when the real issues that they face are acknowledged and valued.

The children of laity are both the victims and the perpetrators of this dangerous behavior. Imagine the healing possibilities that children and youth might discover in the sanctity of the congregation when the real issues that they face are acknowledged and valued. Those with whom we worship can provide a safe sanctuary to nurture and to heal. Likewise, this same setting can serve to discover the causes and redirect the energies of those who injure others through unacceptable and hurtful behavior.

Christ's Promise

I will never leave you or forsake you. So
we can say with confidence, "The Lord
is my helper; I will not be afraid."
—Hebrews 13:5b-6

For the new Christian and the more seasoned Christian, the expectation of Christ's accompanying us on our faith journey is real. We come to believe that the promise to never leave or forsake us is a valid promise. But how do we embrace this promise such that it becomes a mantra for how we respond and participate in our relationships with Christ and each other?

"The Lord is my helper, I will not be afraid." Does this declaration become a statement of truth? Can this declaration be a firmly held belief for the youth who is being bullied in her school, for the newly hired father whose job will be the first to go with the imminent cutbacks, for the recently selected football captain who lives in constant fear of his sexual orientation being discovered, for the divorced mother whose personal assessment of worth is defined solely by her role as a wife, for the business executive whose financial worth has resulted from ill sources of gain? These are real conditions that exist in most congregations. In every congregation, the potential and the resources are present to offer a holy embrace to those who suffer or are simply in need of being heard.

> In every congregation, the potential and the resources are present to offer a holy embrace to those who suffer or are simply in need of being heard.

The natural penchant to celebrate our goodness and successes can be the source of hidden opportunities for healing. The human ugliness that exists is denied the catharsis of repentance through our need to elevate our goodness. Too often, brokenness, pain, and the countless maladies that affect all of life see no place for help within the congregation that seems to continuously espouse its perfection. The Gospel reflects no indication of a prevalence of human goodness.

Through admissions and exposures, lives are changed and brokenness is healed. The extent to which the reality of Christ being our helper is authentically and nonjudgmentally offered in the congregation is a decisive factor in the intimate process of spiritual healing and growth; hence, the relevance of the church in real time amidst real issues.

What the Church Isn't

The church is not the ultimate social setting that substitutes or appeases social awkwardness and feelings of limited self-esteem. The church isn't the place where all ills are healed and all sins forgiven. The church isn't the place that condones missteps and ignores egregious actions. Certainly, there are many things that the church isn't. How affirming it might be to think of the church as all things to all people. Such a role is impossible. Thankfully, the church is and can be so much more as a safe harbor that heals and inspires the human spirit.

What the Church Should Be

At every level of its existence, the church must give evidence to the living out of Christ's commandment:

> Love the Lord your God with all your heart,
> and with all your soul, and with all your mind,
> and with all your strength . . . and love your
> neighbor as yourself.

It is in the human struggle to live out this commandment that the personal discovery is made, that indeed, whatever our missteps and failures, he will never leave us or forsake us and we need not to be afraid.

Chapter One Reflection Exercise

- List three expectations that are communicated to new members of your congregation:

  _____

  _____

  _____

- What is the scheduled follow-up for discussing the expectations?

  _____

- How is the follow-up monitored? _____

- Make a personal contact with the last two persons/families that became members.

- In what way(s) is Jesus's great commandment evident in the life of the congregation? _____

  _____

  _____

- How might it be more evident? _____

- In what ways would church members/families/community benefit from experiencing the great commandment?

  _____

CHAPTER TWO

A Congregational Analysis

Now there are varieties of gifts, but the same Spirit;
and there are varieties of services, but the same Lord;
and there are varieties of activities, but it is the
same God who activates all of them in everyone.
—1 Corinthians 12:4–6

A purposeful and well-organized congregational assessment can be a valuable tool in fostering belonging as a defining characteristic of a congregation. The extent of information sought through a congregational analysis can be considered invasive. The willingness to provide this information will be closely aligned with the individual's sense of belonging and the awareness that any information captured is already known and stored in a variety of different databases. The rationale for obtaining this level of information is to create an environment of trust and to promote an understanding that church membership is an outward manifestation of an expressed relationship with God. Such information provides the church with a knowledge of the whole person so that optimum care can be offered to families and individuals. These acts of care represent both gifts and needs that enrich the Christian experience.

> Preparation of a congregational analysis should be administered with sensitivity and full disclosure of its purpose.

Preparation of a congregational analysis should be administered with sensitivity and full disclosure of its purpose. Congregants need to be apprised of its benefit, enabling the church to better serve through the awareness of needs, gifts, abilities, handicaps, and other circumstances that are valued and protected in a caring, Christian community. Clarity of purpose and discretion is imperative. A breach of confidentiality through carelessness or disregard can have seismic results. Likewise, the care of information and the appropriate partnering of congregants in places of support and growth have vast potential for enhanced spiritual lives and a deeper understanding of the value of the faith community. Comprehensive knowledge of the congregation's composition should be available and maintained with information that includes the following:

1) Total number of members_____
   By gender: Male ____Female ____
   By age categories: 0–6 years____, 7–12 years____,
   13–18 years____, 19–25 years____, 26–32 years_____,
   33–45 years____, 46–55 years_____, 56–65 years____,
   66–75 years____, 76–88 years_____,
   89–100 years_____, 100+ years____

2) Skills, competencies and professions, all listed with individual names (with permission):
   Housewives:
   Contractors:
   Plumbers:
   Electricians:
   Architects:
   Accountants:
   Attorneys:
   Police officers:
   Criminal justice:
   Information technologists, by area of specialty:
   Educators (preschool, elementary, secondary, post-secondary, teacher, administrator, academic area of specialty):
   Linguists:
   Nurses, by area of specialty:
   Physicians, by area of specialty:
   Psychologists, by area of specialty:
   Psychiatrists, by area of specialty:
   Healthcare clinicians, by area of specialty:

Consultants, by area of specialty:
Retirees, career experience:
Maintenance workers:
Carpenters:
Masonry:
Plumbers:
Electricians:
Business owners, by specialty:
College students, listed by schools and majors:
Other:

3) Socio-economic categories:
Homeowners:
Renters:
Homeless:
Divorcees:
Widows:
Widowers:
Felons:
Unemployed:
Other:
Wealth/earning ranges: (For discretionary purposes, individual names must not be provided. The intent here is to identify the number of individuals falling within certain earning ranges. The church's financial secretary, treasurer, or other designated individual(s) or committee will have discrete access to this level of information).
Annual Income of:
   +$250,000_____, $249,999-150,000_____,
   $149,999-80,000_____, $79,999-45,000____,
   $44,999-25,000_____,
   $24,999-15,000_____, $14,999 and under _____.

4) Joined congregation by (listed by name):
Profession of faith_____
Transfer from other denomination_____
Transfer from other congregation/same denomination___
First time member_____

By its very nature, this kind of information changes constantly. Efforts to maintain and update a congregational profile are as important as the information that is captured. Prior to launching a congregational analysis, specific plans for its security and maintenance should be in place and appropriately communicated.

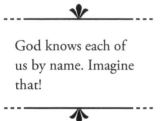

God knows each of us by name. Imagine that!

"I will never leave you or forsake you"—God's commitment to us is permanent. He seeks us out. He never stops searching for us to bring us to him. The notion of our being lost is one that we find within relationships, sometimes, even in the church. God does not accept that we are lost. God knows each of us by name. Imagine that! Of all the people populating the world, God knows each one by name.

Congregations can be Christ-like when every member is known. That may seem an impossible task, especially in very large congregations or when church attendance is irregular. How is it possible for a congregation's membership to know each other? Consider your work environment. How many coworkers are in your immediate area? How many are in your department, division, or housed on the same floor? We know our coworkers because we interact with them. We know our coworkers because we see them with some degree of frequency. We know our coworkers because in some way, they are important to us. This same penchant for familiarity repeats itself in multiple venues: the gym, the senior citizens' center, civic and social groups, the classroom, professional organizations, and sporting events where mothers and fathers interact with other parents. There are no less opportunities to know our Christian faith community as we know our work, social, and professional associates.

Admittedly, the gathering of sensitive information may seem daunting. It is a process that requires care and respect for privacy rights. In our current culture, discretionary information is danger-

Congregations can be Christ-like when every member is known.

ously accessible. Daily findings of how information has been randomly obtained for criminal purposes must indeed give us pause. There must be a trust factor throughout this process. Transparency of purpose is vital with viable evidence of how information is used; and most importantly, how individual congregants are benefited.

Full Disclosure

In conversation with a retired bishop of The United Methodist Church, we discussed the value and importance of knowing what each member contributed financially to the church. The bishop informed me that when serving a church as its pastor this was something he had never known and did not feel that he should have known. In subsequent responsibilities, he had encouraged the pastors under his charge to likewise avoid obtaining church members' financial giving information because of the sensitivity that some people might have regarding the disclosure of financial information. While this position might be assumed for any number of reasons, the absence of such information lends itself to an incredible probability of missed opportunities.

In the previous list of lifestyle categories, somewhat intimate knowledge of our fellow members is explored. Each of these categories provides an insight into an individual or family's joys, celebrations, goals, challenges, problems, and difficulties. Awareness of these conditions connects us as members within a faith community. Awareness and care of each other increases the sense of belonging and the relational manifestation of being cared for, prayed for, supported, and encouraged.

> Awareness and care of each other increases the sense of belonging and the relational manifestation of being cared for, prayed for, supported, and encouraged.

Knowledge about giving to the church is one indication of spiritual health and stability. Money is a measurement of many things. Money signals well-being and its absence can signal shifts in our relationships, lifestyle changes, and potentially difficult times. Knowing about giving consistency and inconsistency is as important as knowing that a job has been lost, a marriage dissolved, a promotion earned, a child is in college, an illness, or legal challenges. Any of these conditions will likely be reflected in our giving. Knowledge about our giving, its regularity or irregularity, can be a decisive indication that something in our lives has shifted, for better or worse.

> Knowledge about giving, its regularity or irregularity, can be a decisive indication that something in our lives has shifted, for better or worse.

Members of the clergy have told me that upon coming to a new church, members of the congregation have informed them that matters of money are not to be broached. "Just preach the word", they were told. In the New Testament there are more than seventy references to matters of money. Had it not been an important part of our spiritual evolution, Jesus would certainly not have given so much time to its mention.

Are medical doctors told by their patients how to be treated with specific conditions and that certain diagnoses are off limits? How physically ill might we be, were we to dictate to our physician what we will be treated for and what we will not accept treatment for? How effective in the classroom can a teacher be when specific subject matter germane to the discipline is removed from the curriculum at the student's request? Of equal importance is the appropriate knowledge of our giving with the understanding that it is an integral component of our spiritual health.

An important caution is noteworthy here. Knowledge of individual members' earnings or assets is not intended as a ploy for asking for contributions. Books, seminars, consultants, and experts in fundraising and capital campaigns abound. It is vital to distinguish between fundraising and the personal discipline of giving as integral to deepening spiritual growth. The awareness of giving practices and potential enhances the individual spiritual relationship and the church's ability to minister to the challenges and opportunities that giving affords.

Broaching sensitive and difficult issues has no better place than the church, and should certainly be addressed with care and discretion. Healing and wholeness are accomplished through acknowledging and naming our brokenness. When the congregation fulfills its role to offer Christ to all, in such a worship space, the familiar prayer, "Almighty God, to you all hearts are open, all desires known, and from you no secrets are hidden," (The Book of Common Prayer, 1979) is embraced in truth and confidence.

As a member of a congregation, there are some common responsibilities that each individual has. When those responsibilities are left unattended or halfheartedly addressed, the congregation suffers. The individual's commitment and participation wane. Likewise, the level of connectedness and belonging suffers. The degree of success in responding to the previous questions about the composition of your congregation through its members is a defining assessment of the extent to which our personal contributions enhance or diminish the relevance of our congregation.

Gift of Belonging

> *For just as the body is one and has many members, and all the members of the body, though many, are one body, so it is with Christ. ...Indeed, the body does not consist of one member but of many. ...But as it is, God arranged the members in the body, each one of them as he chose. If all were a single member, where would the body be? As it is, there are many members, yet one body . . . If one member suffers, all suffer together with it; if one member is honored, all rejoice together with it.*
> —1 Corinthians 12:12, 14, 18, 20 and 26

As this scripture describes order and interdependence, the church, at its best has order and interdependence. Reflecting on your congregation's composition, visualize the various gifts contributed by members. The gifts of administration, song, musical ability, organizational skills, conflict resolution, prayer, visitation, cooking and baking, decorating, Bible study, childcare, eldercare, and children and youth ministries are just some of the gifts that help to maintain the congregation's many ministries. Recognition and affirmation of gifts empower the individual and strengthen the congregation's ministry. Some gifts will be prominent such as worship leader, choir soloist, and Sunday school teacher. Other gifts are less visible such as offering counters, bulletin preparers and folders, and communion sacrament preparers. The roles within the church are endless, as are the gifts of its members.

> Recognition and affirmation of gifts empower the individual and strengthen the congregation's · ministry.

> As the family's strength is maximized by full participation of its members, likewise the church soars in ministry within and without, when its members are engaged fully in Christian discipleship.

Gifts are not always known or recognized. Quite often gifts require cultivation, but even before cultivation, the gift must be discovered. As a family's strength is maximized by full participation of its members, likewise the church soars in ministry within and without, when its members are engaged fully in Christian discipleship. Christian discipleship doesn't occur simply as an outgrowth of church membership. The growth of Christian discipleship is a continuous accomplishment needing to be nurtured, encouraged, and informed.

Personal Assessment Task

Over a two-week period, consider each of the elements cited in the congregational analysis and work to answer each one. Determine who in the congregation can be helpful to populate those categories that are most difficult. Enlist a partner in the membership to accompany you through this process, discussing regularly those areas where you are most and least knowledgeable and be sure to explore why. The why is important because it will help to isolate where interests are strongest. Likewise, the why will reveal those areas in the membership where you are least connected.

Consider this:

Take a moment and list by name members of your congregation. If your congregation is small, you may be able to list most of the members in the following categories. If yours is a large congregation, try and list at least ten families or individuals in each category citing persons with whom you are least familiar:

Two-parent families and the children's names:
Single parent families and the children's names:
Couples married in the church within the last eighteen months:
Couples having celebrated fifty years or more of marriage:
Female members widowed within the past year:
Male members widowed within the past year:
Families of children participating in a new member program or confirmed within the past two years:
The five most recently retired members of the congregation:
Three members having lost a job in the past year:
Three members having started a new job in the past year:
Two members having been divorced within the past year:

Chapter Two Reflection Exercise

- How does the congregation minister to single parents? _____
  _____
  _____

- Are there services within the congregation to assist persons seeking employment?
     If No, how might this be helpful?_____

     _____

     How might employment assistance services be implemented?
     _____

     _____

- When are discussions about money held?_____
     By whom?_____
- What are some personal giving experiences that have enhanced spiritual growth?

  _____

  _____

  _____

  _____

CHAPTER THREE

Leaders Leading

*Now when they saw the boldness of Peter and
John and realized that they were uneducated
and ordinary men, they were amazed and
recognized them as companions of Jesus.*

—Acts 4:13

Jesus CEO: Using Ancient Wisdom for Visionary Leadership by Laurie
Beth Jones[1] is an amazing guide that chronicles Jesus' life from a perspective of leadership. The text covers often complicated situations
in an easy to read format. Its chapters have thought provoking titles,
such as, "He Took One Step at a Time," "He Stuck to His Mission,"
"He Did Not Despise Little Things," "He Called the Question,"
and "He Troubled Himself on Behalf of Others." These are but a
few of the catchy titles that introduce compellingly insightful concepts in this timeless book. The simplicity of the actions affords the
reader an awareness of how our abilities and actions can be Christ-like. The issues and challenges are not insurmountable, and when
approached in basic, committed efforts, ground breaking results can
be accomplished.

Congregations are steeped in leadership resources. Individuals
who lead entire companies, entrepreneurs with creative and implementation skills, Human Resources managers that intercede between
management and hourly employees on issues of safety, equitable pay,
benefits, performance evaluation tools and approaches, pre-kindergarten and day care administrators, teachers and administrators rep-

---

[1]   *Jesus CEO: Using Ancient Wisdom for Visionary Leadership*, Laurie Beth Jones,
    Hyperion, 1995

resenting every tier of education, healthcare professionals from surgeons, general practitioners, anesthesiologists and nurses, lawn and landscaping artisans, architects, and construction workers are members of congregations. The sustainable wealth of every congregation lies in its laity. The wisdom in any congregation is the recognition of its assets in human capital. The health of the congregation depends significantly on the validation of the worth and contributions of its members.

> The wisdom in any congregation is the recognition of its assets in human capital.

The *Congregational Analysis* tool is an indispensable information source to identify the congregation's composition, in effect, its DNA. Leadership assessment helps to identify the gifts and graces that are present in a congregation. When consideration is being made for extending to church members invitations to serve, the depth of knowledge of a congregation's human capital is invaluable. Consultation with a chief executive officer (CEO) in a congregation about methods used to select leadership can be insightful. A Human Resources professional can share valuable knowledge on how decisions are made, variables that need to be considered, pitfalls that can be predisposed, and sensitivity training in addressing the inevitable leadership missteps that occur in religious and secular communities.

> Leadership assessment helps to identify the gifts and graces that are present in a congregation.

It may be offensive to some, but the church **is** a business. Certainly unique in its mission, but a business nonetheless. The excellence of stewardship is paramount to building God's kingdom. An intricate component of leadership, stewardship is responsible for the nurture and oversight of resources entrusted to the care of an organization.

> It may be offensive to some, but the church **is** a business. Certainly unique in its mission, but a business nonetheless.

While seldom easy, the tasks of leadership are vital and necessary for the health of the organization/church.

Modeling leadership requires taking unpopular positions from time to time. In the corporate arena, when performance is ineffective with counter-productive results, the health and stability of the organization requires that decisions be made to sustain and improve the organization. These decisions are generally assessed within the context of the organization's mission. As in the corporate arena, mission statements are commonplace in today's congregations. These statements evolve from a variety of sources. Consultants are frequently called in and given an overview of the congregation's composition, its interests, and what is perceived to be its greatest gift(s). Mission statements are most often the outgrowth of meetings of a select few within the congregation proclaiming to represent the leadership and general thinking of the membership.

The United Methodist Church holds as its mission statement: *making disciples of Jesus Christ for the transformation of the world*. This is a thoughtfully inclusive mission statement. The most decisive measure of leadership for every individual who holds a role of responsibility at each level of the Church is how this mission statement is evident. Leadership should therefore be collectively clear about what a disciple is. Can a disciple be nurtured by someone who is not themselves a disciple? What are the irrefutable characteristics of Jesus Christ that must be borne by those who seek to follow him? "Transformation of the world" is a bold and perhaps even presumptive statement. Transformation suggests moving from one state of existence to another. The *Illustrated Oxford Dictionary* defines transformation as "making a thorough or dramatic change in the form, outward appearance, character."

What is the desired change in form, outward appearance, and character that Christ would have for the world? Without a clear and informed answer to this question, United Methodist congregations might find their respective mission statements lacking in alignment with the denomination's mission mandate. Modeling leadership has a primary characteristic of clarity. Christ's clarity around The United Methodist Church's mission statement might well be explained rather simply in his great commandment: "You shall love the Lord your God with all your heart, and with all your soul, and with all your mind and you shall love your neighbor as yourself." From this, leadership can evolve with specificity. The great commandment permits one to offer examples within the life of the congregation where the commandment is visible and where it is not.

While attention is given here to one denomination's mission statement, the process has universal application. With the proliferation of nondenominational churches, it is important to vet with care and theological grounding the mission of the congregation. This process is vital so that members can responsibly embrace the mission. The great commandment embodies a timeless value that informs and supports what is hopefully the fundamental premise of every congregation's raison d'être.

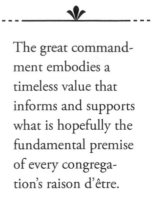

The great commandment embodies a timeless value that informs and supports what is hopefully the fundamental premise of every congregation's raison d'être.

"Truly great companies maintain a set of core values and a core purpose that remain fixed while their business strategies and practices continually adapt to a changing world. They understand the difference between what should never change and what should be open to change, between what is truly sacred and what is not." This statement comes from *The Spirit to Serve*, authored by J. W. Marriott Jr.[2] The Marriott Hotel brand is known worldwide and its repetitive theme is *service*. The foundation of its theme is embedded in its mission and its mission is integrated into every aspect of its training from housekeeping associates to managers to its senior level leaders. From small to large nondenominational churches to congregations of varying sizes within mainstream denominations, each will serve its constituents well with a clarity of mission that invites the presence and participation of every member.

---

[2] *The Spirit to Serve*, J.W. Marriott, Jr. and Kathi Ann Brown, Harper Business, 1997

Many lay persons are employed by companies that anchor their purpose deeply in a mission statement. These persons understand how important clarity, accountability, and affirmation are towards shepherding others in a cohesive direction to accomplish a shared goal. These persons may serve at the highest or lowest rung on the corporate ladder. Likewise, in every congregation, each member can contribute to a shared mission statement with an awareness of the importance and value of their individual contribution.

Even as the church membership numbers in North America are shrinking, Christianity remains the dominant world religion today. When Christ gave the great commission to those who were given the mantle of discipleship to go into all the world to "make disciples of all nations, baptizing them in the name of the Father and of the Son and of the Holy Spirit, and teaching them to obey everything that I have commanded" (Matt. 28:19–20), the mission statement was clear. Over the past two thousand years, strategies and practices have changed to adapt to a changing world. These strategies and practices are seen in the proliferation of denominations: Baptist, Lutheran, Episcopalian, Presbyterian, Methodist, Nondenominational, and Evangelical. Changes have been applied to the ordination of persons, so that they are set apart; flexibility of the worship hour, baptism methods, offerings of sacraments, and the list continues.

Leadership requires adaptability with sensitivity and respect for change while maintaining adherence to the core mission. When the mission is clear and honored, change is less controversial because the clarity of the mission is universally known, even if not completely shared. When new programs are being considered, they are tested against the mission statement. When new leadership is being sought, candidates are evaluated, in part, by their ability to both understand and implement ministry that embraces the mission statement.

Leadership requires adaptability with sensitivity and respect for change while maintaining adherence to the core mission.

Modeling Leadership

The concept of mutual benefit discussed in chapter one, suggests that members look for ways that they can contribute individually to the mission of the church, as well as ways that the church's mission will enhance their lives. Lay leadership can best affect this mutual relationship. This relationship can be addressed by assisting members, new and long time, to find ways to live out the mission of the church, while experiencing spiritual growth through the church's adherence to its mission supported by the Gospel of Jesus Christ.

Effective Leadership Models

- Hospitality: Recall a memory when you entered a room and knew no one. Try and remember how you felt; what concerns you had; what you wanted to happen? _____

  _____

  _____

  _____

  _____

  _____

Hospitality is not reserved for new people. Hospitality is a need that everyone has. On any given day, the most confident person can feel totally alone. Greet someone each Sunday; not just a hello, but engage in conversation with sincerity. And for the visitor, make a point to speak to them, ask their name and if there is something about the church they would like to know or see? Hospitality is never too much or unnecessary. Make it an integral part of every worship experience. Use hospitality in meetings and other gatherings so that belonging is something that everyone feels. Keep the memory of your own need for hospitality as a guide for being hospitable.

- Humility: Galatians 5:22–23 list the fruit of the Spirit. Nine characteristics are given: love, joy, peace, patience, kindness, generosity, faithfulness, gentleness, and self-control. While humility is not listed as one of these, it is perhaps inherent in each fruit of the Spirit. Humility is a derivative of the term, humble. Unfortunately, the definition of humble seems to suggest a less than desirable sense of self, especially in the North American context where assertiveness, visibility, and control are so prominent and celebrated. Some of the descriptive references for humble include: having or showing a low estimate of one's importance, modest pretensions, lowered rank or status. None of these references are particularly inviting in a culture where being seen and heard are perceived as expected characteristics of leadership. Somehow, the presence of humility, integral to the very essence of Jesus' persona has gotten lost.

How often might such acts of humility serve as an invitation to others to share their opinions, to encourage engagement in discussion, to offer an opposing view, or to affirm that one needs not be seated at the head of the table, have ready access to the microphone, or hold an impressive title, or any title to be welcomed and appreciated? Humility reflects gentleness in its willingness to invite others to share their thoughts and feelings without judgment.

> Humility epitomizes generosity through its failure to claim control by earnestly enlisting the expressions of others and valuing those expressions.

Humility epitomizes generosity through its failure to claim control by earnestly enlisting the expressions of others and valuing those expressions. Humility displays an intimate relationship with patience, recognizing that the pace of others' expressions and the differences in which communication can be offered enriches and empowers everyone who is given the privilege of participating.

List three instances in the past two weeks when acts of humility have been demonstrated:

_____

_____

_____

What or where are some additional opportunities for displaying humility?

_____

_____

_____

There is an inherent kindness in the behavior of one who demonstrates humility. The humble person understands that others may feel unworthy or unqualified to serve in a given capacity. Through this understanding, authentic validation evolves. Such validation places everyone as equal with the sensitivity to encourage some while carefully managing the dynamics of the group to offset dominating impulses of assertive personalities. Where humility is a defining mantra, the leader demonstrates a leadership style that does not engage in dominance. Even when it is necessary to make a final decision that will certainly not be favored by everyone, leadership with humility avoids categories of winners and losers.

> Where humility is a defining mantra, the leader demonstrates a leadership style that does not engage in dominance.

- Communication: In today's technology, the methods of communication are endless. Social media provides opportunities to communicate without direct contact. Such nuances as body language or words unspoken that are in direct opposition to what has been verbally communicated cannot be identified through most social mediums. Even when everyone is seated together, the meeting facilitator may be unable to assess with accuracy what is being said or not said. The ability to manage the flow of discussion and to recognize the differences in how others communicate are invaluable leadership gifts.

In more congregations than can be numbered, membership has been diminished by communication failures. Often, the offender, however unintended, never knows that a communication affront has been committed. Matthew 12:36-37 offers a very clear caution about the importance of communication: "on the day of judgment you will have to give an account for every careless word you utter: for by your words you will be justified, and by your words you will be condemned." How often have words been spoken unnecessarily, inaccurately directed, or with tones of accusation, distrust, or devalue? Whatever the mode of communication, electronically or in-person, the importance of word choices, examples used, and potential implications should never be taken lightly. Whatever the medium, words once spoken or transmitted cannot be retrieved.

> In more congregations than can be numbered, membership has been diminished by communication failures.

What example of less than effective communication comes to mind?

_____

_____

What was the effect?

_____

_____

How might the communication have been better?

_____

_____

Lay persons often fail to recognize the subtleties that leadership embodies. A resounding emphasis in all denominations is leadership development as a core need across the ranks of membership. Corporate organizations invest enormous resources in leadership development. No entity within the church has greater exposure to or the demand for effective leadership behavior than laity. And yet, the repetitive expression of the absence of effective leadership receives the most sustained reason for ineffective congregations. Perhaps, closer assessment of needs and ineffectiveness can better identify the best prescription. Leadership development might well have become a catch-phrase without tangible meaning. And as such, leadership development continues to go wanting.

The collective failure of laity to exercise within the church the skills and competencies that define their lives outside the boundaries of the church is astounding. Goal-setting is a rarity in most congregations, and even when the process is implemented, follow-through is often limited. The corporate environment would not successfully exist were specific and attainable goals not used as the fundamental guideline for every expectation. Performance evaluation is a relatively common model for development, assessment, and change in organizations beyond the church. As the composition of the workforce changes, the workplace is increasingly informal and methods of performance evaluation are regularly reassessed. Whatever the outcome of the reassessed design, the certainty remains that accountability helps the individual and the organization to be successful. Regrettably, these intentional accountability practices are rarities, at best, in the congregational setting.

In most congregations there is a committee charged with the responsibility of selecting and inviting persons to serve in certain roles in the life of the congregation. These roles may include administrative functions such as oversight of church property, finances, or staff selection. Other roles relate more programmatically to the ministry of the congregation such as worship, church school leadership, outreach, or mission related initiatives. The scope of these functions may vary significantly. Nonetheless, every congregation, on a relatively regular basis, places persons in positions of leadership. When sharing the specific duties of a responsibility, selection committee members in many instances are uninformed about the specific responsibilities of the function to which individuals are being recruited. Likewise, an incentive when recruiting for a position is often stated as "not being very demanding and only having to meet occasionally." Diminishing the importance of a responsibility diminishes the recruited individual's value.

Modeling leadership certainly resides with the spiritual leader of a congregation or faith community. It is an erroneous assumption, however, that any one individual has all the knowledge or experience necessary to affect the success of an organization or a congregation. When the dominant expectation of leadership lies with the pastor, the congregation is almost certain to experience significant loss when a pastoral change occurs. Likewise, where lay leadership is only occasional or relegated to a select few, stability cannot be accomplished. The congregation is destined to reinvent itself again and again. Lack of stability distracts from commitment to any relationship, whether a personal one, a job, or church membership. Clarity of mission and continuity are sustaining components that undergirds a congregation and shepherds it through inevitable change.

> It is an erroneous assumption, however, that any one individual has all the knowledge or experience to affect the success of an organization or a congregation.

Chapter Three Reflection Exercise

- What is your congregation's leadership selection process?
  _____
  _____
  _____

- How are leaders prepared for their respective responsibilities?
  _____
  _____

- Are mentoring structures in place to assist new leaders?
  Yes_____ No_____
  If yes, how effective are these structures? _____
  If no, what structures might be implemented?_____
  _____

- In what ways are individual skills and competencies affirmed?
  _____
  _____

- How are transitions in leadership managed? _____
  _____
  _____

CHAPTER FOUR

The Collection Plate

*Now the whole group of those who believed
were of one heart and soul . . . everything
they owned was held in common . . . There
was not a needy person among them.*
—Acts 4:32, 34a

So many congregations, actually entire denominations, anchor the
survival and relevance of the church on its financial health. Indeed
Christ spoke often and pointedly about money. Money is an important component in most organizations and relationships. The emphasis on money in the church may well have trumped the more formative reason that people gather in worship settings weekly. The
formative reason for which people commit themselves to other par-
ticipative roles specific to their respective faith community must not
be overshadowed. It would, however, leave a gaping hole in a faith
community's endeavor were money not to be given attention.

Over more than thirty years in a variety of responsibilities as
a volunteer and as an employed lay person by the denomination in
which I hold membership, it has been a privilege and duty to worship in more than four hundred churches fulfilling various responsibilities and invitations. These churches have for the most part been
located in the United States. They have been small congregations
with memberships of two hundred or less, mid-sized congregations
with memberships up to two thousand, and large membership congregations. Without exception, when the collection plate is passed,
in my experience, I have not seen the pastor place an offering or
tithe in the plate. This failed observation in no way suggests that
pastoral participation is not taking place. With the expansive imple-

mentation of electronic giving, this giving method has become increasingly convenient. And certainly, the pastor's contribution to the congregation is demonstrated in countless other ways beyond the corporate worship setting. Nonetheless, the communal ritual of worshiping through giving is a signature moment in the worship experience. Visual participation from the clergy can be both a worshipful and teachable moment.

In addition to the churches of the denomination in which I hold membership, it has also been my privilege to worship in congregations of other Protestant denominations. The absence of overt participation by clergy in the offering has been a consistent observation. To speculate on why this noticeable absence in participation is so prevalent would yield nothing more than a plethora of assumptions. What is not an assumption is that persons in leadership make the most impact when actions follow words; mirroring the kind of behavior desired by those guided by their leadership. Whatever the explanations for why the spiritual leader of a congregation does not visibly participate in what is universally considered a vital element in the life of the church are moot.

> Persons in leadership make the most impact when actions follow words; mirroring the kind of behavior desired by those guided by their leadership.

Why is it moot? Why does any explanation of this behavior have no significance? Quite probably the spiritual leader's reasons for not visibly participating in the offering are known to her or him, and perhaps a smaller group within the congregation. What the majority of the congregation sees is the absence of their spiritual leader's participation in a vital part of the worship experience; reasons of which each member and visitor is free to devise on their own. While the spiritual leader is unavoidably recognized by members and visitors within a congregation, the need for laity to visibly participate in the offering must not be undervalued. Lay persons are fundamental demonstrators of the many facets of being disciples of Jesus Christ. Lay persons relate more often and more intimately to one another and must set the bar of what is expected of others. For laity and clergy, giving is an act of worship, gratitude, and obedience. When this act is a visible demonstration, its importance is shown to the larger body; hence, a teachable moment.

Children and Youth

Some years ago while attending a worship service in Nashville, Tennessee, I observed a simple act during the children's sermon. What was observed offered compelling influence to how easily seeds are planted in fertile soil. Following the end of the children's sermon given by the senior pastor, he joined in a quick rhyme with the children. The rhyme was obviously one with which he and the children were quite familiar. Immediately after repeating the rhyme, the children dropped into the collection plate their offering and skipped excitedly up the aisle to join their parents and family. I remember thinking at the time, "and a little child shall lead them." Few, if any, of the children could explain from a spiritual perspective the significance of their action. Nonetheless, a habit was being formed that might well accompany them throughout their faith journey.

Certainly, this ritual guided by the pastor had some meaning for the children as they each were eager to participate. What an amazing thought: eager to participate in the offering! Quite possibly, these children also had an idea of why their dimes, quarters, and dollars were important. Nothing incites a joy in giving more than a personal awareness of why the gift matters. Perhaps the children gave because they understood from the children's sermons that everything they had was a gift from God and this was a way of giving back a little of what God had given to them. Or maybe they knew that the homeless people they saw in the community received clothes,

Nothing incites a joy in giving more than a personal awareness of why the gift matters.

meals, and sometimes odd jobs that the church provided and their offering helped to make this happen. Perhaps they gave their offering happily because they saw their adult family members regularly place a gift in the offering plate. They may have given their gifts simply from a childlike understanding of what it means to be a member of their congregation.

The importance of children contributing financially to the ministry of the congregation is significant. The contribution can also be so much more than money. Once while serving as youth coordinator, the youth and I cleaned the church several Saturdays during the year. Initially, this started out with much grumbling and speculation from the youth about why these tasks were not left completely with the maintenance staff. As the activity became more routine with the youth polishing the altar, dusting the pulpit and chancel area, arranging hymnals and bibles in the pews, vacuuming throughout the sanctuary, sweeping the choir room, and tidying the kitchen, their sense of that church being the place where they were members took on a different and more relational meaning. An understanding of the church as a living, giving organism that thrived on the care of its members became meaningful to the youth. Years later, when visiting that congregation, it was a joy to see some of those youth, now adults, serving in leadership roles.

> Perhaps they gave their offering happily because they saw their adult family members regularly place a gift in the offering plate.

Giving Units

"Giving units" may not be a familiar term. Many congregations, however, use this term to denote the number of families and individuals from which financial contributions are projected. "Giving units" is an impersonal and unaccountable term. Aside from the impersonal nature of this assessment tool, it completely negates the expectation that financial support is the responsibility of everyone. When the children in the Nashville congregation happily dropped their gifts into the collection plate, they were responding to their relationship with God. Their gift wasn't given as a fraction of the Smith or Benson family's gift. Their contribution was a gift given from each child in response to their personal relationship with God and His church. What an amazing opportunity the church has to teach the joy of giving that expands to needs far beyond the walls of the church.

An irony in the use of the term "giving units" is the pride that congregations and denominations take in sharing their total membership numbers. A congregation will boast of increased membership of 15 percent or 60 new members, while describing its giving sources as a number based on families and individuals. Quite often, the number of giving units will not include the members (families or individuals) who contribute little or nothing financially to the church. The giving unit represents the known contributors. What a deceptive waste! If a congregation has 317 members, it has 317 potential contributors including the children who are old enough to know what money is. This total membership inclusion offers lessons in responsibility and demonstrates the expectation and value of every member to the life of the church.

Categorizing giving as units of the church's membership disenfranchises individual gifts. The wife depends on the husband's contribution as representative of the family. The children and youth do not participate in personal giving because the adult parent represents the "giving unit." As blessings are received individually, our response to God's presence should also be demonstrated individually. The lessons of responsibility as members of families of faith can be greatly diminished when individual giving is piggybacked on another, and personal accountability is not espoused early and as often as possible.

> As blessings are received individually, our response to God's presence should also be demonstrated individually.

The collection plate is one of many symbols in the community of faith. Every member's participation in this part of the faith community is needed. In the congregation where finances are not an issue (and there are some), failure to encourage and expect financial support from every member withholds or lessens a vital element in spiritual growth. In the congregations where grow-ing members in their faith is the priority, the reality that giving to God is a grateful response to His giving to us should be paramount. No one is exempt. No gift is too small, and no gift is too large.

> In the congregation where finances are not an issue (and there are some), failure to encourage and expect financial support from every member withholds or lessens a vital element in spiritual growth.

In addition to receiving gifts, the accountability responsibility looms large. Congregants need to know the details of the church's financial obligations and commitments. This should not be information that is available only to key leadership. While many members may not have expressed interest, there needs to be consistent, easily accessible sources that chronicle the financial structure of the church. Because money can too often be the impetus for suspicion within a congregation, the need for transparency is without question.

The laity is the dominant source of financial support in every congregation. Likewise, the laity should be intimately engaged in the processes of communication and accountability. "I didn't know" can never be an excuse or explanation for failed participation. The stewardship of the church's resources is no less important than the stewardship of resources in our homes, families, and employment.

> Because money can too often be the impetus for suspicion within a congregation, the need for transparency is without question.

Chapter Four Reflection Exercise

- What is your congregation's annual budget?
  _____

- What specific ministries does your congregation support within the immediate community? _____
  _____
  _____
  _____

- What specific ministries does your congregation support beyond the immediate community? _____
  _____
  _____

- Through what methods is the congregation informed of the church's ministry in the community and beyond? _____
  _____

- What ministry contributions are provided other than financial?
  _____
  _____
  _____

- In what ways are children and youth involved in supporting the congregation's ministries? _____
  _____
  _____
  _____

CHAPTER FIVE

Doing Ministry

And what does the Lord require of you
but to do justice, and to love kindness,
and to walk humbly with your God.
—Micah 6:8

Churches undergo great financial strain to create accommodating environments at the expense of failing to inform and demonstrate to its members what the Lord requires.

So much emphasis in recent years has been focused on specific elements of congregational life. Christian bookstores abound with books about church growth, applying every demographic analysis possible to explain, justify, and predict where the church is headed. Inordinate amounts of time is given to inclusive interpretations with worship designs intended to reach every age, ethnicity, race, and gender. Architects specializing in church buildings have sold countless congregations on structural must-haves that will attract prospective targeted members. There is absolutely no end to interpreting financial stewardship. Often financial stewardship is postured on the supposition that gifts to the church are in danger of being usurped by other non-profit organizations with mission statements so attractively crafted that donors will opt to give their previous church dollars to these more compelling missions.

The obsession with competing for time, entertainment, and money may well be the ultimate demise of the church. Care is given to mirror those things that seem to draw big crowds. Sermons can be diluted with feel good clichés. Quite often the likelihood is greater to call for therapy for a behavior, rather than to call a behavior the sin that it is. Churches undergo great financial strain to create accommodating environments at the expense of failing to inform and demonstrate to its members what the Lord requires: "to do justice, to love kindness, and to walk humbly with your God" (Mic. 6:8).

The church works hard not to offend. The church goes to great lengths to make itself a comfortable place, espousing fellowship and belonging. These are important attributes, but hardly the requirements for winning souls to Christ. Regrettably, in the competing quests to bring new people into the church, the fundamental purpose of the church can be compromised. Prospective members don't join and existing members are lost because winning souls to Christ is overshadowed by entertainment and popularity. The expanded parking lot, the colorful murals, the state of the art family life center are only carrots that attract, but hardly spiritual food that sustains.

> The expanded parking lot, the colorful murals, the state-of-the-art family life center are only carrots that attract, but hardly spiritual food that sustains.

"To do justice . . ."

Justice is perhaps one of the most difficult behaviors that can be accomplished. Nonetheless, justice is undeniably expected of those who call themselves followers of Jesus Christ. The opportunities for *doing justice* are endless. Were the funds raised and spent on cosmetic upgrades redirected to partner with other sources to build housing for low-income families, justice might be served for those who have been marginalized. Congregations might encourage its members with legal expertise to offer pro bono work to families facing the residual effects of predatory lending. In countless

> The opportunities for *doing justice* are endless.

ways congregations can confront discrimination and other injustices that impede the most fundamental progress of those whose station in life qualifies them to be counted among "the least of these."

In any given year, multiple occurrences of law enforcement brutality are headlined. People are severely beaten or killed by overzealous police officers. In many of these instances, placement on paid administrative leave is more the norm than the exception. For example, six years after hurricane Katrina decimated much of New Orleans, police officers who shot and killed victims of the hurricane were finally brought to justice. Years of expenses were incurred to defend and orchestrate a masterful cover-up when justice for those killed and their families was the less important goal.

Certainly, tens of thousands of law enforcement officers and criminal justice personnel protect and serve communities and individuals day and night. These men and women daily place themselves in harm's way to insure the safety of citizenry. These performed duties and sacrifices too often go unrecognized and downplayed by the rogue activities of a minority group that disrespects and abuses the cause of justice. Shedding light on the honorable and the dishonorable begs to be addressed.

Indeed, the opportunities to do justice are endless. The absence of the church's active participation in seeking to find justice in those instances where injustice is so blatant deters those who instinctively know that the path of the Christian is not one of ease and inaction. One of the chapters in Laurie Beth Jones's book, *Jesus CEO*, is titled, "He Called the Question." In scripture, Jesus poses seemingly simple questions to the disciples: "Who do people say that I am?" (Mark 8:27); to Peter, "Do you love me?" (John 21:15); to the man who lay at the pool of Bethzatha, "Do you want to be made well?" (John 5:6). In each instance, once the question is asked, the answer requires that some outward manifestation or change in behavior must follow. Perhaps, the church might also engage itself with questions of transformational proportions. Questions like how can this congregation be a catalyst for justice in this community? Or when has an injustice been served in this congregation? Is it possible to rectify that injustice and what can be done to insure that such an injustice will not occur again? These are difficult questions. But the active pursuit of answers demonstrates a concerted effort to respond to what the Lord requires.

Consider this:

- What member(s) of the congregation has felt hurt, disappointment, or anger because of an action that was taken? What can be done to address these feelings? Who should do it? When will it be done?
- Have willing, qualified members been overlooked for a task or responsibility to appease someone else because of their status, influence, or financial contributions? If so, how can this be addressed?
- Who needs to receive an apology?
- Who needs to make an apology?
- What outreach measures can be taken to the member(s) who no longer attends?

Human nature can be tirelessly unforgiving. It is our nature to draw lines of defense with determinants of right and wrong. Being right is often perceived as sufficient justification to move along toward the goal in pursuit, without looking back at any carnage that may have fallen along the way. If an offense occurs, our defense may well be to proceed, ignoring, if not forgetting what has been experienced. No place in scripture do we find a discussion between Jesus and Peter about Peter's denial that fateful night of being one of Jesus' disciples (Luke 22:55–60). Perhaps Peter apologized. Were we in Peter's place, given the opportunity would we tell Jesus how sorry we were? No doubt we would. If we could bring ourselves to face him, a heartfelt apology would be given. It should be so much easier to make the apologies, to right the wrongs within our own faith community, our families, and our work places. It might serve us well to resurrect an old phrase from the past that had much popularity across the church. In earnest, might we ask ourselves in these decisive moments, "what would Jesus do" (WWJD)?

"To love kindness . . ."

Competition abounds in today's culture between the growing number of nonprofit organizations. There are agencies and organizations, large and small, that seek to address the spiraling increase in poor societal conditions. Organizations have been established to give counseling to victims of spousal, sexual, physical, and emotional abuse. Financial and human resources through federal, state, and private agencies are available to curtail child endangerment and its many effects. Assistance is available to aid persons who have overextended themselves financially. Psychologists and psychiatrists of every ilk are in short supply as demands outdistance professional availability.

Persons seeking every possible source of emotional, psychological, and financial assistance are likewise participants in local congregations. The homeless person who comes to the church pantry on Wednesdays between 10:00 a.m. and 3:00 p.m. is not seen as one who has needs outside the hours of the church's availability. Nor is that person likely to be extended an invitation to the Bible Study convening just three hours later, where a light meal will be served.

When "outreach" ministries are offered, the very implication of outreach can be less than inviting. Congregations create elaborate tracking systems to determine the frequency with which persons visit the food bank or clothes pantry and limitations are imposed on the person judged as coming too often. The inventory of unused clothes continues to increase, but the limitations are not lifted. Food is beyond the best before date, but persons who come to receive services are still limited to how much they are given or how often they can visit.

Kindness is a prerequisite to hospitality. Kindness is shown through body language, a casual touch, eye contact, and staying focused long enough with a person to establish that what is being said is important. Kindness disallows judgment as a measure for the authenticity of need. Kindness is a recognizable human interaction that values the other. Kindness speaks caring, patience, and compassion.

> Kindness disallows judgment as a measure for the authenticity of need.

The church has the opportunity, moreover the responsibility, to be kind and not just to those with whom it is familiar. Doing justice and loving kindness may, in some contexts, seem contradictory. When justice is meted with compassion, integrity, consistency, and timeliness the presence of kindness is evident.

Consider this:

- Three observations of acts of kindness at any single gathering in the church

  _____

  _____

  _____

- Identify four persons within the congregation who demonstrate kindness in their interactions with everyone, and thank them

  _____,

  _____,

  _____,

  _____,

- Where has the absence of kindness been a cause of dissension or hurt in the congregation? What measures might be taken to mend fractured relationships?

  _____

  _____

  _____

  _____

"Walk humbly with your God . . ."

It is impossible to walk humbly with God without walking humbly with those we encounter. The often quoted scripture from the twenty-fifth chapter of the Gospel of Matthew referred to in some translations as the "judgment of the nations" clearly states: "just as you did it to one of the least of these who are members of my family, you did it to me." *Three Simple Rules*, a small, powerful book, authored by Bishop Reuben Job[3], puts walking humbly with God in a contemporary context.

---

[3] *Three Simple Rules*, Reuben Job, Abingdon Press, 2007

The first rule, "Do no harm," aligns quite well with doing justice. Guided by an unfailing propensity to never harm another is a natural aversion to injustice. It is impossible to level an injustice without harming another. Unintentionally, members of congregations may be harmed in some way on a regular basis. Disregard for feelings and opinions expressed and failure to value questions raised can harm the individual's sense of acceptance and belonging. Because an injurious action is unintended in no way lessens the degree of its injury. To do no harm requires being engaged with others, and most importantly sensitive to personal feelings and motives.

> Because an injurious action is unintended in no way lessens the degree of its injury.

The second rule: "Do good." Kindness is goodness. A simple show of kindness has the potential to bridge enormous gaps where hurt or disappointment has created chasms of separation. To the lonely widow whose connections with life abruptly snapped with the loss of a lifetime partner, kindness can be the catalyst that brings her back from the brink of despair. To the recently released young woman whose years of incarceration are worn as a badge of isolation, acts of kindness can be the turning points redefining a life that might have been lost. Doing good has remarkable benefit both to the giver and the receiver. No one is immune to the need for kindness and goodness. Thankfully, everyone is blessed with an ample supply of kindness to give.

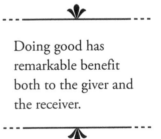

> Doing good has remarkable benefit both to the giver and the receiver.

The third rule: "Stay in love with God." It may sound trite to propose that staying in love with God is the most failproof anecdote for maintaining relationships of patience, respect, and compassion for others. Knowing that God loves each of us, no matter who we are or what we believe or do is a liberating reality.

> Knowing that God loves each of us, no matter who we are or what we believe or do is a liberating reality.

for others. Knowing that God loves each of us, no matter who we are or what we believe or do is a liberating reality. He loves us unconditionally. This knowledge can serve as insulation against relational challenges and difficulties because it helps us to look at ourselves. Realizing that we are often unlovable when we are disrespectful or insensitive to others, we are better able to realize God's unfailing love that sees our faults and loves us anyway.

"For God so loved the world that He gave His only begotten son" (John 3:16) represents the ultimate gift and the ultimate demonstration of love. Our mindfulness of this can serve as a constant mantra that informs our behavior and wills us to be the best we can be. Yes, we do fail. We get caught up in moments of anger, frustration, disappointment, envy, and a litany of other human emotions. Returning, however, to that "peace place" that cautions us against hurtful behavior, we are more likely to try and respond in ways that please God. It is the nature of humankind to please those we love.

Regrettably, in great and small ways, the absence of love can be seen in the congregation. Failure to go to the unmarried, pregnant teen—with words of encouragement when we see the separation that exists between others in the congregation and this young woman—is an overt display of absent love. The pretense of concern for the homeless man who comes into a Sunday worship service and is the benefactor of acts of hospitality, when passing this same man on the street, eyes are averted for fear that a spark of recognition might occur. Our love for God is best demonstrated by our love for each other—no exceptions.

Our love for God is best demonstrated by our love for each other.

Consider this:

- Identify persons within the congregation who are on the margins of society and devise a meaningful, concerted effort for the church to embrace them in tangible ways.
- Sit with someone in the congregation that you do not know and give them something of yourself.
- Where are opportunities to demonstrate God's love in specific ways within the congregation? Do it!

Being the Change

Mahatma Gandhi, one of history's most prolific civil rights leaders through his non-violent resistance, is credited with saying, "Be the change you want to see in the world." Today's religious environment asserts that change is the savior of the church. The saving conditions are postured as more members and more money. Change is presented in many ways with wonderful platitudes to articulate what the church should look like. The constant emphasis is on quantity: quantity of people and quantity of dollars. Real, long term change is best effected one-on-one, embracing those actions that demonstrate what the Lord requires: to do justice, and to love kindness, and to walk humbly with your God.

Enormous amounts of time and financial resources are given to analyzing what the church needs. These results often set forth lists of conditions that are believed to be contributing to a spiraling demise, especially in the Protestant Church. These changes espouse worship formats, casual dress, multiple channels for making financial contributions, the ways visitors are welcomed, building structures that invite ease of access, and programs of ministry that are compatible with a changing social laxity. In effect, the church goes to phenomenal extents to assimilate itself into the ways of the world rather than seeking to draw the world into the church. While adaptation to a changing world is intelligent and wise, care in doing so should always be tempered with the greater purpose of winning souls to Christ.

> While adaptation to a changing world is intelligent and wise, care in doing so should always be tempered with the greater purpose of winning souls to Christ.

Studies are initiated with increasing frequency to determine what the church needs to better attract new members and retain existing ones. Christ's ministry was very specific and his disciples came to be certain of his mission. The mission has not changed. The mission has only become greater with more people to reach and more opportunities to reach them: "Go therefore and make disciples of all nations, baptizing them in the name of the Father and of the Son and of the Holy Spirit, and teaching them to obey everything that I have commanded you. And remember, I am with you always to the end of the age" (Matt. 28:19–20).

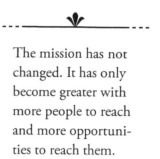

The mission has not changed. It has only become greater with more people to reach and more opportunities to reach them.

"Teaching them to obey everything that I have commanded you" may be a particularly absent activity across the church. From a layperson's perspective, it might be helpful to look at the church for parallels between how laity relates to the church and how laity relates to the workplace. Whether a corporate conglomerate or a small enterprise, there is a purpose for every business. When that purpose is confused or distorted, the stability of that business is at risk and so is survival. Employees know the purpose. Employees who embrace the purpose and are best able to articulate that purpose towards enhancing the success of the business are valued and offer leadership, subtle and overt. When a change in strategy is considered, the impact of the change is weighed to insure that the core mission is not compromised. The entire organization undergoes an assessment to be sure that it will not be harmed and its core mission is protected. Change does not occur for the sake of change. And those who orchestrate change recognize that they are the most vulnerable should the core mission of the organization suffer. These are conditions that define corporate businesses. Lay persons live in this environment and their livelihood survives or dies based on the ability to function effectively within this universal framework.

The church is different. Change can be conceived and implemented with little accountability for the outcome of the change by its initiators. Lay persons join and leave congregations based on the clarity of its mission. A common policy in corporate environments is to have an

Lay persons join and leave congregations based on the clarity of its mission.

exit strategy when an employee leaves. This conversation helps the organization to understand where it has failed the employee and the employee to understand where he or she has failed the organization. This conversation fosters mutual learnings from the separation. The church does not do exit interviews. Members leave and unless relocation is the primary reason, the church has little knowledge and makes minimal effort to discover the cause of separation.

It is as important, if not more important to know why a member leaves a congregation than why a person joins the congregation. Assessment of cause for leaving requires looking at what has been effective and what has been ineffective with a willingness to address change for the overall health and stability of the church. Assessment of causes for leaving suggests that the congregation is always sensitive to whether it is meeting its core mission and understands that change is often painful, but necessary if growth is to be accomplished. In some cases, such a conversation might reverse a member's intention to leave the congregation.

> It is as important, if not more important to know why a member leaves a congregation than why a member joins the congregation.

Failure to assess causes for leaving a congregation sends a message that the congregation is fine and there's nothing to be learned because a member or members have left. Without a doubt, this failure poses costly detriment to the health of the church. This failure diminishes the perceived value of the souls of those who have entrusted themselves to be served and nurtured by the congregation.

In secular work environments, some form of assessment is in place to measure success of accomplished goals. The church can realize tremendous benefit by evaluating its performance with a willingness to listen. Broad and sweeping changes are often employed with limited grassroots assessment of value. Simple questions such as "How will this proposed change impact your spiritual journey?" "Will you be inspired to invite others to share with you in your church's ministry as a result of this change?" "When this change is implemented, how will it increase your growth as a disciple of Jesus Christ?" "Will this change influence your commitment to the church's ministry"? These are the kinds of questions that engage members in the life of the church and deepen the sense of belonging.

When change is implemented without the involvement of those for whom the change is intended, the probability of success is minimal at best. A growing percentage of congregations within The United Methodist Church has limited awareness of the church's overall structure and is not invested in sweeping changes. Members want to know that their congregation values them. A popular television sitcom in the past was *Cheers*. The sitcom's theme song contained a lyric that says, "Where everyone knows your name." This single characteristic made the *Cheers* bar a place where its members came to be welcomed, communicated with, supported and yes, loved. Not a lot different than the church, and yet few churches can describe themselves as being places where everyone's name is known.

Back to Basics

See what love the Father has given us that we should
be called children of God; and that is what we are.
—1 John 3:1

Humankind was created to be in relationship. The Book of Genesis informs us that "in the image of God he created them, male and female, he created them" (chapter 1:27). Relationships continue throughout history. We are engaged in relationships as parents, spouses, siblings, friends, and employees. Relational categories are countless as humankind seeks places of acceptance, challenge, and opportunity. The interesting thing about relationships is that no textbook provides fail proof steps for success. Admittedly, bookstores, the Internet, talk shows, and other informative venues abound with suggestions, if not declarations of "how to" succeed in every imaginable relationship.

The uniqueness of the human mind and spirit prevents a cookie cutter approach. Tradition, cultural mores, language, beliefs, and other conditions of influence circumvent any possibility of irrefutable similarities. Hence, it is largely futile to seek to isolate behavior and dictate the needs and environment that will guarantee a desired outcome.

Humanity exists in a culture of constant change, exacerbated by the immediacy of information, ratcheted to unimaginable levels by technology. Physical and psychological conditions and treatments signal seismic progress. With the exception perhaps of the common cold, practically every human ailment has experienced some degree of success in its treatment. In a world of constant change, understandably the church seeks to move in concert with change in order to maintain its relevance. The critical question is *why* is change sought? Any number of answers may be given to this question.

The church is in need of change to stem the tide of lost members. The church is in need of change to increase its membership. The church is in need of change because communities are changing. The church is in need of change because it is in competition with other social organizations and groups. The church is in need of change because it is losing financial support. It might be helpful to think about your own congregation and its change mantra that has been communicated in the past three to five years. Are its reasons for change the same as some of these cited, or does your congregation have other reasons? What are they?

My congregation is in need of change because_____

_____

If this change is accomplished, what will the congregation be like?

_____

That we should be called children of God; and that is what we are. Of all the relationships that humankind participates in, volun-

> The uniqueness of the human mind and spirit prevents a cookie cutter approach.

tarily or involuntarily, our common role as children of God is the most important. Unlike other relationships, there are some very basic guidelines for what it means to be children of God and what is expected of us. The guidelines transcend culture, ethnicity, social, educational, economic status, language or any other measure or distinction that might be employed. Jesus Christ summarizes, or condenses the guidelines into two: Love the Lord your God with all your heart, mind, soul, and strength; and love your neighbor as yourself (Matt. 22:37–40).

Of all the reasons given for change in today's congregations, too few seem to be for the purpose of adhering to this basic guideline. We seek to change the church to meet the interests of those who attend or those whom we wish to encourage to attend. The church has rapidly embraced a popular ice cream company's strategy, offering a flavor of the month. What a risky strategy this is assuming that everyone will be satisfied by the selected flavor. Unlike any other manmade organization, the church is not made for man, the church exists for God. Our determinants for the relevance of the church may well be off course.

> The church is not made for man, the church exists for God. Our determinants for the relevance of church may well be off course.

Were we to consider God's will rather than our own desires, what might the church look like? Our methods of invitation might be different and the composition of our congregations might look more like a mall with all ages, races, cultures, able, disable, literate, illiterate moving interactively. Teaching would be formative from the basic tenets of the Bible as the springboard from which every message evolved, helping members to understand and recognize the perennial nature of God's Word.

In our many relationships, how prominent do we seek to adhere to God's will? The church's survival and relevance rests squarely in the hearts and on the shoulders of the laity. Certainly, pastors and other spiritual leaders are vital to the church and its health. Without laity, however, for whom would the church exists? How wonderfully profound is this reality. There is no place to lay the burden of ineffectiveness or irrelevance of any congregation other than where it belongs. Given that the church belongs to the laity, in any way that the church is broken, likewise, its fix belongs to the laity.

ABOUT THE AUTHOR

Lynda Byrd is a student of leadership: its strategies, qualities, and application. As a developer and facilitator of leadership skills training in the corporate environment, her experience has transferred well into the religious community. Having served in local congregations to executive positions at the national church level within a leading denomination, Lynda's insight and practical applications reach across the diverse landscape of faith communities. Combining her experiences in the corporate community coupled with a vast exposure to the religious community, Lynda has a lay perspective with a unique view from the pew to the pulpit.

A retired executive, she makes her home in San Antonio, Texas.

The Cat Who Blew the Whistle

Lilian Jackson Braun

JOVE BOOKS, NEW YORK

This Jove Book contains the complete
text of the original hardcover edition.
It has been completely reset in a typeface
designed for easy reading and was printed
from new film.

THE CAT WHO BLEW THE WHISTLE

A Jove Book / published by arrangement with
the author

PRINTING HISTORY
G. P. Putnam's Sons edition / February 1995
Jove edition / March 1996

For information address:
The Berkley Publishing Group, a division of Penguin Putnam Inc.,
375 Hudson Street, New York, New York 10014.

The Penguin Putnam Inc. World Wide Web site address is
http://www.penguinputnam.com

ISBN: 0-515-11824-9

A JOVE BOOK®
Jove Books are published by
The Berkley Publishing Group, a division of Penguin Putnam Inc.,
375 Hudson Street, New York, New York 10014.
JOVE and the "J" design are trademarks
belonging to Penguin Putnam Inc.

PRINTED IN THE UNITED STATES OF AMERICA

16   15   14   13   12   11   10   9

Dedicated to Earl Bettinger,
The husband who . . .

ONE

The engineer clanged the bell. The whistle blew two shrill blasts, and the old steam locomotive—the celebrated Engine No. 9—huff-puff-puffed away from the station platform, pulling passenger cars. She was a black giant with six huge driving wheels propelled by the relentless thrust of piston rods. The engineer leaned from his cab with his left hand on the throttle and his eyes upon the rails; the fireman shoveled coal into the firebox; black cinders spewed from the funnel-shaped smokestack. It was a scene from the past.

Yet, this was a Sunday afternoon in the high-tech present. Thirty-six prominent residents of Moose County had converged on the railway station in Sawdust City to pay $500 a ticket for a ride behind old No. 9. It was the first run of the historic engine since being salvaged and overhauled, and the ticket purchase included a champagne dinner in a restored dining car plus a generous tax-deductible donation to the scholarship fund of the new community college.

When the brass bell clanged, a stern-faced conductor with a bellowing voice paced the platform, announcing, "Train leaving for Kennebeck, Pickax, Little Hope, Black Creek Junction, Lockmaster, and all points south! All abo-o-oard!" A yellow stepbox was put down, and well-dressed passengers climbed aboard the dining car, where tables were set with white cloths and sparkling crystal. White-coated waiters were filling glasses with ice water from silver-plated pitchers.

Among the passengers being seated were the mayors from surrounding towns and other civic functionaries who found it in their hearts, or politics, to pay $500 a plate. Also aboard were the publisher of the county newspaper, the publication's leading columnist, the owner of the department store in Pickax, a mysterious heiress recently arrived from Chicago, and the head of the Pickax Public Library.

The flagman signaled all clear, and No. 9 started to roll, the cars following with a gentle lurch. As the clickety-clack of the drive wheels on the rails accelerated, someone shouted, "She's rolling!" The passengers applauded, and the mayor of Sawdust City rose to propose a toast to No. 9. Glasses of ice water were raised. (The champagne would come later.)

Her black hulk and brass fittings gleamed in the sunlight as she chugged across the landscape. Steel rumbled on steel, and the mournful whistle sounded at every grade crossing.

It was the first run of the Lumbertown Party Train. . . . No one had any idea it would also be almost its last.

Moose County, 400 miles north of everywhere, had a rich history, and railroads had helped to make it the wealthiest county in the state before World War I. Fortunes had been made in mining, lumbering, and transportation, and many of the old families were still there, hanging on to their inherited money or lamenting the loss of it. Only the Klingenschoen millions had escalated into billions, and then—by an ironic quirk of fate—had passed into the hands of an outsider, a middle-aged man with a luxuriant pepper-and-salt moustache and a unique distaste for money.

The heir was Jim Qwilleran, and he had been a hard-working, prize-winning journalist Down Below, as Moose County citizens called the polluted and crime-ridden centers of overpopulation. Instead of rejoicing in his good luck, however, Qwilleran considered a net worth of twelve digits to be a nuisance and an embarrassment. He promptly established the Klingenschoen Foundation to dispose of the surplus in philanthropic ways. He himself lived quietly in a converted barn and wrote the twice-weekly "Qwill Pen" column for the local paper. Friends called him "Qwill," with affection; the rest of the county called him "Mr. Q," with respect.

If a cross-section of the populace were to be polled, the women would say:

"I love his column! He writes as if he's talking to me!"

"Why can't my boyfriend be tall and good-looking and rich like Mr. Q?"

"His moustache is so romantic! But there's something sad about his eyes, as if he has a terrible secret."

"He must be over fifty, you know, but he's in terrific shape. I see him walking and biking all over."

"Imagine! All that money, and he's still a bachelor!"

"He has a wonderful head of hair for his age. It's turning gray at the temples, but I like that!"

"I sat next to him at a Red Cross luncheon once, and he listened to everything I said and made me feel important. My husband says journalists are paid to listen. I don't care. Mr. Q is a charming man!"

"You know he must be a nice person by the way he writes about cats in his column."

And if the men of Moose County were polled, they would say:

"One thing I'll say about Mr. Q: He fits in with all kinds of people. You'd never guess he has all that dough."

"He's a very funny guy, if you ask me. He walks into the barber shop, looking as if he's lost his last friend, and pretty soon he's got everybody in stitches with his cracks."

"All the women like him. My wife goes around quoting his column like it was the Constitution of the United States."

"They say he lives with a couple of cats. Can you beat that?"

"You wonder why he doesn't get married. He's always with that woman from the library."

"People think it's strange that he lives in an apple barn, but what the heck! It's better'n a pig barn."

Qwilleran did indeed live in a converted apple barn, and he spent many hours in the company of Polly Duncan, head librarian. As for the cats, they were a pair of pampered Siamese with extraordinary intelligence and epicurean tastes in food.

The barn, octagonal in shape and a hundred years old, had a fieldstone foundation two feet thick and as high as Qwilleran's head. Framing of twelve-by-twelve timbers rose to a roof three stories overhead. Once upon a time a wagonload of apples could go through the barn door, and bushels of apples were stored in the lofts. Now the interior was a series of balconies connected by ramps, surrounding a central cube of pristine white. There were fireplaces on three sides, and three cylindrical white flues rose to the octagonal roof. It was a lofty perch for cats who enjoyed high places. As for the spiraling ramps, the Siamese considered them an indoor race track, and they could do the hundred-meter dash in half the time required by a human athlete.

One evening in early summer Qwilleran and his two friends had just returned from a brief vacation on Breakfast Island, and he was reading aloud to them when the telephone rang. He excused himself and went to the phone on the writing desk.

"I got it, Qwill!" shouted an excited voice. "I got the job!"

"Congratulations, Dwight! I want to hear about it. Where are you?"

"At the theatre. We've just had a board meeting."

"Come on over. The gate's open."

The home of the Pickax Theatre Club had been carved out of the former Klingenschoen mansion on the Park Circle. Behind the theatre a fenced parking lot had a gate leading to a patch of dense evergreen woods that Qwilleran called the Black Forest. It was a buffer between the traffic on the Park Circle and the apple barn. Within minutes Dwight's car had negotiated the rough track through the woods.

"Glad everything worked out so well," Qwilleran said in greeting. "How about a glass of wine to celebrate?"

"Just a soft drink," said the young man. "I'm so high on good news that anything stronger would launch me into space. How do you like my new facade?" He stroked his smooth chin. "My new bosses don't go for beards. I feel suddenly naked. How would you feel without your moustache?"

"Destitute," Qwilleran said truthfully. His moustache was more than a facial adornment, more than a trademark at the top of the "Qwill Pen" column.

As Qwilleran carried the tray of drinks and snacks into the lounge area, Dwight pointed to the top of the fireplace cube. "I see you've got your ducks all in a row."

"I haven't heard that expression since the Army. How do you like them? They're hand-painted, hand-carved decoys from Oregon. Polly brought them back from her vacation."

"What did she think about Oregon? I hear it's a beautiful state."

"I doubt that she saw much of the landscape," Qwilleran said. "She was visiting a former college roommate, who's now a residential architect, and it seems they spent the whole time designing a house for Polly. She's going to build on a couple of acres at the east end of my orchard."

"I thought she wanted to keep her apartment on Goodwinter Boulevard."

"That was her original idea when they started converting the boulevard into a college campus. She thought she'd enjoy living among students. But when they began paving gardens for parking lots, she changed her mind."

"They should've made one large parking lot at the entrance and kept a grassy look on campus," Dwight said.

"God forbid anyone would have to walk a block from his car, Dwight. Rural communities live on wheels. Only city types like you and me know how to use their legs. . . . But tell me about the new job."

Dwight Somers, a publicity man from Down Below, had come north to work for a prosperous Moose County developer. Unfortunately the job fizzled, and the community that had benefited from his creativity and vitality was in fear of losing him.

"Okay," he began. "I told you I was having an interview with a PR firm in Lockmaster, didn't I? They want me to open a branch for them in Pickax, and we have a highly promising client for starters. Do you know Floyd Trevelyan in Sawdust City?"

He referred to an industrial town that was considered unprogressive and undesirable by Pickax standards, although it had a larger population and a thriving economy.

"I'm not acquainted with anyone in Sawdust

City," Qwilleran said, "but I know the phone book is full of Trevelyans. This barn was part of the Trevelyan Apple Orchard a hundred years ago."

"Well, this guy is president of the Lumbertown Credit Union in Sawdust City—good name, what?—and it's a really going institution. He and his family have a big house in West Middle Hummock with acreage. He also happens to be a railroad nut, and he has a model train layout that's worth half a mil. That's not all! Now he's into rolling stock—a steam locomotive and some old passenger cars. He intends to use them for charter excursions."

"What will he use for tracks?"

"The old SC&L Line still hauls slow freight up from Down Below. No problem there. Floyd's idea is to rent his train out for dinners, cocktail parties, business functions, weddings, tourist excursions—whatever. We're calling it the Lumbertown Party Train. The civic leaders in Sawdust City are hot for tourism, like everyone else around here, and they've given him a few perks—helped him get a liquor license, for one thing."

"Does he expect to make any money on this venture?" Qwilleran asked, remembering the dashed hopes of Dwight's previous employer.

"Well, in Floyd's case it's a hobby or maybe a calculated loss for tax purposes. He's spent a mint on equipment, but he seems to have it to spend, so why not? It all started when he stum-

bled across this SC&L engine in mothballs.
Steam locomotives are almost impossible to
find, he says, and here was one with local connections. A great find! He's spent hundreds of
thousands to restore it, starting with the removal of pigeon droppings. After that he
bought a dining car, and then an Art Deco club
car, and then a private railcar that had belonged
to a textile magnate. The PV had fabulous ap-
pointments, but everything was in bad shape,
and he spent a fortune to renovate the three
cars. Amanda's Studio of Design supervised the
renovation. How's that for a plummy contract?
Maybe Amanda will retire now, and Fran
Brodie can take over."

"Is it old family money he's sinking into this
project?" Qwilleran asked. "I know there are
some well-heeled Trevelyans as well as some on
public assistance."

"No way! Floyd came up from a working
class branch of the Trevelyan clan, but he inherited upwardly mobile genes from his pioneer
ancestors. He started out as a carpenter and
parlayed his toolbox into the largest construction firm in the county. Luckily he got in on the
ground floor of the Moose County revival
when federal funds were pouring in."

"Do you mean to say that a builder in Sawdust City was doing more business than XYZ
Enterprises?" Qwilleran asked in astonishment.

"Believe it or not, XYZ didn't even exist
until Exbridge, Young and Zoller formed a syn-

dicate and bought out Trevelyan Construction. Floyd took their millions and opened the Lumbertown Credit Union. He was tired of the blue-collar image, and this move made him a white-collar VIP in his hometown—sort of a local hero. For offices he built a building that looks like an old-fashioned depot. The interior is paneled with narrow boards, highly varnished, and he even got a couple of old, uncomfortable waiting-room benches. To cap it all, he has model trains running around the lobby. The depositors love it! They call it the Choo-Choo Credit Union, and the president is affectionately called F.T. . . . How do you feel about model trains, Qwill?"

"At the risk of sounding un-American, I must say I never caught the fever. As a kid I received an oval track and four cars for Christmas. What I really wanted was a baseball mitt. After the cars went around the track six or eight times, I was a very bored first baseman. Let's assume that my whole life has been colored by that one disappointment. . . . Still, I wouldn't object to writing a column on toy trains, if your client will cooperate."

"We call them *model* trains," Dwight informed him. "The adult hobbyists outnumber the kids, if my statistics are accurate."

"I stand corrected," said Qwilleran, who had a journalist's respect for the right word.

"Do you realize, Qwill, that serious collectors will fight for vintage models? Floyd paid over a thousand dollars for a ten-inch locomotive in the original box."

"Would he be interested in an interview?"

"Well, he's not exactly comfortable with the media, but I'll coach him. Give me a couple of days, and then you can call him at the Lumbertown office. His home in West Middle Hummock is called The Roundhouse, and it's two miles beyond the fork, where Hummock Road splits off from Ittibittiwassee. You can't miss it. His mailbox is a locomotive. Don't use his address; he's antsy about theft. You should see his security system!"

"When does the Party Train make its debut?"

"In a couple of weeks. Three weeks max. What I'm planning is a blastoff that'll attract the best people in the county and get publicity around the state. How would you react to a trial run at $500 a ticket, with proceeds going to charity? Everything would be first-class: champagne dinner with Chateaubriand, fresh flowers, live music—"

Qwilleran interrupted. "Give the proceeds to the scholarship fund of the new college, and I'll buy two tickets. I'll also twist Arch's arm until he buys a couple . . . Refresh your drink, Dwight?"

"No, thanks. I'll coast along with what I have . . . Hey, these snacks are good! What are they? They look like dry dog food."

"A friend sent them from Down Below—her own invention. She calls them Kabibbles."

"She should package these and sell them."

As he spoke, two slinky fawn-colored bodies with brown extremities were creeping silently toward the coffee table and the bowl of Kabibbles. Eyes that were celestial blue in daytime glistened like jet in the artificial light. Their concentration on their goal was absolute.

"No!" Qwilleran thundered, and they rose vertically on legs like springs before running away to contemplate their next maneuver. Their names were Koko and Yum Yum. The male, whose real name was Kao K'o Kung, had a lean, strong body with musculature that rippled beneath his silky fur; he also had a determination that was invincible. Yum Yum was daintier in size and deportment, but she knew how to get what she wanted.

"How did the cats like Breakfast Island?" Dwight asked.

"They don't care where they are," Qwilleran replied, "as long as they get three squares a day and a soft place to sleep."

"What's going to be done about the mess on Breakfast Island?"

"It hasn't been officially announced, but XYZ Enterprises will forfeit their equity in the resort, and the Klingenschoen Foundation will restore the south end of the island to its natural state. That includes reforestation and beach nourishment. Mother Nature is expected to do the rest."

"A major undertaking, if you ask me," said Dwight.

"But worth it."

"What about the Domino Inn and the other bed-and-breakfasts?"

"The plan is to have them function as youth hostels, elder hostels, and a summer campus for the new college. The islanders will continue to live in their secluded village, and the exclusive summer estates will have their taxes raised. . . . Now tell me about the theatre club, Dwight. What happened at the board meeting tonight?"

"We decided to go out on a limb and do a summer production for the first time. I'm recording secretary and always tape the minutes. Want to hear it?"

Dwight took a small recorder from his pocket and placed it on the coffee table. After a few seconds of fast-forwarding, familiar voices could be heard. Though distorted by the limitations of the device, they were recognizable: Larry Lanspeak, owner of the department store . . . Fran Brodie, interior designer . . . Scott Gippel, car dealer, who served as treasurer of the club . . . Dwight's own voice . . . and Junior Goodwinter, young managing editor of the newspaper.

LARRY: Now for new business. Considering the influx of tourists, should we do a summer play?

JUNIOR: The campers and fishermen and boaters have no place to go in the evening, except bars. Not even a movie house.

GIPPEL: I'm for giving it a shot. Let's grab some of those tourist dollars. Let's do a Broadway comedy with lots of belly laughs.

JUNIOR: Or a good mystery.

DWIGHT: Or a campy melodrama, like *Billy the Kid,* that'll get the audience booing the villain.

LARRY: Or a musical with a small cast, like *The Fantasticks.*

FRAN: I'd like to see us do *Midsummer Night's Dream.*

GIPPEL: You're nuts! That's Shakespeare!

LARRY: Yes, but it has comedy, romantic love, glamorous court scenes, and magic. What more can you ask?

JUNIOR: You can have a lot of fun with *Dream.* I played Puck in college.

LARRY: All the costumes for *Henry VIII* are in the basement. We could use them for the court scenes.

DWIGHT: *Thrift, thrift, Horatio!*

FRAN: How about using students for extras, as we did in *Henry?*

GIPPEL: Now you're talkin' turkey! All their friends and relatives will buy tickets. I say: Go for it. How many kids can we use?

FRAN: There's no limit to walk-ons. High-schoolers can play the lords and ladies, and junior high kids can do the fairies.

GIPPEL: *Fairies?* Are you kidding? You'd better make them little green men. Kids don't go for fairies. I've got three at home, and I know.

DWIGHT: Three little green men? Or three kids?

(Laughter)

FRAN: I like the idea of little green men! Let's do it! I'd love to direct.

Dwight turned off the recorder. "What do you think of it, Qwill?"

"Sounds okay to me, but Polly will have a fit if you convert Shakespeare's fairies into extraterrestrials. She's a purist."

"That detail isn't finalized, but we're going ahead with auditions. Off the record, we're precasting Junior as Puck and the Lanspeaks as the duke and his bride. They'll also double as Oberon and Titania. They've done the roles before, and we've got to take a few shortcuts if we want the show on the boards before Labor Day."

It was eleven o'clock, and the Siamese had come stalking back into the room. They stared pointedly at the visitor.

Suddenly he said, "Well, I'd better head for the hills. Thanks for everything."

"Glad your career has taken a propitious turn, Dwight."

"And that's not the only good news. I had a date with Hixie last night, and everything's coming up roses."

"You're lucky! She's great fun." It was an appropriate match. Hixie Rice was another transplant from Down Below, and she was in charge of public relations for the newspaper. Qwilleran put on a yellow baseball cap hanging near the kitchen door and accompanied his guest to his car. "We have an owl in the woods," he explained, "and if he sees a good head of hair, he might think it's a rabbit. I'm quoting Polly, the ornithology expert."

"Well, I'm safe," Dwight said, passing a hand over his thinning hair. He cocked his head to listen. "I can hear him hooting. Sounds like Morse code—long and short hoots."

As the happy young man drove away, Qwilleran watched the taillights bouncing through the ruts of the Black Forest and wondered what had happened to Hixie's previous heartthrob. He was a doctor. He owned a cabin cruiser. He had a beard. Qwilleran walked around the barn a few times before going indoors; it was pleasantly warm, with a soft breeze. He listened and counted.

"Whoo-o-o hoo hoo . . . hoo hoo hoo . . . whoo-o-o."

Qwilleran decided to call him Marconi and write a "Qwill Pen" column about owls. Fresh topics were in short supply in the summer. Sometimes the newspaper had to rerun his more popular columns, like the one on baseball and the one on cats.

When he went indoors, all was quiet. That was not normal. The Siamese should have been parading and demanding their nightly treat with ear-piercing yowls. Instead, they were assiduously washing their paws, whiskers, and ears, and the bowl on the coffee table was empty. Stuffed with Kabibbles, they staggered up the ramp to their apartment on the top balcony. Qwilleran, before he called it a day, wrote a thank-you note to a woman named Celia Robinson.

TWO

When Qwilleran wrote his thank-you note for the Kabibbles, he sat at his writing table in the library area—one side of the fireplace cube that was lined with bookshelves. For serious work there was a writing studio on the balcony, off-limits to the Siamese, but the bookish, friendly atmosphere of the library was more comfortable for writing notes and taking phone calls. For this brief letter to Celia Robinson he used a facetiously bombastic style that would send her into torrents of laughter. She laughed easily; it took very little to set the dear woman off.

Dear Celia,

I find it appropriate to pen an effusive expression of gratitude for the succulent delights that arrived today to tantalize my taste buds and heighten my spirit. Your Kabibbles are receiving rave reviews from connoisseurs in this northern bastion of gastronomy. I suggest you copyright the name and market them. You could become the Betty Crocker of the twenty-first century! Perhaps you would grant me the distribution franchise for Moose and Lockmaster counties. Let me know your new address so I can order Kabibbles in ten-pound sacks or twenty-gallon barrels.

Gratefully,
Q

No one in Pickax knew about Qwilleran's whimsical acquaintance with Celia Robinson, not even Polly Duncan—especially not Polly, who was inclined to resent the slightest intrusion on her territory. The cross-country acquaintance had begun when Junior Goodwinter's grandmother died suddenly in Florida. Through long-distance conversations with her next-door neighbor, Qwilleran conducted an investigation into the death, and he and Celia developed a chummy rapport. He called her his secret agent, and she called him Chief. He sent her boxes of chocolate-covered cherries and the paperback spy novels that she liked; she sent him homemade brownies. They had never met.

The case was closed now, but Qwilleran had an ulterior motive for continuing the connection: She enjoyed cooking. Fondly he envisioned her relocating in Pickax and catering meals for himself and the cats. It was not an improbability; she wanted to leave the retirement village in Florida. "Too many old people" was her complaint. Celia was only sixty-nine.

Qwilleran posted the letter in his rural mailbox the next morning, walking down the orchard wagon trail to the highway, Trevelyan Road. The trail was the length of a city block. It ran past the skeletons of neglected apple trees, between other trees planted by squirrels and birds in the last hundred years, alongside the remains of the old Trevelyan farmhouse that had burned down, and past the two acres where Polly would build her new house. After raising the red flag on the oversized mailbox, he took a few minutes to consider the construction site. The fieldstone foundation of the old house was barely visible in a field of waist-high weeds. An abandoned lilac bush was doing nicely on its own, having grown to the size of a two-story, three-bedroom house, and it still bloomed in season. When the wind direction was right, its fragrance wafted as far as the apple barn.

Polly wanted to preserve the old stone foundation—for what purpose she had not decided. She kept asking, "Shall I build in front of it, or behind it, or beyond it? I can't build on top of it."

Qwilleran had tried to make suggestions, but her questions were merely rhetorical; she was an independent person and had to make her own decisions. As head librarian she had a brilliant reputation. She was efficient and briskly decisive. She charmed the members of the library board, improved the collection, controlled the budget, coped with the quirks of an old library building, staged events, and solved the personal problems of her young assistants with kindness and common sense. In facing her own dilemmas, however, she melted into a puddle of bewilderment.

Returning from the mailbox, Qwilleran became aware of two pairs of blue eyes staring at him from an upper-level window of the barn. He waved to them and kept on walking— through the Black Forest to the Park Circle, with its important buildings and multi-lane traffic. The proximity of town and country was one of the attractions of living in a small city (population 3,000). On the perimeter of the Park Circle were two churches, the courthouse, the K Theatre, and a building resembling a Greek temple: the public library.

Qwilleran walked briskly up the stone steps of the library—steps rounded into gentle concavities by a century of feet. Now added to the feet of book-subscribers were the feet of video-borrowers, and Qwilleran doubted that the steps would last another half-century. In the main room he headed directly toward the stairs to the mezzanine, nodding pleasantly to the young clerks who greeted him as Mr. Q. They also glanced mischievously at each other, amused at the sight of the middle-aged friend of their middle-aged boss paying a call in broad daylight. The relationship between the head librarian and the richest man in the northeast-central United States was a subject of constant conjecture in Pickax.

Qwilleran bounced up the stairs, noting the familiar sight of Homer Tibbitt at one of the reading tables, surrounded by books and pamphlets. Although well up in his nineties, the county historian spent every morning at the library, pursuing some esoteric research project. Or perhaps he was avoiding his overly attentive wife, as the giggling clerks surmised. In her eighties, Rhoda Tibbitt could still drive, and she chauffeured her husband to and from his life's work.

Polly was seated in her glass-enclosed office in front of a deskful of paperwork. When she spoke, her serenely low-pitched voice gave Qwilleran a shudder of pleasure as it always did, no matter how often they met or how many hours they had spent together the evening before.

"Morning," he said with an intimate nuance.

He never used terms of endearment, except to Yum Yum, but he could infuse a two-syllable greeting with warmth and affection. He slid into a hard, varnished oak chair, library-style circa 1910.

Polly said, "You look especially vibrant this morning, dear."

"I'm a veritable fountain of news," he announced as he launched into his report on Dwight's new job, the Party Train, and the theatre club's decision to do *A Midsummer Night's Dream*. He avoided mentioning that the fairies might be updated. He even revealed Dwight's date with Hixie Rice as a kind of romantic milestone on the social scene. Outsiders might call it gossip, but in Pickax this was legitimate sharing of information. Good news, rumors, bad news, scandal, and other data somehow reached the library first, and Polly's assistant, Virginia Alstock, was tuned in to the Moose County grapevine for its dissemination.

Today Polly's reactions were subdued. She seemed preoccupied, glancing frequently at the stack of manuals on home building that occupied a corner of her desk.

The title on top of the pile was *How to Build a Better House for Less Money,* and he asked, "Are you making any progress with your house plans?"

"I don't know," she said with a world-weary sigh. "It's all so confusing. In Oregon, Susan did sketches for a one-story house that would integrate with the terrain. No basement. Heating equipment in a utility room next to the laundry. . . . But these books say that a two-story house is more economical to build and to heat, and it would give Bootsie a chance to run up and down stairs for exercise."

"Build a one-story house with a basement and let him run up and down the basement stairs," Qwilleran suggested with simple logic. Bootsie was the other male in Polly's life, a husky Siamese. He was grossly pampered, in Qwilleran's opinion.

"I'm not fond of basements. I've seen too many that leak," she objected. "I was thinking of a crawl space with good insulation. What do you think, Qwill?"

"You're asking the wrong person. I'm only a journalist; I leave the house building to the house builders. Why not line up a professional firm like XYZ Enterprises?"

"But it's so large and commercial, and I've lost respect for them since the fiasco on Breakfast Island. It's my belief that a small builder gives more personal attention to one's needs and ideas. Mrs. Alstock's in-laws in Black Creek hired a young man. He finished on schedule and very close to the estimated cost. We should encourage young people in the trades, don't you think? He works out of Sawdust City."

"Hmmm," Qwilleran mused, having heard that the Sawdusters were all roughnecks who threw bottles through tavern windows on Saturday nights. "What is his name?"

"He's a Trevelyan—another of those 'hairy Welshmen,' as they're called, but I have no objection to long hair and a shaggy beard if he does a good job."

"Want me to check him out for you? The paper has a stringer in Sawdust City."

"Well . . . thank you, Qwill, but . . . Mrs. Alstock is taking me to see her in-laws' house tomorrow night, and Mr. Trevelyan will be there. I'll have my sketches with me, and if he impresses me favorably—"

"Find out if he eyeballs the construction from the sketches," Qwilleran suggested, remembering the underground builder he had encountered in Mooseville.

"Oh, no! In Pickax the plans and specifications must be drawn up by an architect in order to obtain a building permit."

Changing the subject abruptly, Qwilleran said, "I'm keeping you from your work. How about dinner tonight at the Old Stone Mill?"

"I'd love to, dear, but I've called a special meeting of the library board. We'll have dinner at the hotel, then come back here to discuss the paving of the parking lot. We've had it out for bids."

Teasingly he said, "I hope your literary ladies enjoy the inevitable chicken pot pie and lemon sherbet, spelled 'sherbert' on the menu."

Polly smiled, recognizing his genial thrust at

the hotel's cuisine and the library's frugal allowance for board members' meals. "You're welcome to join us," she said coyly.

"No thanks, but why don't you get the board to budget a few dollars for cushions for these chairs?"

"Go away," she said affectionately, waving him out of her office. She was wearing the ring he had given her for Christmas—a fiery black opal rimmed with tiny diamonds. He knew that she was wearing it to impress the "literary ladies."

Leaving Polly's office, Qwilleran stopped to say hello to Homer Tibbitt. The old man's eyes were glazed after poring over his books, and he blinked a few times before he could recognize the face.

"Tell me, Homer. How can you sit on these hard chairs for so many hours?" Qwilleran asked.

"I bring an inflated cushion," said the historian. "Also a thermos of decaf, but don't tell Polly. The sign says: No food or beverages. I take my brown bag into the restroom every hour or so and have a swig."

Qwilleran nodded with understanding, knowing there was a shot of brandy in Homer's decaffeinated coffee. "How are you feeling these days?" The old man was wheezing audibly.

"I suffer the usual tweaks and twinges of advancing age, plus a touch of bronchitis from these dusty, mildewed records." He slapped his chest. "My tubes whistle. You can hear me all over the building. I'm trying to do a paper *(whistle)* on Moose County mines, 1850 to 1915."

"What do you know about the Trevelyan family?"

"They go back six generations, all descended from two brothers who came from Wales *(whistle)* to supervise the mines. Second generation built sawmills and founded Sawdust City." Mr. Tibbitt stopped for a coughing spell, and Qwilleran rushed to the water cooler for a cup of water. "Sorry about that," the old man apologized when the coughing was relieved. "Now, where was I?"

"Sawdust City," Qwilleran reminded him. "The Trevelyans."

"Believe it or not, that ugly little town was the county seat originally, when Pickax was only a bump in the road. When they switched government functions to Pickax because of *(whistle)* its central location, the Sawdusters rose up in arms and tried to secede from Moose County. All they accomplished was an independent school system."

"Do you know a Floyd Trevelyan, Homer? He's president of the Lumbertown Credit Union in Sawdust City."

"Can't say that I do. We Pickaxians are unmitigated snobs, you know. Are you aware you're living *(whistle)* in the old Trevelyan orchard? No one would touch the property for generations until you came along—a greenhorn from Down Below, heh heh heh."

"Because of snobbery?" Qwilleran asked.

"Because of the Trevelyan curse," the historian corrected him. "The apple trees withered, the farmhouse was struck by lightning, and the farmer hanged himself."

"Who pronounced the curse?"

"Nobody knows."

"For your information, Homer, Polly is building a house where the farmhouse used to be."

"Well, don't tell her *(whistle)* what I said."

"That's all right. She's not superstitious."

"Just the same, don't tell her," the old man warned.

After leaving the library, Qwilleran continued his walk downtown, making a few unscheduled visits for the purpose of sharing information:

To Scottie's Men's Store to look at summer shirts. Nothing caught his fancy, but he chatted with the proprietor and told him about the Party Train.

To Edd's Editions, a shop specializing in pre-owned books from estate libraries. Eddington Smith was interested to hear about the Party Train because he had several books on railroads. Qwilleran bought one on the digging of the Panama Canal.

To the office of the newspaper which, for

strange reasons, was named the *Moose County Something*. His longtime friend from Down Below, Arch Riker, was publisher and editor-in-chief and was pleased to hear about the Party Train.

To Toodle's Market to buy six ounces of sliced roast beef from the deli counter and two packages of macaroni and cheese from the frozen food chest. In the checkout line he stood behind Wally Toddwhistle's mother, who made costumes for the theatre club. She asked if he'd heard about *A Midsummer Night's Dream*, and he asked if she'd heard about the Party Train.

Returning to the barn, he found it good to be greeted by importunate yowls and waving tails, even though he knew the cats' real motive. He diced roast beef for them and heated both packages of macaroni and cheese for himself. Dicing, thawing, and pressing the button on the computerized coffeemaker were his only kitchen skills.

After dinner the three of them gravitated to the library area for a session of reading. Qwilleran's growing collection of old books was organized according to category: biography, classic fiction, drama, and so forth. He added his new purchase to the history shelf. Yum Yum waited patiently for him to sit down and make a lap; Koko was alert and awaiting his cue.

"Book! Book!" It was one of several words understood by Kao K'o Kung, among them:

treat, brush, leash, and NO! The cat surveyed the expanse of shelving before jumping up and teetering on the edge of the classic fiction collection. He sniffed the bindings critically, then pawed *Swiss Family Robinson* with enthusiasm.

A curious choice, Qwilleran thought. He realized it was mere coincidence but a provocative one, Koko having a unique sense of association. Yet, the connection between an 1813 Swiss novel and the inventor of Kabibbles was too absurd even for a willing believer like Qwilleran.

He sprawled in his favorite lounge chair and propped his feet on the ottoman. Yum Yum hopped lightly into his lap and turned around three times counterclockwise before settling down. Koko took his usual position on the arm of the chair, sitting tall.

Qwilleran opened the book, which he had bought for its illustrations, and said, "This is a book primarily for young people but is suitable for cats of any age. There are chapters on . . . let's see . . . whales, turtles, ostriches, and bears. You'll like it. Chapter One: *Shipwrecked and Alone.*"

Yum Yum was the first one to sigh and close her eyes; then Koko started swaying drowsily; finally Qwilleran, mesmerized by the sound of his own voice, read himself to sleep.

One afternoon, before his appointment with the president of the Lumbertown Credit Union,

Qwilleran drove to Sawdust City out of sheer curiosity. The town itself might be material for the "Qwill Pen" column. He knew only that it was the industrial hub of the county, straddling the mouth of the Ittibittiwassee River, where pollution was an ongoing problem. Although freight trains made regular runs to points Down Below, most manufactures were shipped by truck. Their tires constantly tracked mud from unpaved side streets onto the highway, giving the town the nickname of Mudville. Nevertheless, there was a healthy job market there, and Sawdust City was home to 5,000 working-class residents whose soccer team regularly trounced others in the county.

Outside the town limits Qwilleran noticed an athletic field with a running track, one softball diamond, and three soccer fields with goal nets—no tennis courts. There was also an extensive consolidated school complex with its own football stadium.

On Main Street there was plenty of downtown traffic as well as cafés, gas stations, churches, a storefront library, gun shops, pawnbrokers, apparel shops with racks of clothing on the sidewalk, taverns, and a video store. The Lumbertown Credit Union occupied a new version of an old depot, while the real railway station was a neglected relic on the outskirts of town, surrounded by tracks, boxcars, trucks, and warehouses. The residential neighborhoods were notable for their neat lawns, swarms of

schoolchildren on summer vacation, basketball
hoops, barbecues, and satellite saucers. In every
sense it was a thriving town. Whether it would
be material for the "Qwill Pen" was question-
able. Qwilleran knew only that Sawdust City
stood in sharp contrast to West Middle Hummock, where the Lumbertown president lived.
This was the most fashionable of the Hummocks with the largest estates, owned by families like the Lanspeaks, the Wilmots, and—in
happier days—the Fitches. When Qwilleran set
out to interview Floyd Trevelyan his route lay
out Ittibittiwassee Road between stony pastures
and dark woods, past abandoned mines and
ghostlike shafthouses. After passing the Buck-
shot Mine, where he had suffered a nasty tum-
ble from his bike, he reached a fork in the road.
Ahead was Indian Village, a more or less
swanky complex of apartments and condomini-
ums. Hummock Road branched off to the left,
forming a triangular meadow where car-poolers
left their vehicles. Share-the-ride had been a
Moose County custom long before the first energy crisis; it was the neighborly thing to do
and an opportunity to keep abreast of rumors.
Beyond the meadow the road passed a blighted
hamlet or two before emerging in a landscape
of knobby hills, bucolic vistas, architect-designed
farmhouses, and no utility poles. All cables
were underground, and the road curved to
avoid cutting down ancient trees.

Then there was a rural mailbox shaped like a

locomotive and a sign hanging between railroad ties announcing "The Roundhouse." There was nothing round about the residence that perched on a hill at the end of the drive. It was a long, low contemporary building with wide overhangs and large chimneys—almost brutal in its boldness—and the rough cedar exterior was stained a gloomy brownish-green.

Qwilleran parked at the foot of a terraced walkway and climbed wide steps formed from railroad ties, then rang the doorbell and waited in the usual state of suspense: Would this interview make a great story? Or would it be a waste of his time?

The man who came to the door, wearing crumpled shorts and a tank top, was obviously one of the "hairy Welshmen" for whom Sawdust City was famous. Although seriously balding toward the brow, his head was rimmed with hair that was black and bushy, and although his jutting jaw was clean-shaven, his arms and legs were thickly furred. So also was his back, Qwilleran discovered upon following him into the foyer.

His initial greeting had been curt. "You from the paper?"

"Jim Qwilleran. Dwight Somers tells me you have a railroad empire on the premises."

"Downstairs. Want a shot or a beer?"

"Not right now, thanks. Let's have a look at the trains first. I'm completely ignorant about model railroading, so this visit will be an education." Following the collector toward a broad staircase to the lower level, Qwilleran quickly appraised the main floor: architecturally impressive, poorly furnished. On the way downstairs he tossed off a few warm-up questions: How long have you been collecting? How did you get started? Do you still have your first train?

The answers were as vapid as the queries: "Long time . . . Dunno . . . Yep."

The staircase opened into a large light room with glass walls overlooking a paved patio and grassy hillside. The opposite wall formed a background for a table-height diorama of landscape and cityscape. There were buildings, roadways, rivers, hills, and a complexity of train tracks running through towns, up grades, across bridges, and around curves. A passenger train waited at a depot; a freight train had been shunted to a siding; the nose of a locomotive could be seen in the mouth of a tunnel.

"How many trains do you have?" Qwilleran asked, producing a pocket tape recorder.

"Six trains. Thousand feet of track." The hobbyist started toying with a bank of controls at the front edge of the layout, and the scene was instantly illuminated: the headlight of the locomotive in the tunnel, the interior of the passenger coaches, and all street lights and railway signals. Then the trains began to move, slowly at first, and gradually picking up speed. One train stopped to let another pass. A locomotive chugged around a curve, with white smoke pouring from its smokestack. It blew its whistle as it approached a grade crossing and stopped at the station with a hiss of steam.

Qwilleran was impressed but said coolly, "Quite realistic!"

An engine pulled cars up a grade to cross a bridge while another passed underneath. Trains backed up as cars were coupled. A train of boxcars, tank cars, and gondolas stopped to give right-of-way to a diesel speeding through with passenger coaches and an observation car.

"Watch 'em take those curves," Trevelyan said proudly. He operated the remote controls with practiced skill, switching tracks, unloading coal from hopper cars, and dumping logs from a flatcar. In a freight yard with seven parallel tracks he had a switch engine shifting boxcars. "You hafta be quick to figure how fast they go, what route to take and which turnouts to switch. . . . Wanna try it?"

"And derail the whole railroad? No thanks," Qwilleran said. "Did you play with trains when you were a kid?"

"Me? Nah, my folks were too poor. But I had the real thing in the backyard. Our house, it was next to the track, and I knew every train schedule and all the crews. The engineers, they always clanged their bell and waved at me. Man! Did I feel like a big shot! Saturdays I'd go down to the yard and watch 'em switchin'." I wanted to stow away in a boxcar, but I knew my pop would lick the devil outa me."

"I suppose you wanted to grow up to be an engineer," Qwilleran said.

"Funny thing, I wanted to be a crossin' guard and sit in a little shack high up, lookin' down the tracks and workin' the gate. That's a kid for you!"

Above the confusion of mechanical noises in front of him, Qwilleran heard an elevator door open at the far end of the room and turned to see a frail woman in an electric wheelchair coming hesitantly in their direction. Although she was in Trevelyan's line of vision, he ignored her. He was saying, "There was four of us kids. Pop worked in the plastic plant till the chemicals killed 'im. I took Vocational in school. English and that kinda stuff, you could shove it! I could build things and tinker with motors, so who needed English? Summers I got jobs with builders. Finally got to be a contractor myself, licensed and all that."

The woman in the wheelchair was fixing her gaze eagerly on Qwilleran, and he mumbled a polite good-afternoon.

In a faltering voice she said, "You're Mr. Q. I see your picture in the paper all the time."

It was the kind of ambiguous comment that beggared reply, but he bowed courteously.

Trevelyan went on talking. "Like I said, I went as far as I could go with model trains. I'm into somethin' bigger now. Did Dwight tell you we're gonna—"

The woman interrupted shrilly. "My pop was an engineer!"

The man scowled and waved her away with an impatient hand. Obediently she wheeled back to the elevator, leaving Qwilleran to wonder who she might be. Her age was difficult to guess, her face and figure being ravaged by some kind of disease.

The trains were still running and performing their automatic ballet, but Qwilleran had all the information he could use and had even learned some railroad terms:

Roundhouse: a round building where locomotives were serviced in the Steam Era
Hog: locomotive
Hoghead: engineer
Wildcat: a runaway locomotive
Consist: a train of cars (accent on first syllable)
Gandy dancer: member of a section gang repairing rails
Whittling: taking a curve at high speed and braking the wheels
Rule G: the SC&L rule against drinking

Trevelyan said, "We don't worry about Rule G around this man's railroad yard. How's about wettin' your whistle?" He opened the door to a well-stocked bar. "Whatever you want, we got it."

"What are you drinking?" Qwilleran asked.

"Whiskey and soda."

"I'll take the same without the whiskey."

His host gave him an incredulous glance, then shook his head as he poured plain soda. They carried their glasses outdoors and sat on the patio while the railroad buff talked about the Lumbertown Party Train and the $500 tickets.

"How many can you seat in the dining car?" Qwilleran asked.

"Thirty-six at a shot. We figure to have a double shift, two o'clock and six o'clock. We figure we can sell out."

"How long will the ride last?"

"We figure we can kill three hours on the rails, round trip, with a layover at Flapjack."

"How did you go about buying your rolling stock?"

"Went to train museums, read PV magazines, answered ads."

"PV meaning . . . ?"

"Private varnish—all about private railroads. But I found my hog in a scrapyard in Sawdust City. She was a mess! I almost cried. As soon as those SC&L sharpies saw I was hooked, they upped the price outasight. I didn't care. I hadda have that baby! Spent another bundle to fix 'er up. Diesels—you can have 'em. Steam is where it's at—for me anyway."

"What's the big attraction?"

The collector shrugged. "A hog's nothin' but a firebox and a big boiler on wheels, but what a sight when she rolls! Raw power! My Engine No. 9 is a 4-6-2."

"You'll have to explain that," Qwilleran said.

Without a word Trevelyan went into the train room and returned with a framed photo of No. 9. "Four small wheels in front keep the engine on the rails. The six big babies with piston rods are the drivin' wheels; they deliver the power. The two in back hold up the firebox and the engineer's cab. Dwight tells me you signed up for the first run. Tell him to show you through my PV; it's a palace on wheels! . . . How long did you know Dwight?"

"Ever since he arrived from Down Below. He's a real pro—knows his job—good personality."

"Yeah, nice fella . . . How come he isn't married?"

"I don't know. Why don't you ask him?" Qwilleran replied in a genial tone that masked his annoyance at the prying question. Then he changed the subject. "There's a town south of Pickax called Wildcat, and I often wondered why. Any railroad connection?"

"Sure is! A runaway train was wrecked on the trestle bridge there in 1908—worst wreck ever! Old railroaders still talk about it."

"Are their recollections being recorded?" Qwilleran asked. "Is there a railroad library in

Sawdust City? Are any old engineers still living?" He was feeling an old familiar urge. With a little research and some oral histories from retired railroad personnel, plus stories handed down in their families, he could write a book! It would capture the horror of train wrecks as well as the nostalgia of the Steam Era when trains were the glamorous mode of transportation and locomotive engineers were the folk heroes. Homer Tibbitt, who had grown up on a farm, still remembered the haunting sound of a steam whistle in the middle of the night. He said it had filled him with loneliness and nameless desires. He doubted that it could be equaled today by the honking of a diesel, or the roar of a jet, or the whining tires of an eighteen-wheeler on a freeway.

"Ready for another drink?" the host asked. "I am."

Qwilleran declined, saying he had to meet a newspaper deadline, but on his way out of the house he asked casually, "Do you happen to know a Trevelyan who's a house builder?"

"My son," was the prompt reply. "Just starting out on his own."

"Does he know his stuff? A friend of mine is thinking of hiring him."

"Sure, he's a whizbang! Learned the trade from me. I taught him the whole works. I said to both my kids: The trick is to start early and work hard. That's what I did."

"You have another son?"

"A girl. She took bookkeepin' in high school. Works in my office now."

Strange family situation, Qwilleran thought as he drove away from The Roundhouse. There was the unkempt president of a successful family business. Then there was the undistinguished furniture in a pretentious house. And how about the shabbily treated woman in a state-of-the-art wheelchair? Who was she? She seemed too old to be his wife, too young to be his mother. Was she a poor relative or former housekeeper living on his charity? In any case, the man should have made some sort of introduction or at least acknowledged her presence. The financial success that had vaulted him from Sawdust City to West Middle Hummock had hardly polished his rough edges.

On the way home Qwilleran stopped at Toodles' Market for a frozen dinner and six ounces of sliced turkey breast. He was not surprised when Yum Yum met him at the kitchen door, slinking flirtatiously, one dainty forepaw in front of the other.

"There she is! Miss Cat America!" he said. "Where's your sidekick? Where's Koko?"

The other cat came running, and the two of them sang for their supper—a duet of baritone yowls and coloratura trills, the latter more like shrieks. After Qwilleran had diced their favorite treat and arranged it on their favorite plate, Koko made a dive for it, but Yum Yum looked at the plate sourly and veered away with low-ered head.

Qwilleran was alarmed. Was she ill? Had she found a bug and eaten it? Was it a hair ball? Had she swallowed a rubber band? He picked her up gently and asked, "What's wrong with my little sweetheart?" She looked at him with large eyes filled with reproach.

Meanwhile, Koko had polished off two-thirds of the repast, leaving the usual one-third for his partner. Qwilleran, with Yum Yum still in his arms, picked up the plate and placed it on the kitchen counter. Immediately she squirmed from his grasp, landed on the counter, and de-voured the turkey.

"Cats!" he muttered. "They drive you crazy!"

THREE

Qwilleran wrote a thousand words about Floyd Trevelyan's model trains and walked downtown to the office of the *Moose County Something* to file his copy. Junior Goodwinter had a managing editor's ability to read at the rate of fifty words a second, and he scanned the "Qwill Pen" copy in its entirety before Qwilleran could pour himself a cup of coffee.

"You seem pretty enthusiastic about this guy's trains," the editor said.

"The trick is to sound that way whether you are or not," Qwilleran retorted. "I like to increase the reader's pulse beat. . . . Actually, I was impressed by the train layout but not enthusiastic."

"How about putting some of your fake enthusiasm into an extra assignment?"

"Like what?"

"You know, of course," Junior began, "that the club is doing *Midsummer Night's Dream.* We want to run a short piece on each of the leads—about eight inches with a head shot. It's not supposed to be a blurb for the play or a bio of the actor; it's a miniature think-piece on the actor's perception of both the role and the theme of the play."

"All that in eight inches?"

"Only you can do it, Qwill. Your style is concise and pithy. What's more, your readers devour anything and everything you write, and you'll get a by-line on each piece—also free coffee for life."

Junior was wheedling him, and Qwilleran was succumbing to the flattery. "How many pieces would there be?"

"Nine or ten. Since you live behind the theatre, it'll be easy to drop in during rehearsal and catch the actors on their break. We'll alert them to start thinking about it. Someone like Derek Cuttlebrink does more thinking about his costume than about the essence of his role."

"How is he cast?"

"He's doing Nick Bottom, the weaver."

"That's a good one for him. He'll enjoy hee-hawing like a donkey."

"He'll be a howl! As soon as he walks on stage he'll bring down the house."

Derek, a resident of Wildcat, was a waiter at the Old Stone Mill. With his outgoing personality, engaging candor, and impressive height (six-feet-eight, going on nine) he was a favorite with restaurant diners, theatregoers, and impressionable young women.

"When do you want to start the series?" Qwilleran asked.

"Soonest. We're rehearsing five nights a week. . . . And say! Do you keep in touch with that Chicago heiress you brought over from Breakfast Island?"

"I didn't bring her over; she happened to be on the same boat," Qwilleran said tartly. "Why do you ask?"

"Well, she's joined the club, and she's helping with costumes. She has some good ideas."

That's appropriate, Qwilleran thought. Her own wardrobe was straight out of *Arabian Nights*.

"Also," Junior went on with relish, "she and Derek are hitting it off like Romeo and Juliet. If it's true that she has an annual income of $500,000, Derek's on the right track for once in his life."

Qwilleran huffed into his moustache. "Don't place any bets. In my opinion, she's a mighty flighty young woman. . . . See you at rehearsal."

"Before you leave the building," Junior called

after him, "our esteemed editor-in-chief wants to see you."

Arch Riker had the florid complexion and paunchy figure of a veteran journalist who has been a deskman throughout his career and has attended too many press luncheons. When Qwilleran appeared in the doorway, he was sitting in his high-back executive chair and swiveling in deep thought. "Come in. Come in," he said, beckoning. "Help yourself to coffee."

"Thanks. I haven't had one for the last three minutes. What's up, Arch?"

"Good news! . . . Sit down . . . After we ran our editorial on the Lumbertown Party Train, all tickets for the kickoff sold out, for both sittings! At $500 a ticket, that's pretty good for a county in the boonies. It was a stroke of genius, of course, to earmark the proceeds for college scholarships."

"The charity angle was Dwight Somers's idea, not that of the train owner," Qwilleran said. "Trevelyan doesn't strike me as a great philanthropist."

"Dwight just called and suggested we run a profile on the guy," Riker said. "What say you?"

"I've just handed in a column on his personal collection of model trains, and I think that's enough for now."

"I agree. We can cover the actual event from the social angle. . . . So you met Floyd-boy! What's he like?"

"Not your average bank president. He's a rough-hewn, self-made man who started as a carpenter. He's sunk a fortune in his Party Train, and his model collection is incredible! What makes a guy want to own more, bigger, and better than anyone else? I've never understood the urge to collect. You never got bitten by the bug either, did you?"

"Once!" Riker admitted. "When I was married to an antique collector, I collected antique tin like a madman. It's strange how suddenly I lost interest when wife, house, and cats went down the drain, *k-chug!*"

Qwilleran nodded solemnly, remembering his own bitter past, when he himself almost went *k-chug!*

His friend was in a talkative mood. "Mildred wants me to start another collection of something, so it'll be easier to buy me Christmas presents. I tell her I don't need Christmas presents. Every day in my life is Christmas since we took the plunge. . . . Qwill, why don't you and Polly—"

Qwilleran interrupted. "Don't—start—that—again, Archibald!"

"Okay, okay. At least you two will be within whistling distance when she builds her house. How's it coming?"

"She's hired the son of Floyd Trevelyan to build it. He's based in Mudville. His father says he's good."

"What else do you expect a parent to say?"

Riker remarked caustically. "Personally, I'd think twice before hiring a Sawduster to fix a leaky faucet!"

"Well . . . you know Polly . . . when she makes up her mind!"

About two weeks later, on a Sunday afternoon, Qwilleran and Polly drove to Sawdust City and met Arch and Mildred Riker on the railway platform. Well-dressed patrons were arriving from all parts of the county, and curious Sawdusters watched as the strangers' cars were whisked away and parked by young men in red jumpsuits. It was the first valet parking in the history of Mudville. The weather was warm enough for the women to wear sheer summer dresses and cool enough for the men to wear light blazers. The one exception was Whannell MacWhannell of Pickax, sweltering in his pleated all-wool kilt and full Scottish regalia.

Surprisingly, the Chicago heiress was there with the waiter from the Old Stone Mill, and Riker said, "Derek must have been getting some good tips lately."

Qwilleran said, "Last week I saw him buying her a hot dog at Lois's. This must be her turn to treat."

Today, as always, she was theatrically dressed—the only woman wearing a hat. The high-crowned straw wound with yards of veiling and accented with a cabbage rose was vintage Edwardian. Furthermore, she was incredibly thin by Moose County standards. Polly, who wore size sixteen, guessed her size to be a four, or even a two.

Also attracting attention was a young woman in a pantsuit. In Moose County the custom was skirts-on-Sunday, but this eye-catching beauty in a well-cut summer pantsuit made all the women in skirts look dowdy. She was with Floyd Trevelyan. He himself was well groomed and properly dressed for the occasion. Was she his wife? His daughter? They were not mingling with the crowd.

Newspaper photographers and a video cameraman added excitement, and a brass band was blaring numbers like "Chattanooga Choo Choo" and "Hot Time in the Old Town Tonight." Riker recognized the trombone player, who worked in the circulation department of the *Moose County Something*.

Polly said, "I do hope they're not going on the train with us."

Commemorative programs had been handed to the passengers waiting on the platform, and Mildred said, "Can you believe this? They brought the crew out of retirement for this historic run. The engineer is eighty-two; the brakeman is seventy-six; the fireman is sixty-nine— all veterans of SC&L."

Riker said, "I hope I can shovel coal when I'm sixty-nine."

"Dear, you couldn't even shovel snow last winter," his wife said sweetly.

"Do you suppose anyone had the foresight to check the engineer's vision and blood pressure? Has the fireman had an EKG recently? Will there be a doctor on the train?"

"Where's the hog?" Qwilleran asked, exhibiting his knowledge of railroad slang.

There had been no sign of the locomotive, except for puffs of steam rising from behind a warehouse. Then abruptly the music stopped, and the brasses sounded a fanfare. As the chatter on the platform faded away, No. 9 came puffing and whistling around a curve. The crowd cheered, and the band struck up "Casey Jones."

Old No. 9 was a magnificent piece of machinery, towering above the passengers on the platform. Its noble nose had a giant headlight; the black hulk and brass fittings glistened in the sunlight; the piston rods were marvels of mechanical magic as they stroked the huge driving wheels; even the cowcatcher was impressive. Leaning from the cab and waving at the waiting crowd was an aging engineer with tufts of white hair showing beneath his denim cap. He was beaming with pride.

Mildred, who had an artist's eye, called the locomotive a masterpiece of sensitive beauty and brute strength. "No wonder they called it the Great Iron Horse!"

When the freshly painted coaches came around the bend, her husband said, "They're still the same old moldy, muddy green."

"That's a perfectly acceptable color," Mildred

said. "I can mix it on my palette with chrome oxide green and cadmium red deep, with a little burnt umber to muddy it."

Dwight Somers, overhearing the conversation, informed them that the traditional Pullman green was designed to hide mud and soot.

"What do you know about the engineer?" Polly asked.

"He was an SC&L hoghead for fifty years. Many times his skill and bravery saved lives, and he only jumped once. He'd tell his fireman to jump, but Ozzie Penn was like the skipper who stays with his ship, braving it out."

"That's comforting to know," Riker said. "I trust they gave him a gold watch when he retired."

Then the conductor swung down the steps of the first car and shouted "All abo-o-oard!"

Qwilleran had reserved a table for four in the center of the dining car, where woodwork gleamed with varnish, tablecloths were blindingly white, and wine glasses sparkled. There was a hubbub of delight as the diners were seated. Then came one of those long, unexplained waits inflicted on train passengers. The wags in the crowd made wild conjectures: "They ran out of coal. . . . The fireman slipped a disc. . . . The chef forgot his knives. . . . They're sending out for more ice cubes."

Eventually the bell clanged, the whistle screamed and, as the train started to move, an army of waiters in white coats surged down the aisle with bottles of champagne. Everyone applauded.

Qwilleran, riding backward, saw Floyd Trevelyan at an end table with his attractive companion, and their body language was not that of a husband and wife or father and daughter. Also in his line of vision were Carol and Larry Lanspeak with a fresh-faced young woman and the bearded doctor who had been Hixie Rice's escort for the last six months. All four seemed inordinately happy, leading Qwilleran to mumble a question to Polly. She replied that the young woman was Dr. Diane, the Lanspeaks' daughter, who had escaped the medical madness Down Below and had returned to Moose County to go into practice with Dr. Herbert.

Polly said, "I'm transferring my medical records to Dr. Diane. I didn't like the man who replaced Dr. Melinda."

The train was rolling along at a comfortable excursion clip through typical Moose County landscape: fields of potatoes and pastures dotted with boulders and sheep.

The waiters kept pouring champagne, and Qwilleran produced a bag of snacks to accompany the drinks. "I'd like you to taste these," he said. "A friend of mine made them."

"Who?" Polly asked too quickly.

"A woman I know in Florida." He was purposely taunting her with incomplete information.

"They're very good," Riker said. "I'll have another handful."

"They're rather salty," Polly murmured.

Mildred, who wrote the food column for the newspaper, said they were actually croutons toasted with parmesan cheese, garlic salt, red pepper, and Worcestershire sauce.

Qwilleran said, "Koko and Yum Yum think they're the cat's meow."

The food expert nodded. "They detect the anchovy in the Worcestershire."

In a far corner of the car, out of the path of the bustling waiters, a white-haired accordionist was playing show tunes with the blank demeanor of one who has played the same repertoire at thousands of banquets.

Polly said, "His lack of passion is refreshing. We attended a Mozart concert in Lockmaster where the string ensemble was so passionate, they almost fell off their chairs."

"I watched their antics," Qwilleran said, "and forgot to listen to the music."

"It's the same way in art," Mildred declared. "The artist is becoming more important than the art. I blame the media."

"We get blamed for everything," Riker said.

They discussed the curriculum at the Moose County Community College: No music. No art. Plenty of English, accounting, data processing, office systems, and business management. Introductory courses in psychology, economics, history, sociology, etc. No cosmetology. No real estate. No tennis.

Polly said, "They're making giant strides

with the remodeling of the campus. The administration offices are staffed and operating, and I introduced myself to the president. Dr. Prelligate is a very interesting man."

"In what way?" Qwilleran asked bluntly.

"He combines a solid academic background with a most congenial personality. He's from Virginia and has that ingratiating Southern charm."

"I adore Southern men," Mildred said girlishly. "Is he married?"

"I don't believe so."

"But *you are!*" Riker informed his wife.

Polly had more to report. "Dr. Prelligate's staff has been feeding a dirty orange-and-white stray who looks exactly like Oh Jay. I phoned the Wilmots and learned that Oh Jay disappeared last November, right after they moved from Goodwinter Boulevard."

Riker said, "That's called 'psi trailing.' He's been on the road nine months, panhandling and living off the land! That's a fifteen-mile hike!"

"Well, the Wilmots said he can stay on campus," Polly said in conclusion, "and he's going to be the college mascot."

"And the school colors," Qwilleran guessed, "will be orange and dirty white."

The soup course was served: jellied beef consommé. It was rather salty, according to Polly. The Chateaubriand was an excellent cut of beef, and everyone agreed that neither the meat nor the chef could have come from Mudville.

Meanwhile, the cars rolled gently from side

to side, the whistle blew at grade crossings, and the conversation in the dining room was animated. Eventually the landscape became craggy, and there were dramatic views never seen from the highway. The tracks ran through the town of Wildcat, then down a steep grade to the Black Creek gorge, and across a high bridge. Now they were in Lockmaster County with its rolling hills and lush woods. By the time the cheesecake and coffee had been served, the train pulled into Flapjack, an early lumbercamp converted into a public recreation park.

The TV crew from Minneapolis was waiting. They wanted to video the train owner with his handsome companion on the observation platform of the private car, but Trevelyan vetoed that. He preferred to put on a striped railroad cap and lean out of the engineer's cab. In addition, there were sound bites of the Chicago heiress in her soufflé of a hat and Whannell MacWhannell in his kilt, each describing the thrill of riding behind old No. 9.

Polly told the portly Scot that he cut a magnificent figure in his tartan, and she wished Qwilleran would buy a kilt.

"Your man has the right build," Big Mac assured her, "and his mother was a Mackintosh, so he's entitled."

Riker explained with the authority of an old friend, "It's the idea of wearing a skirt that bugs Qwill, and you'll never convince him otherwise."

Qwilleran was relieved when Dwight Somers

put an end to the kilt claptrap by inviting them to see the private railcar. "The corporate jet of its day!" he said.

No one was prepared for its splendor: the richly upholstered wing chairs in the lounge, the dining table inlaid with exotic woods, the bedrooms with brass beds and marble lavatories. All of the woodwork was carved walnut, and the window transoms and light fixtures were Tiffany glass.

Dwight said, "The Lumbertown Party Train would be great for a wedding. Have the ceremony in the club car and the reception in the diner en route to Flapjack. Then uncouple the private car and leave the newlyweds on a siding for a week, with access to the golf course, riding stables, hiking trails, and so forth. At the end of the week the train returns with the wedding guests whooping it up in the club car, and they all huff-puff-puff back to Moose County and live happily ever after. . . . You should keep it in mind, Qwill," he added slyly.

Ignoring the remark, Qwilleran asked with mock innocence, "Is the woman with Floyd his bookkeeping daughter?"

"No, that's his knee-crossing secretary," Dwight said with a polite leer. "He met her in Texas while he was shopping for rolling stock."

"Was she a cheerleader?"

"Something like that" was the cryptic reply.

The brass bell of No. 9 clanged, and the commanding voice of the conductor swept the passengers back on board. As the train chugged north, waiters handed out souvenir whistles— long wooden tubes that duplicated the shrill scream of a steam locomotive. For a while the dining car reverberated with ear-splitting noise. Then the accordionist started playing requests. Mildred asked for "The Second Time Around." Qwilleran requested "Time After Time" for Polly. She might not know the lyrics, but the melody was unmistakably affectionate.

By the time the train rumbled through the outskirts of Pickax, the excitement was winding down, and conversation reverted to the usual: "Are you going to the boat races? . . . Have you tried the new restaurant in Mooseville? . . . How are your cats, Qwill?"

"After a lifetime of sharing a dinner plate with Koko," he replied, "Yum Yum suddenly demands separate dishes. I don't know what's going on in that little head."

Mildred said, "She's had her catsciousness raised."

Qwilleran groaned, Polly shuddered, and Arch said, "There are good puns and bad puns, and that's the worst I've ever heard. . . . Conductor! Throw this lady off the train!"

Then he asked Polly about her house.

"They're supposed to pour the concrete this week. Once the trenches are dug for the footings, they don't lose any time because a rainstorm could cause an earthslide. It's all so exciting! I've always lived in small, rented units, but now I'll have a guestroom and family room and two-car garage."

"Who's your builder?"

"The name on the contract is Edward P. Trevelyan. He's a big shaggy fellow with a full beard and a mop of black hair, and his grammar is atrocious! Incidentally, his father owns this train."

Finally No. 9 whistled at the grade crossings of Sawdust City, and the historic ride ended with a great hissing of steam. The valets in red jumpsuits ran for the parked cars, and the passengers drove back to Pickax, Mooseville, West Middle Hummock, and Purple Point. Qwilleran drove Polly home to Goodwinter Boulevard, now cluttered with paving equipment, piles of lumber, and other signs of campus renovation.

Polly said, "This has been a delightful afternoon, dear."

"Glad you enjoyed it. You look particularly attractive today."

"Thank you. I'm feeling more relaxed now that work on the house has actually started. It bothers me, though, that I can't understand the architect's plans with their abbreviations and arcane symbols. I'd appreciate it if you'd come up and look at the blueprints."

When Qwilleran finally left Polly's apartment, it was eleven p.m. and time for the nightly news. He tuned in the car radio in time to hear the WPKX announcer say, ". . . paid

$500 a ticket to ride behind the historic No. 9 steam locomotive on the SC&L Line, netting the Moose County Community College more than $16,000 for scholarships. Popular-priced excursions on the new Party Train will be announced, according to spokesperson Dwight Somers. . . . In local baseball, Lockmaster walloped Pickax nine to four, with the Safecrackers hitting two homers, one with bases loaded. . . . Next, the weather, after this late bulletin from Sawdust City: A surprise move by the state banking commission has padlocked the Lumbertown Credit Union, pending a state audit. No further details are available at this time."

FOUR

The morning after the train ride and the afterglow at Polly's apartment, nothing disturbed Qwilleran's deep sleep until the telephone rang at nine o'clock. He had slept through the yowling demands coming from the top balcony; he had slept through the rumble of the cement-mixing truck down the lane. He thought it was predawn when he said his sleepy hello into the bedside phone.

"What's the matter? Aren't you up yet?" Arch Riker shouted at him. "All hell's breaking loose! Didn't you hear the news from Sawdust City?"

"Only on the radio last night," Qwilleran replied with a lack of energy or interest. "Any more news?"

"Only that Floyd Trevelyan can't be reached for clarification. It sounds like a bust! It must be a major case to warrant surprise action like this—on a Sunday, for Pete's sake!"

Always grouchy before his first cup of coffee, Qwilleran replied with irritable sarcasm, "I can imagine a SWAT team of bookkeepers in business suits and knit ties, armed with portable computers, parachuting down on the Lumbertown office and kicking in the doors."

"You're not taking this seriously," the publisher rebuked him. "Consider the timing! It happened while the evening excursion was in progress. The Capitol gang evidently knew the schedule of the Party Train."

"Thanks to Dwight Somers's hype, everyone in three states knew the schedule."

"Anyway, we'll soon find out what it's all about. Junior is contacting the state banking commission, and Roger's on his way to Sawdust City, via Trevelyan's home in West Middle Hummock. We'll have a story for the front page, and if my hunches are right, it'll bump the Party Train to page three. . . . Talk to you later."

Now that Qwilleran was awake, more or less, he pressed the Start button on the coffeemaker and shuffled up the ramp to release the Siamese from their loft. As soon as he opened their door, they shot out of the room like feline cannonballs and streaked down to the kitchen. Qwilleran followed obediently.

"Yow-ow-ow!" Koko howled upon arriving at the feeding station and finding the plate empty.

"N-n-now!" echoed Yum Yum.

As Qwilleran opened a can of red salmon, crushed the bones with a fork, removed the black skin, and arranged it on *two plates,* he thought, Cats don't fight for their rights; they take them for granted. They have a right to be fed, watered, stroked on demand, and supplied with a lap and a clean commode . . . and if they don't get their rights, they quietly commit certain acts of civil disobedience. . . . Tyrants!

The two gobbling heads were so intent on their salmon that even the loud bell of the kitchen phone failed to disturb them.

This time the call was from Polly. "Qwill, did you hear about the state audit in Sawdust City? What do you think of the timing?"

"It looks fishy," he said, having gulped his first cup of coffee and geared up his usual cynicism. "Any crank can call the hotline to the state auditor's office and blow the whistle on a state-regulated institution. One of the universities was investigated for misuse of funds, you remember, and it was a false alarm—the work of an anonymous tipster. In Trevelyan's case, the tip could be a spiteful hoax perpetrated by a customer who was refused a loan."

"That's terrible!" she said.

"In a way," he said, "it's better to embarrass the management than to barge into the office with a semiautomatic and wipe out innocent depositors."

"Oh, Qwill! Things like that don't happen up here."

"Times are changing," he said ominously.

There was a pause on the line before she said softly, "I slept beautifully last night. It was a wonderfully relaxing day and evening—just what I needed. I've been worrying too much about my house."

"No need to worry, Polly. I'll keep an eye on the action at the end of the trail—when I go down to the mailbox—and I'll keep you informed."

"Thank you, dear. À bientôt!"

"À bientôt."

Qwilleran poured another mug of the blockbuster brew he called coffee and sat down at the telephone desk to call a number in Indian Village. "Dwight, this is Qwill," he said soberly.

"Oh, God! Oh, God!" the publicity man wailed. "What the hell's going on? I didn't hear the news until this morning, on the air. I called Floyd's number in West Middle Hummock, but he wasn't home."

"Who answered?"

"His wife. She sounded as if she didn't know

anything had happened, and I didn't want to be the messenger bringing bad news."

"I didn't meet his wife when I was there."

"She usually stays in her room, confined to a wheelchair. I don't know exactly what her problem is, but it's one of those new diseases with a multisyllabic name and no known cure. What a shame! All that money, and she can't enjoy it."

"Hmmm," Qwilleran murmured with a mixture of sympathy and curiosity. "So what happened? Could she tell you where he was or when he'd be back?"

"Well, she's quite frail and speaks in a weak voice that's hard to understand, but I gathered that he came home last night and went out again. Just between you and me, I think it's not unusual for him to stay out all night. Anyway, the nurse took the phone away from Mrs. T and told me not to upset her patient. So I asked to speak to the daughter, but she wasn't home either. The way it works: A nurse comes every morning, a companion every afternoon, and the daughter stays with her mother overnight."

"Sad situation," Qwilleran said. "Do you know anything about matters in Sawdust City?"

"No more than you do. You know, Qwill, I worked my tail off, getting that show on the road yesterday—"

"And you did a brilliant job, Dwight. Everything was perfectly coordinated."

"And then this bomb dropped! Talk about suspicious timing! It couldn't be purely coincidental."

"Is Floyd mixed up in politics?"

"Why do you ask?"

"Has he made any enemies in the state bureaucracy? Did he support the wrong candidate for the legislature?"

"Not that I know of. Maybe he distributed a little judicious graft here and there; he had no trouble getting a liquor license for the train, you know. But no. He's bored with politics. If it doesn't have steel wheels and run on steel tracks, he's not interested."

Qwilleran said, "I'm sorry about this for your sake, Dwight. Let's hope it's a false alarm."

"Yeah . . . well . . . it was a kick in the head for me, after I'd tried so hard to create a favorable image for Floyd *and* Lumbertown *and* Sawdust City."

"One question: Was Floyd a passenger on the six o'clock train?"

"No, he had to go home and take care of his wife—*he said!* I went on both runs, and I've had enough accordion music to last my lifetime!"

"Arch has the staff digging for facts, so it'll be in the first edition if anything develops. If you hear any rumors, feel free to bounce them off a sympathetic ear. And good luck, whatever the outcome, Dwight."

"Thanks for calling, Qwill. How about lunch later in the week when I've finished licking my wounds?"

When the *Moose County Something* appeared, the front page was not what Qwilleran had been led to expect. The Party Train had the banner headline:

JOY IN MUDVILLE
OLD NO. 9 ROLLS AGAIN!

The Lumbertown crisis was played down with only a stickful of type in a lower corner of the page: Sawdust C.U. Closed for Audit. Either there was no alarming development, or the editor had chosen not to throw the depositors into panic. That was small-town newspaper policy. Riker, with his background on large metropolitan dailies, preferred the eye-grabbing, heart-stopping, hair-raising headline; Junior Goodwinter, born and bred 400 miles north of everywhere, had other ideas, rooted in local custom. He always said, "Don't try to make bad news worse."

Qwilleran was pondering this viewpoint over a ham sandwich at Lois's Luncheonette when Roger MacGillivray blustered into the restaurant and flung himself into the booth where Qwilleran was reading the paper.

"I suppose you're wondering why we didn't play it up," the young reporter said.

"You're right. I did . . . Why?"

"Because there was nothing to report! Junior was stonewalled when he called the commission, and no one in Mudville would talk to me. Two state vehicles were parked behind the Lumbertown building, and there was a notice plastered on the front door with some legal gobbledy-gook, but the doors were locked front and back, and the dirty dogs completely ignored my knocking. Also they refused to answer when I called from a phone booth. Before I left, I got a shot of the building exterior with some old geezers standing on the sidewalk in a huddle. I also got a close-up of the official notice on the door, and another one of the license plate on a state car. . . . How's that for brilliant photojournalism?" he finished with a bitter laugh.

"They didn't use any photos," Qwilleran said, tapping his newspaper.

"I know, but you have to hand in *something,* just so they know you've been there."

"Could you see through the window?"

"I could see auditors at work stations, that's all. But then I talked to the old geezers and got some man-on-the-street stuff, which I phoned in, and which they didn't print."

"Maybe later," Qwilleran said encouragingly. "What did the old geezers say?"

"Well! It was an eye-opener, I thought. First of all, they like Floyd. He's the local boy who was captain of the high school football team, started to work as a carpenter, and made millions! They like the interest he pays. They like the electric trains in the lobby. They think this underhanded action on the part of vipers in the state capitol is unfair and probably in violation of the Constitution. They don't trust government agencies."

"Did you try to reach Floyd's secretary?"

"Yeah, but no luck. When I asked the old geezers about her, they sniggered like schoolkids. Anyway, they told me she lives in Indian Village, so I phoned out there. No answer. I went to Floyd's house. He wasn't there, and no one would talk or even open the door more than an inch. It's been a frustrating day so far, Qwill. On days like this I'd like to be back in the school system, teaching history to kids who couldn't care less."

After his conversation with Roger, Qwilleran did a few errands before returning home. Whenever he walked about downtown, he was stopped by strangers who read the "Qwill Pen" or recognized him from the photo at the top of his column. They always complimented him on his writing and his moustache, not necessarily in that order. In the beginning he had welcomed reader comments, hoping to learn something of value, but his expectations were crushed by the nature of their remarks:

"I loved your column yesterday, Mr. Q. I forget what it was about, but it was very good."

"How do you think all that stuff up?"

"My cousin in Delaware writes for a paper. Would you like me to send you some of her clippings?"

"Why do you spell your name like that?"

Now, whenever he was complimented, he would express his thanks without making eye contact; it was eye contact that led to monologues about out-of-state relatives. Instead, he would say a pleased thank-you and turn his head aside as if modestly savoring the compliment. He had become a master at the gracious turnoff. Fifty percent of the time it worked.

On this day the situation was quite different. While he was waiting in line to cash a check at the Pickax People's Bank, a security guard hailed him. "Hi, Mr. Q."

Immediately the young woman ahead of him in the line turned and said, "You're Mr. Qwilleran! Reading your column is like listening to music! Whatever the subject, your style of writing makes me feel good." There was not a word about his moustache.

Surprised and pleased, he made eye contact with a plain young woman of serious mien, probably in her early twenties. "Thank you," he said graciously without turning away. "I write my column for readers like you. Apparently you know something about the craft. Are you a teacher?"

"No, just a constant reader. I have one of your columns pasted on my mirror. You gave three rules for would-be writers: write, write, and write. I'm a would-be, and I'm following your advice." There was not a word about sending him a manuscript for evaluation and advice.

"Have you thought of enrolling at the new college?" he asked. "They're offering some writing courses . . . and there are scholarships available," he added, with a glance at her plain and well-worn shirt, her lack of makeup, her limp canvas shoulder bag.

"I'd like to do that, but I'm rather tied down right now."

"Then I wish you well, Ms. . . . what is your name?"

Her hesitant reply was mumbled. It sounded like Letitia Pen.

"P-e-n-n, as in Pennsylvania?" he asked and added with humorous emphasis, "Is that a *pen name*?"

"It's my own name, unfortunately," she said with a grimace. "I hate 'Letitia.' "

"I know what you mean. My parents named me Merlin, and my best friend was Archibald. As Merlin and Archibald we suffered the slings and arrows of outrageous first-graders."

"It's not as terrible as Letitia and Lionella, though. That's the name of my best friend."

"At least you could do a nightclub act. Can you sing? Dance? Tell jokes?"

Letitia giggled. The two of them were the only ones in the bank line who were enjoying the wait. The man behind Qwilleran cleared his throat loudly. The bank teller rapped on the counter to get Letitia's attention and said, *"Next!"*

Ms. Penn turned and stepped quickly to the window, saying a soft "I'm sorry."

Qwilleran advanced a few steps also, shortening the long line behind them; the bank was always rushed on Mondays and Fridays. Ahead of him his constant reader seemed to be withdrawing a substantial sum. He could see over her shoulder. The teller counted the bills twice.

"Fifty, a hundred, hundred-fifty, two hundred, two-fifty . . ."

"I'd like an envelope for that," said Ms. Penn.

"There you are," said the teller. "Have a nice day, Ms. Trevelyan."

"Constant reader" stuffed the money into her shoulder bag and left the bank hurriedly.

That, Qwilleran observed, was a curious development. Why would she choose not to give her right name? Before leaving the bank, he consulted the local telephone directory and found seventy-five Trevelyans but no Letitia. There were no Penns at all—not that it mattered; it was one of the pointless things he did to satisfy his idle curiosity. After that, he walked home with a lighter step, buoyed by the knowledge that his twice-weekly words were not totally forgotten and might even be doing some good. He walked via the back road to pick up his mail and check Polly's building site.

There were no trucks and no workmen, but concrete had been poured and smoothly troweled. She had decided on a crawl space instead of a basement, and on a poured foundation instead of concrete block—this after extensive reading on the subject. On one of their recent dinner dates she had explained, "A poured foundation gives a stronger wall with less danger of cracks and leaks. Did you know they are supposed to leave a groove in the footings to tie in a poured concrete wall?" And after dinner they had visited the building site to check the grooves.

Now the walls had been poured, and Qwilleran phoned Polly at the library to report.

"Thank you for letting me know," she said. "Now I feel the project is finally under way."

"Yes, you have something concrete to show for all your planning," he said lightly.

"I wonder how long it takes to dry before they can start the framing. Mr. Trevelyan uses platform framing construction. I must phone him tomorrow morning to see if he spaces the joists on twelve-, sixteen-, or twenty-four-inch centers."

"I'd go with twelve-inch, considering the way Bootsie goes around stamping his feet," Qwilleran said in another attempt to amuse her.

With worry in her voice she said, "Will I regret my decision to eliminate the fireplace? It makes a charming focal point, but it adds to the initial cost and then creates extra work if one burns wood, and I would never consider the gas-fired type."

"Be of good cheer," he said. "I have three fireplaces, and you're welcome to come and enjoy one or more at any hour of the day or night. I'll chop the wood, keep the logs burning, and haul the ashes. Reservations should be made an hour in advance." He was doing his best to divert her, without success, and the conversation ended with frustration on Qwilleran's part.

He turned from the telephone to his stack of mail. An envelope with an Illinois postmark caught his eye:

Dear Chief,

I got your letter about the Kabibbles and almost died laughing. Glad you like them. I'll send some more. You can see by the envelope I've left Florida. I'm back on my son's farm. Sorry to say, I don't get along too good with my daughter-in-law—she's such a sourpuss—and you may think I'm crazy, but I'm thinking of moving to Pickax. It sounds very nice. I know you get lots of snow, but I love to throw snowballs at the side of a barn. I'd need to somehow find a furnished room because I sold everything when I moved to Florida, and maybe

I could find a part-time job—cleaning houses or waiting on tables. I'd like to sort of give it a try for a year anyway.

What do you think?

Yours truly
Celia Robinson

She gave a phone number, and Qwilleran called immediately without waiting for the evening discount rates as he was prone to do. The phone rang and rang, and he let it ring while fragments of thought teased his brain: Celia could cook . . . Did he need a live-in housekeeper? . . . No, he liked his privacy . . . Some macaroni and cheese, though . . . Some meatloaf for the cats . . .

He was wondering about Celia's mashed potatoes when a woman's harassed voice shouted a breathless hello.

In a menacing monotone he said, "I'd like to speak to Mrs. Celia Robinson."

"She's out back, collecting eggs. Who's calling?"

"Tell her it's the Chief."

"Who?"

"Chief of the Florida Bureau of Investigation," Qwilleran said with his talent for impromptu fabrication.

The receiver was put down abruptly, and a woman's voice could be heard shouting, "Clay, go and get Grandma quick. Tell her to hurry!"

There was a long wait, and then he could hear Celia's laughter before she reached the phone. "Hello, Chief," she said happily. "You must've got my letter."

"I did indeed, and it's a splendid idea! Your grandson can spend Christmas with you, and you can have snowball fights. How is Clayton?"

"He's fine. Just got back from science camp. He won a scholarship."

"Good! Now to answer your questions: Yes, you'll have no trouble finding part-time work. Yes, you can find a furnished apartment. There's one close to downtown, if you don't mind walking up a flight of stairs."

"I don't want to pay too much rent."

"No problem. The owner will be only too happy to have the premises occupied."

"Could I bring my cat? You remember Wrigley, from Chicago."

"By all means. I'll look forward to meeting him." He waited for her merry laughter to subside before asking, "Do you have transportation?"

"Oh, you should see the cute little used car I bought, Chief! It's bright red! I bought it with your check. I didn't expect you to send so much. It was fun helping you."

"You performed a valuable service, Celia. And now . . . Don't waste any of our glorious summer weather. Plan on coming soon. I'll send you the directions."

"Oh, I'm all excited!" she crowed, and he could hear her happy laughter as she hung up.

The apartment he had in mind was a four-room suite in the carriage house behind the former Klingenschoen mansion, now the K Theatre. It was imposing in its own right, being constructed of glistening fieldstone with carriage lanterns at all four corners and four stalls for vehicles. Qwilleran had lived there while his barn was being remodeled, and it was still equipped with his basic bachelor-style furnishings in conservative colors.

After talking to Celia, he tore into action, his first call being to Fran Brodie at the design studio. She had selected the original furnishings and also those in the barn.

"Fran, drop everything—will you?—and do a quick facelift on my old apartment . . . No, I'm not moving back into it. A woman who was a friend of Euphonia Gage in Florida has been advised by her doctor to move up here for the salubrious climate."

"Well! I never heard anything like that!" Fran exclaimed. "Perhaps we should open a health spa. What kind of person is she?"

"A fun-loving grandmother, who has a cat and drives a red car. . . . Yes, I agree the place needs some color—and some feminine fripperies, if you'll pardon the political faux pas. The cats' old hang-out should be made over into a guestroom for her teenage grandson, and my Pullman kitchen should be replaced by a full-scale cooking facility, with an oven big enough to roast a turkey. How fast can you do this? She'll be here in ten days."

"Ten days!" Fran yelped into the phone. "You're a dreamer! Free-standing appliances are no problem, and we can get stock cabinets from Lockmaster, but there's the labor for installing countertops, flooring, lighting—"

"Offer the workmen a bonus," Qwilleran said impatiently. "Get them to work around the clock! Send me the bill." He knew Fran liked a challenge; she prided herself on doing the impossible.

Breaking the news to Polly required more finesse, however. He called her at home that evening. "How did everything go today?" he asked pleasantly. "I see they painted the yellow lines on the library parking lot."

"Yes, but that wasn't the main event of the day," she said. "Mr. Tibbitt's seat cushion developed a slow leak and whistled every time he moved. It could be heard on the main floor, and the clerks were in hysterics. It *was* rather amusing in a bawdy way." Polly trilled a little discreet laughter.

Finding her in a good mood, Qwilleran broached the real subject on his mind. "I know your assistant likes to moonlight on her day off. Would she be willing to act as mentor for a new resident of Pickax?"

"What would it entail?"

"Driving someone around town and pointing

out the stores, churches, restaurants, civic buildings, medical center, and so forth. Information on local customs would be appreciated—also city ordinances, like 'No whistling in public.' And she might throw in some current gossip," he added slyly, knowing that Virginia Alstock was the main fuse in the Pickax gossip circuit.

"Who is this person?" Polly asked crisply.

Expecting the third degree, Qwilleran roguishly teased her with piecemeal replies. "A friend of Junior's grandmother in Florida."

"Why would anyone in his or her right mind leave the subtropics to live in the Snow Belt? Is this person male or female?"

"Female."

There was a brief pause. "Where is she going to live?"

"In my old apartment."

"Oh, really? I didn't know it was available for rent. How did she find out about it?"

"The subject of housing arose in a telephone conversation, and I offered it to her."

There was another pause. "You must know her quite well."

"As a matter of fact," he said, thinking the game had gone on long enough, "she was instrumental in solving the mystery surrounding Euphonia's death."

"I see. . . . How old is she?"

"Polly, I never ask a lady her age. You know that."

There was an audible sniff. "Approximately."

"Well . . . old enough to have a teenage grandson . . . and young enough to like snowball fights."

"What is this woman's name?"

"Celia Robinson, and I'll appreciate it, Polly, if you'll alert Mrs. Alstock. Mrs. Robinson will be here in about ten days."

Qwilleran chuckled to himself after hanging up the receiver. He could imagine the gabby Mrs. Robinson and the gossipy Mrs. Alstock having lunch at Lois's Luncheonette.

For the next few days he made discreet inquiries, wherever he went, about parttime work for a newcomer. One day he met Lisa Compton in the post office. She worked at the Senior Care Facility, and her husband was superintendent of schools; between them they could provide answers for most questions.

Qwilleran mentioned his quest, and Lisa asked, "Does this woman have a warm, outgoing personality?"

"She's got it in spades," he said.

"Do you know about our new outreach program? It's called Pals for Patients. We supply Pals to homebound Patients; the Patients pay us, and we pay the Pals, minus a small commission for booking and collecting. Patients who can't afford to pay are subsidized by the Klingenschoen Foundation. You probably know all about that."

"That's what you think," Qwilleran said. "No one tells me these things. . . . Was the program your brainchild?"

"No, it was Irma Hasselrich's last great idea. I merely implemented it," said Lisa. "What's your friend's name?"

Qwilleran hesitated, knowing that a bulletin would flash across the Pickax grapevine: *Mr. Q has a new friend.* He explained his hesitation by saying glibly, "Her last name is Robinson. Her first name is Sadie or Celia—something like that. We've never met. She was a dear friend of Euphonia Gage in Florida, who said Celia—or Sadie—had an exceptionally warm and outgoing personality."

"Okay. Send her to me when she arrives. We'll put her name on the list."

"She'll appreciate it, I'm sure. How's your grouchy old husband, Lisa?"

"Believe it or not, he's happy as a lark. You know Lyle's perverse temperament. Well, he's tickled to see Floyd Trevelyan in trouble. They've been enemies ever since Floyd sued the school board for expelling his son."

As it turned out, Floyd was in more trouble than anyone imagined, and the *Moose County Something* could gloat over its first front-page coverage of a financial scandal.

The Lumbertown Credit Union was closed indefinitely and its assets frozen, pending a hearing before the state banking commission on charges of fraud.

Millions of dollars belonging to depositors were allegedy missing.

Also missing were the president of the institution and his secretary.

FIVE

News of the Mudville scandal broke in mid-morning, enabling the *Moose County Something* to remake the front page. Arch Riker phoned Qwilleran for help with rewrites and phones. "And listen, Qwill: Stop at Toodles' and pick up a few bottles of champagne."

Suffused with a newsman's urge to disinter the story behind the story, Qwilleran left in a hurry, although not without waving good-bye to the Siamese. He told them where he was going and when he might return, as if they cared. After their breakfast they could be infuriatingly blasé. Yum Yum merely sat on her brisket and gave him a glassy stare; Koko walked away and was heard scratching in the commode.

At the newspaper office the mood was one of jubilation. Rarely did breaking news break on their deadline. Ordinarily the public heard it first from the electronic media—sketchily, but first. Not until the next day would the newspaper come in a poor second. True, they were able to publish photos, sidelights, background facts, quotes from individuals involved, and opinions from casual observers. After all, the *Moose County Something* claimed to be the north-country newspaper of record. "Read all about it" was their slogan, recalling the cry of the old-time corner newshawker.

When the presses were finally rolling, the champagne corks popped in celebration. If Qwilleran remembered his own exuberant days of champagne-squirting Down Below, it was without any wishful pangs of yearning. He was simply glad to be where he was when he was— and who he was.

Eventually Riker's booming voice announced, "Enough hilarity! Back to reality!" The staff calmed down and went to work, and Qwilleran went on his way, leaving his car in the parking lot and walking around town to do his own snooping.

First he went to the police station to see his friend Andrew Brodie, but the chief was absent—probably meeting with state and county lawmen to organize a manhunt, and woman-hunt.

Qwilleran's next stop was Amanda's Studio of Interior Design on Main Street. Amanda was not there, but Fran Brodie was holding the fort attractively, sitting at a French writing table with her long slender legs crossed and her double-hoop earrings dangling. She had been one of the seductive young women who pursued Qwilleran when he arrived in Pickax to claim his inheritance. Only Polly Duncan remained in the running; in this case, he had done the pursuing. Fran was still a friend and confidante, however. He admired her talent as a designer, her dedication to the theatre club, and her strawberry blond hair. Also, she was the daughter of the police chief and an occasional source of privileged information.

When he entered the shop, she saw him immediately and turned her face away, groaning loudly—a bit of theatre-club pantomime.

"Is it as bad as all that?" Qwilleran asked. He knew that the studio had handled the renovation of the Party Train.

"That rat owes us tens of thousands!" she wailed. "Amanda's at the attorney's office right now. Floyd had signed a contract for the work, and we never dreamed he'd run out on it."

"Were the rail coaches the only work you'd done for him?"

"No. The first was the Lumbertown office,

and he liked it. Maybe you've seen how we duplicated the atmosphere of an old railway depot. He had just sold his construction firm to XYZ Enterprises and had tons of money. He paid the bill in thirty days."

"And what about his house in West Middle Hummock? I had a glimpse of it when I interviewed him about the model trains. The interior didn't look like you; it looked like Mudville thrift shop."

"Well, *he said* his wife didn't want any professional help with the house. That meant one of two things: Either he'd rather spend the money on model trains, or Mrs. T was too ill to care. We accepted that. Apparently Floyd himself didn't care how the house looked as long as the bar was well stocked. I don't know who drinks all that stuff. I think they never have company. Maybe Floyd has drinking buddies from Sawdust City. . . . But then, he commissioned us to do the interiors of the PV and the diner and the club car, and believe me, they needed a lot of doing!"

"You did a beautiful job, Fran."

"Well, why not? He was willing to spend a fortune . . ."

"And you thought you were on the gravy train," Qwilleran said sympathetically.

Fran groaned again. "I'm afraid Amanda will have a stroke. You know how excitable she is."

"Did you work directly with Floyd on the cars?"

"No. With his secretary—or assistant—or whatever she is. Nice person. Good to work with. Nella Hooper has fine taste. When Floyd wanted something flashy, she toned him down."

"I saw her on the Party Train. Very attractive. Know anything about her background?"

"Only that she's from Texas. She never wanted to talk about herself, and I know when not to ask questions. Floyd had me do her apartment in Indian Village and gave me carte blanche to spend money. She wanted a southwestern theme."

"How about your father, Fran? Has he had anything to say about the embezzlement?"

"It's too soon."

"Or the disappearance of the principals?"

"Too soon."

The way it worked: The police chief would come home from his shift and talk shop with his wife at the kitchen table; then, when Fran made her daily phone call to her mother, Mrs. Brodie would pass along some tidbit of information in strict confidence; later, if Qwilleran dropped into the studio looking genuinely concerned and utterly trustworthy, Fran would feel free to confide in him. She was aware that he had helped the police on several occasions, behind the scenes.

"It's too early for any scuttlebutt," Fran said, "although I haven't called home yet. Why don't you come to rehearsal tonight? By that time I might have heard something."

"Will Derek Cuttlebrink be there?" Qwilleran asked. "He's on my list of leads to interview."

"He'll be there. So will his latest girlfriend."

"You mean—Elizabeth Appelhardt?"

"She prefers to be called Elizabeth Hart now."

"I must say they're an odd couple."

"But they're good for each other," Fran said. "She's talked him into enrolling at the college, and Derek is gradually nudging her into the mainstream. When you first brought her from the island, she was in a world of her own."

"Please! I didn't bring her here," Qwilleran said gruffly. "She happened to be on the same boat."

"Whatever," the designer said with raised eyebrows. "She's started wearing natural makeup and patronizing my hairdresser, and now she looks less like a character in a horror movie."

"I hear she's joined the club. That'll be good for her."

"Good for us, too! She has some fresh ideas for costumes and staging, although I expect some opposition from our older members."

"Any other news?"

"I'm doing an apartment in Indian Village for Dr. Diane—country French, lots of blue. She seems to have replaced Hixie in Dr. Herbert's life, but here's an off-twist: When Hixie broke her foot, she stayed with Dr. Herbert's mother until she could walk, and now Dr. Diane is staying with his mother until her apartment is ready."

Qwilleran said, "I'm sure there's some underlying significance to that fact, but it escapes me. . . . I like that paperweight. What is it supposed to be?" He pointed to a fanciful chunk of tarnished brass on Fran's desk.

"That's Cerberus," Fran told him. "The three-headed dog that guarded the gates of Hades in ancient mythology. Amanda picked it up at an estate sale in Chicago. It belonged to a wealthy meatpacker."

The detail was meticulous, even to the snakes that formed the dog's mane and tail. Qwilleran often bought a small object in the design studio; it pleased Fran, and it was advantageous to please the daughter of the police chief.

"If you like it," she said, "I'll give you a price on it and shine it up for you."

"I like it," he said, "but I have some other stops to make. How about shining it up and bringing it to the rehearsal tonight?"

As Qwilleran left the studio, he was chuckling to himself in anticipation of the cats' reaction to the grotesque bauble. They were always aware of any new item that arrived in their territory.

His next stop was the office of MacWhannell

& Shaw. There was a question he wanted to ask an accountant.

Big Mac, as he was called, met him with a welcoming hand. "Just thinking about you, Qwill. We're planning Scottish Night at the lodge, and we'd like you to be our guest again."

"Thank you. I enjoyed it last year—even the haggis."

"I was telling the committee that your mother was a Mackintosh, and Gordie Shaw said you ought to join the clan officially, as a tribute, you might say, to her memory. The Shaws had Mackintosh connections, you know."

The suggestion hit Qwilleran in a tender spot. He had grown up with a single parent, and now that he was maturing he realized how much she had done for him. He could forget the piano lessons, and drying the dishes, and two-handed games of dominoes; he owed her a great deal. "What would it entail?" he asked.

"According to Gordie, you apply for membership, pay your dues, and receive a periodic newsletter. After that you probably start attending Scottish Gatherings and Highland Games."

"Sounds okay," said the writer of the "Qwill Pen" column, sensing a source of material. "Ask Gordie to send me an application."

"But I've been doing all the talking," the accountant said. "Is there anything I can do for you?"

"Just answer a question, Mac. How do you

react to the Lumbertown fraud—or alleged fraud?"

"Fortunately, I have no clients who would be affected, but I sympathize with the Sawdusters. When a white-collar crime is committed in a blue-collar community, it seems particularly reprehensible—to me, that is. Don't ask me why."

"At the risk of sounding financially naive, may I ask how a guy like Trevelyan can abscond with millions belonging to his customers? I'm sure he doesn't carry it out in a suitcase."

"Basically, he has to be a crook," said MacWhannell, "but if you're talking about ways and means, well . . . there are such practices as juggling the books, forging documents, falsifying financial statements, and so forth."

"Floyd is, or was, a carpenter by trade," Qwilleran pointed out. "Would he have such educated tricks in his toolbox?"

"Sounds as if there was an accomplice, doesn't it? This will be an interesting case. With today's crime information networks, he'll be found soon enough."

Leaving the accountant's office, Qwilleran passed the department store and saw Carol Lanspeak on the sidewalk, waving her arms and shouting. She was directing the setup of a clothing display in the main window, giving terse but loud instructions to an assistant inside the glass, while the young woman mouthed replies.

Catching Qwilleran's reflection in the plate glass, Carol turned and explained, "The one inside the window can hear the one outside, but not vice versa." She waved to her helper and told her to take a break. "This is our last window before back-to-school, Qwill. How time flies! And oh! Weren't you shocked by the news from Sawdust City? Some of our employees live there, and they're Lumbertown depositors. What will happen? When this has occurred elsewhere in the country, it's been a real disaster."

Qwilleran said, "If the guy is a swindler and a fugitive, can't his assets be liquidated to cover debts and embezzled funds? He has a big house in the Hummocks near you, and a model train layout that's worth a mint, and the Party Train. That alone must be valued in the millions."

"But the justice system is so slow, Qwill! And the victims are families with children, and factory workers subject to layoffs, and retirees with nest eggs on deposit. What will they do when emergencies arise?"

"Well, let me tell you something surprising," Qwilleran said. "This morning I was helping to man the phones at the paper, when our reporters were calling in man-on-the-street opinions, and the victims, as you call them, weren't blaming Trevelyan; they were blaming the government for deception and injustice! They called it a plot, a conspiracy, a dirty trick! They refused to believe that Floyd would take their money and skip. They said he'd been a high school football hero and a good carpenter; his picture hung in the lobby of the credit union; he paid daily interest; he was crazy about trains."

Carol shook her head. "Everyone in Sawdust City must be nutty from exposure to industrial pollution."

Before leaving for the rehearsal that evening, Qwilleran started to read the first few scenes of *A Midsummer Night's Dream* aloud. Both cats enjoyed the sound of his voice, whether he was reading great literature or the baseball scores. On this occasion Koko was particularly attentive and even got into the act a few times.

The first scene opened with an indignant father hauling his disobedient daughter before the duke for reprimand. *Full of vexation am I, with complaint against my daughter, Hermia.*

"Yow!" said Koko.

"That's not in the script," Qwilleran objected.

After the father had raved and ranted, the duke argued with gentle reasonableness. *What say you, Hermia? Be advised, fair maid.*

"Yow!" Koko said again.

The young woman was being forced by law to marry a man of her father's choosing, or enter a convent, or die. *Therefore, Hermia, question your desires.*

"Yow!"

Qwilleran closed the book. He said, "This is

getting monotonous, if you don't mind my saying so." Later, as he walked through the Black Forest to the theatre, he construed Koko's responses as infatuation with a certain sound. To a cat, "Hermia" might have a secret meaning. Then again, Koko might be playing practical jokes; he had a sense of humor.

The K Theatre, originally the Klingenschoen mansion, was a great three-story mass of fieldstone, transformed into a two-hundred-seat amphitheatre. From the lofty foyer a pair of staircases curved up to the lobby, from which the seating sloped down to the stage. When Qwilleran arrived, the cast was doing a run-through without the book, while the director watched from the third row and scribbled notes. Other cast members were scattered throughout the auditorium, waiting for their scenes. Quietly he took a seat behind Fran Brodie.

The "rude mechanicals" were onstage: tinker, tailor, joiner, bellowsmaker, carpenter, and the six-foot-eight weaver, who delivered the final line of the scene: *Enough: Hold, or cut bowstrings.*

"Break! Take five!" Fran called out.

Qwilleran tapped her on the shoulder. "That line about bowstrings—I've never quite understood it."

"I take it to mean 'cooperate—or else,' but I don't know its origin. Ask Polly. She'll know."

Actors wandered up the aisle to get a drink

of water in the lobby or stopped to ask Fran a question. As soon as she and Qwilleran were alone, she said in a low voice, "They've picked up Floyd's car. It was in that meadow where car-poolers park. It had been there all week, and the sheriff was aware of it, but Floyd wasn't on the wanted list then."

"Do you suppose someone tipped him off about the audit? Who could it be?"

"It looks as if an accomplice drove in from Indian Village and picked him up—Nella, for example. They're both missing."

"But how would she know about the audit?"

"Interesting question."

"If they're headed for Mexico," he said, "they've had a headstart of three days. She'd know a lot about Mexico, being from Texas."

"Wherever they went, they'll be found easily enough." Fran looked at her watch. "Time for the next scene. Don't go. I have more to report. . . . And do you know what? I brought your paperweight and left it in my car."

"Why don't you drive down to the barn when you're through here. I'll pour. You can bring the paperweight."

"Elizabeth Hart will be with me. Do you mind? I'm her ride tonight."

"That's fine. She's never seen the barn. . . . Is it okay to interview Derek now?"

"Sure. He won't be called for fifteen minutes."

Before interviewing the young actor,

Qwilleran checked his bio in the most recent playbill:

DEREK CUTTLEBRINK. Veteran of five productions. Best-remembered roles: the porter in *Macbeth* and the villain in *The Drunkard*. Lifelong resident of Wildcat. Graduate of Pickax High School, where he played basketball. Currently employed as a waiter at the Old Stone Mill. Major interests: acting, camping, folk-singing, girls.

The last of these was only too true. At performances in the K Theatre there was always a claque of Derek's girlfriends and ex-girlfriends and would-be girlfriends, ready to applaud as soon as he walked on stage. Whatever the source of his magnetism, his turnover in female companions was of more interest than the Dow Jones averages in Pickax. Tonight Derek was sitting with his latest, Elizabeth Hart, in the back row, where they could whisper without disturbing the proceedings on stage.

Qwilleran asked her if he might borrow Derek for a brief interview in the lobby.

"May I listen in?" she asked.

"Of course."

The eccentric young woman he had met on Breakfast Island had improved her grooming, but her taste for exotic clothing had not changed. While other club members were in grungy rehearsal togs, Elizabeth wore an embroidered vest and skullcap, possibly from Ecuador, with a balloon-sleeve white silk blouse and harem pants. Their bagginess camouflaged her thinness. The interview was taped:

QWILLERAN: You're playing the role of Nick Bottom, the weaver. How do you perceive Mr. Bottom?

DEREK: You mean, what's he like? He's a funny guy, always using the wrong words and doing some dumb thing, but nothing gets him down. People like him.

ELIZABETH: (interrupting) His malapropisms are quite endearing.

DEREK: Yeah. Took the words right outa my mouth.

QWILLERAN: How does Bottom fit into the plot?

DEREK: Well, there's a wedding at the palace, and for entertainment they've got a bunch of ordinary guys to put on a play. Bottom wants to direct and play all the roles himself.

ELIZABETH: His vanity would be insufferable, if it weren't so ingratiating.

DEREK: Yeah. You can quote me. The players rehearse in the woods, and one of the little green men turns me into a donkey from the neck up. The joke of it is: the queen of the greenies falls in love with me.

ELIZABETH: She's a bewitcher who is bewitched.

DEREK: That's pretty good. Put it in.

QWILLERAN: How do you feel about little green men in a Shakespeare play?

DEREK: No problem. He called 'em fairies; we call 'em greenies. They're all aliens, right?

QWILLERAN: What is your favorite line?

DEREK: I like it when I roar like a lion . . . *Arrrrgh! Arrrrgh!* And at the end I have a death scene that's fun. *Now die, die, die, die, die.* That always gets a laugh.

Qwilleran, having completed his mission, more or less, returned to the barn through the Black Forest, listening for Marconi. It was still daylight, however, and Marconi was a night owl.

Yum Yum was waiting at the kitchen door. He picked her up and whispered affectionate words while she caressed his hand with her waving tail. Koko was not there. Koko was in the foyer, looking out the window.

The formal entrance to the barn was a double door flanked by tall, narrow windows. These sidelights had sills about twenty inches from the floor, a convenient height for a cat who wanted to stand on his hind feet and peer through the glass. There was something out there that fascinated Koko. With his neck stretched and his ears pricked, he stared down the orchard trail. Surveyors had been there and lumberyard trucks and carpenters' pickups and a cement mixer, but that was daytime activity, and there was no action after four-thirty. Yet Koko watched and waited as if expecting something to happen. His prescience was sometimes unnerving. He could sense an approaching storm, and a telephone about to ring. He often knew what Qwilleran was going to do before Qwilleran knew.

Koko also had a sense of right and wrong. The decoys on the fireplace cube, for example, were lined up facing east. One day Mrs. Fulgrove came to clean and left them facing west. Koko threw a fit!

On this summer evening he watched and waited, while Qwilleran listened to the tape of Derek's interview; to make an eight-inch thinkpiece out of it would require all his fictive skills. Only once was Koko lured away from the window, and that was when Derek roared like a lion.

A run-through without the book was always a long rehearsal, and it was dark when Qwilleran's guests arrived. As soon as the car headlights came bobbing along the wooded road, he floodlighted the exterior of the barn to play up its striking features: a fieldstone foundation ten feet high, three stories of weathered shingle siding, and a series of odd-shaped windows cut in the wall of the octagonal building. Visitors were usually awed.

Qwilleran put on his yellow cap and went to meet the two women, and as he opened the passenger's door Elizabeth stepped out and looked around. "You have an owl," she said. "It sounds like a great horned owl. They hoot in clusters. We had one in our woods on the island, and we used to count the hoots. The pattern varies with the season and the owl's personal agenda."

"Shall we go indoors? I'm thirsty," Fran said impatiently.

The interior was aglow. Indirect lighting accented the balconies and the beams high overhead; downlights created mysterious puddles of light on the main floor; a spotlight focused on a huge tapestry hanging from a balcony railing. Appropriately, the design was an apple tree.

As Fran gazed around in admiration, Elizabeth went looking for the cats.

Fran said, "I've been here a hundred times, and I never cease to marvel at Dennis's genius. His death was a flagrant waste of talent. If he had lived, would he have stayed in the north?"

"I doubt it," Qwilleran said. "His family was in St. Louis."

"I can't find Koko and Yum Yum," Elizabeth complained.

"They're around here somewhere, but we have an abundance of somewhere in this place. Shall we go into the lounge area and have a glass of wine or fruit juice?"

Koko, having heard his name, suddenly appeared from nowhere, followed by Yum Yum, yawning and stretching her dainty hindquarters.

"They remember me from the island!" Elizabeth said with delight, as she dropped to her knees and extended a finger for sniffing.

Fran followed Qwilleran into the kitchen to watch him prepare wine spritzers.

"What did you want to tell me?" he asked quietly.

In a low voice she said, "The police have been questioning Floyd's associates, and they've discovered something that I consider bizarre. Have you heard of the Lockmaster Indemnity Corporation? They were supposed to be private insurers of depositors' funds in the Lumbertown Credit Union, but they're broke! They can't cover the losses!"

"How can that be? Sounds to me as if they're part of the scam."

"I don't know, but they'd transferred their assets to their wives' names. They call it estate planning. Dad calls it dirty pool."

"I'd say your dad is right. If they get away with it," Qwilleran said, "there's something radically wrong in this state!"

As he carried the tray into the lounge area—two spritzers and one club soda—Elizabeth rose gracefully from the floor. "We've been having a significant dialogue," she said. "They're glad to see me."

All five of them sat around the large square coffee table, where Qwilleran had placed three small bowls of Kabibbles. There was also a copy of that day's *Moose County Something*. Fran commented on the in-depth coverage of the scandal, and Qwilleran gloated over the journalistic feat, while Elizabeth listened politely. She was known to have a high I.Q. and an interest in esoteric subjects, as well as a sizable trust fund, but she had no idea what was happening in the world. She avoided reading newspapers, finding them too depressing.

After a few minutes the host steered the conversation to her realm of interest. He said, "I hear you're working on costumes for the play. What do you have in mind for the fairies?"

"We call them greenies," she replied, "and the assumption is that they come from outer space. We know, of course, that extraterrestrials have been visiting our planet for thousands of years."

"I see," he said.

"For our production they'll wear green leotards and tights, green wigs, and green makeup. We have to get parental approval for the young people to wear green makeup. The effect will be surreal, and Fran is coaching them in body movements that will make them appear amiable and slightly comic."

"How about the king and queen of the . . . greenies? Oberon and Titania usually wear something regal."

"They'll have glitter: green foil jumpsuits

with swirling capes of some gossamer material—and fantastic headdresses. I really love this play," she said with eyes dancing.

Qwilleran remembered how dull her eyes had been when he first met her on the island. Moose County—or Derek—had a salutary effect. "Do you have a favorite character? If you were to play a role, what would you choose?" He expected her to choose Titania in green foil.

Her reply was prompt. "Hermia."

"Yow!" said Koko, whose ears were receiving the conversation even while his nose was tracking the Kabibbles.

"I can relate to her parent problem," Elizabeth explained, "although in my case it was my mother who insisted on ordering my life."

Fran said, "We'd have the greenies arriving in a spacecraft, if it were feasible, but we don't have the stage machinery. Larry thinks they should appear in puffs of stage smoke. Pickax audiences love stage smoke. But I'd like to see something more high-tech. Elizabeth has an idea, but I can't figure out the logistics. Tell Qwill about your pyramids, Elizabeth."

She turned to Qwilleran. "Do you know about pyramid power?"

"I've read about it—quite a long time ago."

"It's nothing new. It dates back thousands of years, and my father really believed in it. He had little pyramids built for my brothers and me, and we were supposed to sit in them to make wonderful things happen. I thought it was magic, but my mother said it was subversive. She had them destroyed after Father died." Her voice drifted off in a mist of nostalgia and regret.

Fran said, "Wally Toddwhistle can build us a portable see-through pyramid out of poles. For a scene change we'd black out the house briefly, and when the stage lights came on, there'd be a pyramid in the forest. Wouldn't it be wonderful if the poles could be neon tubes?"

Qwilleran questioned whether the audience would understand the magical implications of such a pyramid, and Fran said it would be explained in the playbill.

"How many playgoers read the program notes?" he asked. "Most of them are more interested in the ads for Otto's Tasty Eats and Gippel's Garage. That's been my observation based on preshow chitchat. How does Larry feel about it?"

"He thinks it'll clutter the stage without contributing dramatically, but we haven't given up yet, have we, Elizabeth?"

Qwilleran offered to refresh their drinks, but Fran said it was time to leave. On the way out, she handed him a black felt-tip pen. "Where did you find this?" he asked.

"On the floor near the coffee table."

"Yum Yum's at it again! She's an incorrigible cat burglar." He returned the pen to a pewter mug on the telephone table and escorted the women to their car, first putting on his yellow cap. When they had driven away, he walked around the barn a few times, reluctant to go indoors on this perfect midsummer night. With a little suspension of disbelief one could imagine Puck and the other greenies materializing from the woods in a puff of smoke . . . A high-pitched yowl from the kitchen window reminded him that he was neglecting his duty.

"Treat!" he announced as he opened the kitchen door.

Yum Yum responded immediately, but . . . where was Koko? When he failed to report for food, there was cause for alarm. Qwilleran went in search and found him on the large square coffee table—not eating the Kabibbles, not playing with the wooden train whistle, not sniffing the book on the Panama Canal. He was sitting on the *Moose County Something* with its front-page treatment of the Mudville scandal and two-column photo of the president. It was the same as the portrait hanging in the lobby of the Lumbertown Credit Union.

Koko's attitude indicated something was wrong—and not just the embezzlement. Qwilleran felt a tingling sensation on his upper lip and tamped his moustache with a heavy hand. Koko was trying to communicate. Perhaps the tipoff had been a hoax. Perhaps the auditors were trying to cover up their own mistake. Perhaps Trevelyan was being, so to speak, railroaded.

As if reading the man's mind, Koko slowly

rose on four long legs, his body arched, his tail bushed. With whiskers swept back and eyes slanted, he circled the newspaper in a stiff-legged dance that sent shivers up and down Qwilleran's spine. It was Koko's death dance.

SIX

Following Koko's macabre dance on the coffee table, Qwilleran brooded about its significance. He had seen that performance before, and it meant only one thing: death. And it pointed to Floyd Trevelyan. To Qwilleran's mind it pointed to suicide. The arrogant, self-centered, self-made man would self-destruct rather than suffer the humility of capture, trial, and imprisonment. He was too rich, too cocky, too vain, too autocratic to return to his hometown in handcuffs.

Qwilleran made no mention of his theory to

Polly when they had dinner Saturday night. His fanciful suspicions were always politely dismissed by the head librarian, whose mind was as fact-intensive as the *World Almanac*. He had never told her about Koko's supra-normal intuition either, nor his unique ways of communicating. By comparison her beloved Bootsie was a Neanderthal cat!

They had dinner at Tipsy's restaurant in North Kennebeck without referring to the scandal that had electrified Moose County. Polly had other concerns: Would her house be ready in time for Thanksgiving? Would the fumes of paint and vinyl and treated wood—the "new house smell"—be injurious to Bootsie's sensitive system? Qwilleran's attempts to change the subject were only temporary distractions from the major issues: insulation and roofing.

"Have you met Eddie Trevelyan?" she asked.

"Not formally," he replied. "When I walk to my mailbox, he looks up and waves, and I say 'Lookin' good' or something original like that. He has a helper called Benno—short, stocky fellow with a ponytail—and a beautiful chow dog who comes to work with him everyday and sits in the bed of Eddie's pickup or in the shade of a tree. I tell him he's a good dog, and he pants for joy with his tongue hanging out. His name is Zak, I found out."

There were other details that he thought it wise to omit; Polly would only worry. There were the cigarette butts all over the property. There was the "essence of barroom" that Eddie exuded much of the time.

"At first the men—they're both young—seemed to be enjoying their work, bantering back and forth," Qwilleran reported. "But now there's an air of tension that's understandable. To see one's parent, a leading citizen, suddenly branded as a thief must be hard to take. Eddie keeps nagging Benno to 'get the lead out' and pound more nails. It occurs to me that he's rushing the job in order to collect his second payment. When is it due?"

"When the house is weathered-in. Oh, dear! I hope this doesn't mean he'll be cutting corners."

"If his operating capital is tied up in the credit union, he may be strapped for cash to meet his payroll and pay bills. Has he dropped any hints?"

"No, he hasn't, and I talk to him on the phone every morning, early, before he gets away."

The next day, after Sunday brunch at Polly's apartment, they drove to the building site. Polly was appalled by the cigarette butts; she would tell Mr. Trevelyan to get a coffee can and pick them up. The future rooms were a maze of two-by-fours; she thought the rooms looked too small. Rain was predicted, and she worried that the roof boards would not be installed in time.

Polly's constant worrying about the house

caused Qwilleran to worry about her. "Why don't we take a pleasant break," he suggested, "and drive to the Flats to see the wildfowl. They might be nidulating, or whatever they do in July." This was a noble concession on his part; she was an avid bird watcher, and he was not. "We might see a puffin bird," he added facetiously.

"Not likely in Moose County," she said with a bemused smile, "but I really should go home and study the blueprints, in order to figure out furniture arrangement."

After dropping her off, Qwilleran went home to the barn, grateful for the company of cats who never worried. Both were pursuing their hobbies. Yum Yum was batting a bottle cap around the floor, losing it, finding it, losing it again—until she flopped down on her side in utter exhaustion. Koko was standing on his hind legs in the foyer, gazing down the orchard trail. Did he know that a chow came to work with the builder every day? Had Zak ventured up the trail to the barn? In any case, it seemed abnormal for a four-legged animal to spend so much time on two legs.

"Come on, old boy! Let's go exploring," he suggested. "Leash! Leash!"

Yum Yum, recognizing the word, scampered up the ramp to hide. Koko trotted to the broom closet, where the harnesses were stored, and purred while the leather straps were being buckled. Then, dragging his leash, he walked purposefully to the front door. When it was opened, however, he stood on the threshold in a freeze of indecision. He savored the seventy-eight-degree temperature and the three-mile-an-hour breeze; he looked to right and left; he noted a bird in the sky and a squirrel in a tree.

"Okay, let's go. We don't have two days for this excursion," Qwilleran said, picking up the leash and shaking it like reins. "Forward march!"

Koko, an indoor cat in temperament and lifestyle, stepped cautiously to the small entrance deck and sniffed the boards, which were laid diagonally. He sniffed the spaces between the boards. He discovered an interesting knot in the wood and a row of nailheads. In exasperation Qwilleran grabbed him and swung him to his shoulder. Koko was quite amenable. He liked riding on a shoulder. He liked the elevation.

Everyone had advised Qwilleran to "do something" about the orchard, a tangle of weeds and vines choking neglected apple trees. Many had lost their limbs for firewood; others had fallen victim to storms.

"Why don't you clean out that eyesore?" Riker had said. "Plant vegetables," Polly suggested. "Have a swimming pool," Fran Brodie urged.

At the building site, Qwilleran allowed the excited cat to jump down but held a firm hand on the leash. It was not the skeleton of the house that interested Koko, nor the tire tracks where the builders parked their pickups, nor the spot under a tree where Zak liked to nap in the shade. Koko wanted only to roll on the floor of the future garage. He rolled ecstatically. Both cats had discovered this unexplainable thrill at their Mooseville cabin, where the screened porch was on a concrete slab. They rolled on their backs and squirmed voluptuously. Now Koko was inventing new contortions and enjoying it immensely.

"Let's not be excessive," Qwilleran said to him, jerking the leash. "If that's all you want to do, let's go home."

On the way back to the barn he had an idea: He would add a screened porch on a concrete slab for the Siamese, where they could have a sense of outdoor living and roll to their hearts' content. Eddie could build it after he finished Polly's house. It would not be attached to the barn; that would only destroy the symmetry of the octagonal structure. It would be a separate summer house—a pergola—like the one he had visited on Breakfast Island, and like the one he had built in the Potato Mountains.

Yum Yum met them at the door and sniffed Koko with disapproval; he had been out having fun, and she had been left at home.

"That's what happens," Qwilleran advised her, "when you elect to be asocial." At any rate, he hoped the jaunt had satisfied Koko's curiosity and there would be no more absurd trail gazing. It was a futile dream. Soon the cat was back in the foyer, standing on two legs at the window, watching and waiting.

Ordinarily Qwilleran would have shrugged off Koko's aberration, but he was feeling edgy. There was the itch of suspicion without the opportunity to scratch. There was the uneasy feeling that Koko knew more than he did. And there was frustration caused by too much of Polly's house and not enough of Polly.

He was still feeling cranky the next day when he walked downtown to hand in his thousand words on the aurora borealis. The colorful phenomenon in the midnight sky was a tourist attraction, although locals took it for granted, and some thought "Northern Lights" was simply the name of a hotel in Mooseville.

Looking more than usually morose, Qwilleran walked through the city room where staffers sat in front of video display terminals and stared blankly at the screens. In the managing editor's office, the slightly built Junior Goodwinter was further dwarfed by the electronic equipment surrounding him.

When Qwilleran threw his copy on Junior's desk, the young editor glanced at the triple-spaced typewritten sheets and said, "When are you getting yourself a word processor, Qwill?"

"I like my electric typewriter" was the belligerent reply, "and it likes me! Are you implying that a word processor would make me a better writer? And if so, how good do you want me to be?"

"Don't hit me!" said the younger man with an exaggerated cringe. "Forget I said it. Have a cup of coffee. Sit down. Take a load off your feet. Will you be at the softball game tonight?"

"I haven't decided" was the curt answer. Polly usually accompanied him to the annual event, but he doubted she could tear herself away from her blueprints.

Junior threw him a copy of Monday's paper. "Read the third bite," he said.

A new feature on the front page was a column of brief news items of twenty-five words or less, each preceded by a single word in caps: ARRESTED, or HONORED, or LEAVING, or PROMOTED. Other newspapers labeled such a column "Briefs" or "Shorts." Hixie Rice, who had been responsible for naming the paper the *Something,* wanted to call the new front-page column "Undies." The editorial committee decided, however, on "Bites."

Qwilleran read the third bite:

SHOT: Police are investigating the shooting of a watchdog in West Middle Hummock Sunday night. The animal was penned in a dog-run on Floyd Trevelyan's estate.

"What do you deduce from this?" he asked Junior.

"That victims of the embezzlement are finally transferring their hostility from the government to the embezzler. Roger's been hanging out in Mudville coffee shops, and he says the emotions range from gloomy self-pity to vengeful rage. Someone was trying to get back at Floyd by killing his dog."

"Stupid!" Qwilleran murmured.

"And now read the first letter on the ed page, Qwill."

To the Editor:

I am writing in behalf of the Sawdust City High School Summer Camp Fund, which enables seniors to spend a week in the woods, living with nature, studying ecology, and learning to share. For twenty-four years this has been a tradition at our school.

This year forty-seven students have spent their junior year selling cookies, washing cars, chopping wood, and cleaning garages to earn money for the camping experience. They deposited their earnings regularly in the Lumbertown Credit Union and watched them earn interest—a worthwhile lesson in thrift and financial management. Next week they were to shoulder their backpacks, hike into the woods, and pitch their tents.

How can we explain to them that there will be no campout for the new senior class? How can we explain that $2,234.43 of their own money is being withheld by order of the government?

Elda Mayfus-Jones
Faculty Sponsor
SCHSSCF

Qwilleran finished reading and said irritably, "Why doesn't Ms. Mayfus-Jones just tell them their uncle Floyd is a crook, and he spent their $2,234.43 on toy trains to run around his office lobby?"

"You're in a grouchy mood today," Junior said. "I thought the K Foundation could afford to stake these kids to the money until their deposits are released."

"The Foundation could afford to send all forty-seven brats on a round-the-world cruise!" Qwilleran snapped. "All they have to do is apply. It's in the telephone book under K. That's between J and L." He started to leave without finishing his coffee.

"Hey!" Junior called after him with a grin. "If the kids get their money, you can go camping with them for a week and write a 'Qwill Pen' series!"

Qwilleran stomped from the room. As he passed the publisher's office, Riker beckoned to him. "I've just been talking to Brodie. How come they haven't caught that guy? They nabbed the Florida crooks right away, and they were pros! Floyd is only a small-town conniver. Why haven't they found him?"

"They'll never find him."

"What makes you think so? Do you know something we don't know?"

Qwilleran shrugged. "Just a hunch." If he were to mention Koko's input, it would only lead to an argument. Riker thought he took the cat's abstract messages too seriously. "You seem to be giving the scandal a lot of space, Arch."

"We're trying to keep the public outrage alive, spur the manhunt, and goad the banking commission into action. Our stories are being picked up by major newspapers around the state. We've assigned Roger to the Mudville beat exclusively until something breaks, one way or the other . . . So! . . . Where are you going from here, Qwill?"

"Home."

"How's Polly's house progressing?"

"Slowly, and that's what concerns me, Arch. She worries about it too much. She worries unnecessarily. I'm afraid she's headed for a nervous collapse."

His friend nodded sympathetically.

"Polly's so desk-bound that she's not getting any exercise—not even fresh air. She didn't even want to go bird watching yesterday."

"Are you bringing her to the game tonight?" Riker asked.

"Are you kidding? That's the last thing in the world she'd want to do!"

Chatting with his old friend bolstered Qwilleran's flagging spirits somewhat, and walking a few miles helped dispel his gloom. He took the long way home and, in doing so, passed the photo studio of John Bushland. His van was in the parking lot, meaning that the photographer was shooting a subject in the studio or developing film in the darkroom.

Bushy, as the nearly bald young man liked to be called, was a recent transplant from Lockmaster, and it was evident that he was doing well. The van was new. The lobby, it was obvious, had been professionally designed. On the walls were framed photographs from Bushy's prize-winning Scottish series. There was even a receptionist in the lobby, and she was not badlooking. True, she seemed to be doing invoices and correspondence as well as phones, but she was a pleasant addition to the lobby.

Qwilleran said to Bushy, "Your business seems to be thriving."

"Yeah, they keep me busy all right: studio portraits Wednesdays and Saturdays by appointment only; commercial work at my own pace; free-lance assignments for the newspaper."

"Your photo of Trevelyan on the front page—wasn't it the same one that hangs in the Lumbertown lobby? You made him look good!"

"I'll say I did! If the police use it for their Wanted poster, they'll never catch the guy! You see, I was shooting his train layout for a hobby magazine, and the editor wanted a head-shot of Floyd. I tried a candid, but it made him look like the wild man in a carnival. So I got him to put on a shirt and tie and do a formal sitting in the studio. His secretary came along. She's a knockout, but she drove me crazy, telling Floyd to turn his head, or raise his chin, or not look at the camera. Finally I asked her to wait in the lobby while I took the picture. That didn't make points with her boss, but I got a good portrait."

"Interesting sidelight," Qwilleran said. . . . "Are you going to the game tonight?"

"Should I?" asked the newcomer to Pickax.

"It's the sporting highlight of the year!" Qwilleran said seriously, as if it were true. "Take your receptionist."

Once a year there was a softball game between the Typos and the Tubes—two scrub teams composed of newspaper staffers and hospital personnel. Compared to the regular league games, their efforts were ludicrous, and the only spectators were family members and fellow employees, but everyone had a good time. On this occasion, Qwilleran was in no mood to attend the game alone, but he knew Roger MacGillivray would be on the sidelines, hurling scurrilous insults at the Tubes. Roger was the on-the-spot reporter in Mudville.

The softball field had been merely a bare spot in the landscape west of Pickax until the K Foundation added two more diamonds, a soccer field, bleacher seats, and a pavilion. Now it was named Goodwinter Field, after the founders of the city. A Goodwinter was playing shortstop this year—Junior, the managing editor. Others were recruited from the city room, sports department, and photo lab. Their bright red T-shirts and baseball caps made a lively scene when they were in the field. The hospital team, composed mostly of technicians, wore T-shirts in operating-room green and happened to win every year.

Most of the spectators sat in the second and third rows of the bleachers. Junior's wife was there with a baby in a car tote and a small boy who couldn't sit still. Bushy had brought his receptionist, who was more attractive than Qwilleran had previously thought. Arch and Mildred Riker were there, of course, wearing red baseball caps with the MCS logo.

"Where's Polly?" Mildred asked.

Hixie Rice and Dwight Somers were a chummy duo seated apart from the others, a development that was duly noted by the matchmakers at the game. She waved to Qwilleran and called out, "Where's Polly?"

When he saw Roger arriving and heading for the pavilion, he followed him. "Nice piece in the paper today, Roger."

"Thanks. I finally learned how to make no-news sound like news."

"The shooting of the dog was a bizarre twist."

"Right! The natives are restless. Someone threw a brick through the Lumbertown office window this afternoon, and when they talk about F.T., the initials stand for something else."

The cry of "Batter up" sent the two men scurrying to the bleachers with their soft drinks. At Qwilleran's suggestion they climbed to the top row. "Better view," he explained. More privacy, he thought.

The sun was still high in the sky, where it belonged on a summer evening in the north country. The play on the field was leisurely. The sports fans were appropriately rude.

During a lull in the game, Qwilleran asked, "How did you find out about the dog?"

"The family reported it to the police, and I went out to their house. They're not supposed to talk to the media, and the nurse wouldn't let me in, but then the daughter saw me and said it was all right. She was in my history class when I was teaching—an A-plus student. When I'd assign a chapter, she'd augment it with research in the library.... *Sock it to 'im, Dave! Break his bat!* . . . She should've gone on to college."

"Why didn't she?"

"They wanted her at home to take care of her invalid mother. I think she's a lonely and frustrated girl. I could tell she wanted to talk to me, lawyer or no lawyer. We went out on the patio and reminisced about high school—had a few laughs."

"Could you tell how she was reacting to the publicity and the pressure?"

"She was all broken up about the dog. He was a chow. His name was Zak, spelled Z-a-k. *Dead on second! Good mitt, Juny!* . . . Finally she told me, off the record, that the dog really belonged to her brother, but the lawyer wanted the public to think he was Floyd's."

"So all the dog lovers would feel sorry for his client," Qwilleran suggested.

"Right! Her brother lives in an apartment where they don't allow pets, so he kenneled Zak at his parents' house, nights. Served a double purpose. Everybody in the country has a watchdog. . . . *Make it three, Dave. You're hot!*"

Dave made it three, the green shirts trotted onto the field, and the red shirts took their turn at bat.

"Was Floyd's son in any of your classes?" Qwilleran asked.

"All I can say is: He occupied a seat. A student he was not! He and his buddy from Chipmunk were always in trouble."

"What kind of trouble?"

"Fighting . . . carrying knives . . . underage drinking . . ."

"Any drugs?"

"Alcohol was the chief problem then. That was a few years ago, you know. Eddie and the other kid were expelled. . . . *Okay, Typos! Murder those bedpan pushers!*"

From the third row Riker bellowed, *"Send those bloodsuckers to the morgue!"*

Nevertheless, at the end of the sixth, the score stood 12 to 5 in the Tubes' favor. Qwilleran watched with mild enthusiasm; he preferred hardball to softball. He liked the overhand or sidearm pitch, the crack of a real baseball, the long run to first, and *nine* innings. At the next lull he asked Roger, "Does Floyd's daughter think the shooting was connected with the charge against her father?"

"She didn't say, and I didn't ask. Sensitive subject."

"What time did the shooting take place?"

"About two in the morning. Her mother was awake and heard the shot. She rang for her daughter."

"Did anyone hear the dog bark at the prowler?"

"I guess not."

The game ended at 13 to 8, and Roger stood up, yelling. *"Good try, guys! Next year we'll anesthetize those tube jockeys!"*

When Qwilleran returned to the barn after the game, Yum Yum was curled up like a shrimp in his favorite lounge chair, asleep. Koko was in the foyer, looking out the window.

"If it's Zak you're waiting for, give up!" Qwilleran told him. "He won't be coming around anymore. . . . Let's have a read. Book! Book!"

After one last intense look down the trail, Koko tore himself away from the window and did some educated sniffing on the bookshelves. Finally he nosed *The Panama Canal: An Engineering Treatise.*

"Thank you for reminding me," said Qwilleran, who had forgotten to open the book since bringing it home.

It contained many statistics and black-and-white photos of World War I vintage, and although Qwilleran found it quite absorbing, Yum Yum quickly fell asleep, and Koko kept yawning conspicuously.

"To be continued," Qwilleran said as he replaced the book on the history shelf.

SEVEN

After the ballgame and the Panama Canal session, Qwilleran phoned Polly at her apartment. "Did you read the front page today?" he asked. "Did you see the item about the Trevelyan dog?"

"Wasn't that a senseless, uncivilized thing to do?" she replied vehemently. "What did they hope to accomplish? It won't bring the fugitive back! It won't compensate them for their financial losses!"

"And it wasn't even Floyd's dog," Qwilleran told her. "It belonged to his son, your builder."

"That's even worse!"

"He's the chow who came to work with the crew every day—a beautiful animal, friendly and well-behaved."

"Are there any suspects, have you heard?"

"Not as yet, I guess. Police are investigating."

"Oh, dear," Polly sighed. "One evil only leads to another."

Qwilleran changed the tone of his voice from objective to warmly personal. "And how is everything with you and Bootsie?"

"We're well, thank you. And what did you do today, dear?"

"Well, this evening I watched the Tubes trounce the Typos in the annual ballgame. I knew you'd be too busy to go, but everyone wanted to know where you were." This was stretching the truth; there had been only two inquiries, although everyone was probably wondering why the richest bachelor in the northeast central United States was alone. Hope sprang eternal in the breasts of several hundred single and soon-to-be-single women in Moose County.

"I'm sorry, dear," Polly said. "I know I haven't been good company recently. I've had so much on my mind."

"That's all right," he said and then added naughtily, "Celia Robinson arrives tomorrow, and I feel obliged to spend some time with her. She doesn't know anyone up here."

There was an eloquent pause before Polly said coolly, "That's very hospitable of you."

"You'll meet her sooner or later, although I think she's not your type. She splits infinitives."

"I'll look forward to meeting her." Polly's voice dripped icicles.

"Well, I'll let you get back to your blueprints."

"Thank you for calling . . . dear."

"I'll keep in touch. Don't let the house get you down, Polly."

Qwilleran hung up with a pang of misgiving. He had deliberately irked Polly by mentioning Celia, and he recognized it as an act of unkindness to vent his own frustration. It was like shooting the embezzler's dog, he realized.

Tomorrow, he told himself, he might call and apologize; then again, he might not.

The next day was sunny with little breeze and temperatures higher than usual. An Anvil Chorus of ringing hammers at the end of the trail indicated that the carpenters were working feverishly. After coffee and a roll, Qwilleran walked down to the building site. There were now three men on the job, all wearing sweatbands and no shirts. Their perspiring backs glistened in the sun.

Qwilleran called to them, "Could you guys use some cold drinks? I live at the end of the trail. Be glad to bring a cooler down here."

"Got any beer?" asked the helper with a ponytail.

"No beer!" Eddie ordered. "No drinkin' on the job when you work for me . . . *Benno*!" The way he spoke the man's name was a reprimand in itself.

Qwilleran went home and loaded a cooler with soft drinks, which he delivered by car. The trio of workers removed their nail aprons and dropped down under a tree—Zak's tree—and popped the cans gratefully.

After a couple of swallows, Eddie set down his drink and started sharpening a pencil with a pocketknife.

Qwilleran said, "I notice you sharpen that pencil a lot."

"Gotta have a sharp pencil when you measure a board," the carpenter said, "or you can be way off."

"Is that so? It never occurred to me. . . . Where's your dog? Is it too hot for him today?"

The two helpers looked at their boss questioningly, and Eddie said with a glum scowl, "He won't be comin' with me no more. Some dirty skunk shot him, night before last."

"You don't mean it!" Qwilleran said in feigned surprise. "Sorry to hear it. Was it a hunter, mistaking him for a wild animal?"

Furiously Eddie said, "Wasn't no accident! I could kill the guy what done it!"

Qwilleran commiserated with genuine feeling and then said he'd leave the cooler and pick it up later.

Eddie followed him to the car. "D'you live in

the barn up there? Somebody in my family built it, way back. This was his orchard. I see you fixed up the barn pretty good. I poked around one day when there wasn't nobody home, 'cept a cat lookin' at me out the window. At first I thought it was a weasel."

"Would you like to see the inside of the barn when you've finished work today?" This was a rare invitation. Qwilleran discouraged ordinary sightseers.

"Would I! You bet!" the young man exclaimed. "We quit at four-thirty. I'll drive up and bring your cooler back."

"Good! We'll have a drink." Qwilleran knew how to play the genial host.

Before driving back up the trail, he picked up his mail and noticed with foreboding a bulky envelope from the accounting firm. It suggested tax complications with pages of obscure wordage in fine print. When he opened it, however, out fell a large swatch of plaid cloth in bright red—the Mackintosh tartan. He felt the quality. It was a fine wool, and the red was brilliant. An accompanying note from Gordie Shaw stated that custom-made kilts could be ordered from Scottie's Men's Store. There was also an application for membership in the Clan Mackintosh of North America. It was simple enough; the dues were low; his mother's clan affiliation qualified him for membership. It was something he would have to think about seriously—the membership, not the kilt. He left the envelope on the telephone desk where it would catch his eye and jog his decision.

Qwilleran planned to stay home all day, waiting for an important phone call. Celia Robinson was driving up from Illinois and was instructed to telephone upon reaching Lockmaster.

Throughout the day there were frenzied sounds of building at the end of the trail: the clunk of two-by-fours, the buzz of a tablesaw, the syncopated rhythm of hammers. Qwilleran admired a carpenter's skill in sinking a nail with three powerful blows. His own attempts started with a series of uncertain taps, a smashed thumb, and a crooked nail, which he tried to flatten by beating it into the wood sideways.

At about two o'clock the phone rang, and Koko's uncanny sense knew it was important; he raced to the telephone and jumped on and off the desk. Qwilleran followed, saying, "I'll take it, if you don't mind."

A cheery voice said, "I'm in Lockmaster, Chief, and I'm reporting like you said. Permission requested to proceed." This little charade was followed by a trill of laughter.

"Good! You're thirty miles from Pickax, which is straight north," he said crisply. "When you reach the city limits, it's three more blocks to a traffic circle with a little park in the center. Look for the K Theatre on your right. It's a big fieldstone building. Turn into the driveway. I'll be watching for you. Red car, did you say?"

"Very red, Chief," she said with a hearty laugh.

Qwilleran immediately jogged through the woods to the carriage house to check its readiness. The windows were clean, the phone was connected, and the rooms had been brightened with framed flower prints, potted plants, and colorful pillows. He added a copy of the *Moose County Something* to the coffee table. The kitchen was miraculously complete, even to red-and-white checked dishtowels. In the bedroom there was a' floral bedspread; in the guestroom, a Navajo design. He thought, Nice going, Fran!

Qwilleran went downstairs, just in time to see a red car pulling into the theatre parking lot. The driver rolled down her window and gave him a wide, toothy smile. "We made it!"

"Welcome to Pickax," he said, reaching in to shake her hand.

She was a youthful-looking, gray-haired woman whose only wrinkles were laugh lines around the eyes and smile creases in the cheeks.

"You look just like your picture in the paper, Chief!"

He grunted acknowledgment. "How was the trip?"

"We took it easy, so as not to put a strain on Wrigley. Most of the way he was pretty good." In the backseat a black-and-white cat peered mutely through the barred door of a plastic carrier. "One motel in Wisconsin didn't take pets, but I told them he was related to the White House cat, so they let him stay."

"Quick thinking, Celia."

"That's something I learned from you, Chief—how to make up a neat little story. . . . Where shall I park?"

"At the doorway to the carriage house—over there. I'll carry your luggage upstairs, but first we'll show the apartment to Wrigley, to see if it meets with his approval."

Celia laughed merrily at this mild quip. "I'll carry his sandbox and water dish."

As they climbed the stairs, Qwilleran apologized for the narrowness of the flight and the shallowness of the treads. "This was built a hundred years ago when people had narrow shoulders and small feet." This brought another trill of laughter, and he thought, I've got to be careful what I say to this woman; she's jacked up.

Upstairs she gushed over the spaciousness and comfort of the rooms, while Wrigley methodically sniffed the premises that had once been home to two Siamese.

"Now, while I'm bringing up your luggage," Qwilleran instructed Celia, "you sit down and make a list of what groceries you need. Then I'll do your shopping while you take a rest."

"Oh, that's too much trouble for you, Chief!"

"Not at all. I have an ulterior motive. Did you bring your recipe for chocolate brownies?"

She laughed again. "I brought a whole shoe-box of recipes!"

He had a reason for wanting to shop alone. Otherwise it would be all over town that Mr. Q was buying groceries in the company of a strange woman who laughed at everything he said and was not at all like Mrs. Duncan.

"This evening," he said in a businesslike way, "it will be my pleasure to take you to dinner, and tomorrow a pleasant woman by the name of Virginia Alstock will drive you around and give you a crash course in what Pickax is all about."

"Oh, Chief! I don't know what to say. You're so kind!"

"Don't say anything. Get to work on that list. I have a four-thirty appointment."

"*Yes, sir!*" she said with a stiff salute and torrents of laughter.

Qwilleran himself was a chuckler, not a laugher, and on the way to Toodles' Market he began to wonder how much of Celia's merriment he could stand. He pushed a cart up and down the aisles briskly, collecting the fifteen items on her list. At the checkout counter the cashier expressed surprise.

"Gonna do some cooking, Mr. Q?"

Ordinarily he checked out a few ounces of turkey or shrimp and a frozen dinner. Tonight he was buying unusual items like flour, potatoes, bananas, and canned cat food. "Just shopping for a sick friend," he explained.

He delivered the groceries to the carriage house and returned to the barn just as Eddie Trevelyan's pickup came bouncing up the trail. The young man, in jeans and a tank top, jumped out of the cab and gestured toward the decrepit orchard. "Y'oughta do somethin' about them weeds and rotted trees."

"What would you suggest?" Qwilleran asked amiably.

"I could clean 'em out with a bulldozer and backhoe, pave the road, and build a string of condos." He glanced toward the front window. "There's the weasel again. You sure he's a cat?"

"Sometimes I'm not sure *what* he is" was the truthful answer.

"Hey, this is some barn, ain't it?"

"Wait till you see the interior. Come in and have a drink."

As soon as they went indoors, Koko came forward with mouth open and fangs bared, emitting a hostile hiss. His stiffened tail was straight as a fencer's sword.

"Does he bite?" the visitor asked, drawing back.

"No, he's overreacting because you think he's a weasel. Sit down and make yourself comfortable. Sit anywhere," he added, noting the young man's reluctance to step on the unbleached Moroccan rug or sit on the pale, mushroom-tinted furniture. "What's your drink?"

"Shot 'n' a beer's okay." He sank into a capacious lounge chair and stared in awe at the balconies, catwalks, ramps, and giant fireplace cube.

"How do you like it?" Qwilleran called from the bar.

"Piece o' work, man!"

"I heard about the house you built for the Alstocks in Black Creek. It's been highly praised."

"Yeah ... well ..." Eddie was uncomfortable with the compliment.

At the barn the drinks were usually served on a tray, but on this occasion Qwilleran carried the beer can and shot glass by hand. "How are you getting along with Mrs. Duncan?" he asked.

"She's okay, but she worries too much. She's always on my back about somethin'." He downed the whiskey. "Hey, I don't know your name."

"Qwilleran. Jim Qwilleran."

"I think I heard it somewheres."

"Could be. . . . I noticed you had an extra helper today."

"The job'll go faster now."

"Who's your regular man? You two seem to work well as a team."

"Benno. He's from Chipmunk. I knew him in high school. We both took Vocational. What do you do?"

"I'm a writer. I write books ... about ... baseball." It was the whitest lie Qwilleran could devise on the spur of the moment. He could get away with it because Eddie obviously did not read the *Moose County Something*.

"I like soccer," Eddie said, and Qwilleran became an instant soccer enthusiast.

After the builder's second shot of whiskey, he seemed more relaxed. "Wotcha think of my dog?"

"Beautiful chow! Friendly personality! What was his name?"

"Zak."

"Good name. Who came up with that?"

"My sister."

"Did she get along with Zak, or was he strictly a man's dog?"

"Zak liked everybody. But him and me, we were like buddies. He was a joker, too. I'd take him out on a job, and he'd hang around all day till I started to pack up. Then he'd take off, and I'd hafta chase him. The louder I yelled, the faster he'd run, like he was laughin' at me. He liked to run, di'n't like to be chained. He had a long dog run at my folks' house. That's where they got 'im. Right between the eyes. Musta come outa the kennel to see who was prowlin' around."

"Did he bark? Shouldn't he have barked?"

"Di'n't nobody hear any barkin'."

"Where was his body found?"

"Right near the fence."

Qwilleran smoothed his moustache. "So he was evidently shot at close range, and he didn't bark. Sounds as if the shooter was someone he knew."

Eddie's delayed response and nervous eye-balls gave the impression that he knew more than he was telling. "Zak knew lotsa people."

Qwilleran was at his sympathetic best: the concern in his eyes, the kindly tilt of his head, the way he leaned toward his listener, the gentle tone of his voice. "How's your mother feeling these days?"

Eddie looked startled. "D'you know her?"

"We've met, and I feel very bad about her illness. Does she have good medical care?"

"Aw, the doctors don't know nothin'. There's one doctor that has a cure, but he's in Switzerland."

"Is that so? Have you thought of taking her there?"

"Yeah, my sister and me, we thought about it, but . . . we di'n't have the dough. The trip, y'know . . . the treatment . . . stayin' there a long time . . . outa sight! I dunno . . ."

"How about another drink?" Qwilleran suggested.

"Nah, I gotta hit the road."

"Some coffee? I could throw a burger in the microwave."

"Nah, I gotta meet a guy in Sawdust."

As the contractor drove away in his pickup, Koko ambled inquisitively into the room as if saying, Has he gone?

"That was impolite to hiss at a guest," Qwilleran reprimanded him, though realizing the cat had never before seen such a hairy human. He himself was pleased that he had concealed his connection with the media, while establishing a contact with the Trevelyan family that could be pursued without arousing suspicion. He made a mental list of procedures:

—Continue to take an insulated chest of cold drinks to the building site.

—Talk soccer with the crew during their break; read the soccer news in the daily paper.

—Attend a soccer game.

—Show interest in the house construction and ask dumb questions.

Qwilleran's ideas concerning the shooting of the dog were crystallizing. The perpetrator (a) had a grudge against Floyd and (b) knew where and how the dog was kenneled, although (c) he was unaware that he was shooting someone else's pet. One distasteful idea came to mind: The crime was purposely committed to encourage public sympathy for Floyd. The notion was not completely farfetched in this stronghold of dog owners.

In any case, since Zak had not barked and was shot at close range, the shooter was obviously someone he knew, and yet . . . that could be anyone. Zak was friendly to a fault.

Regarding the police investigation of the shooting, Qwilleran assumed that they knew all of the above but had more important matters to investigate, such as the whereabouts of the embezzler himself.

Something Eddie had said now started a new train of thought: Floyd might have stashed the stolen money in Swiss banks; he might now be in Switzerland and not Mexico as everyone assumed; he might be arranging to fly his wife there for treatment. This theory, Qwilleran realized, had its flaws, but if it were viable, why had Koko performed his death dance? Baffled, he decided to table the matter and take Celia Robinson to dinner.

First he had to feed the cats. He often reflected that he was retired from the workplace, had no family responsibilities, and was the richest man in the northeast central United States. Yet his entire life was structured around the humble routine of feeding the Siamese, brushing their coats, entertaining them, doing lap service, and policing their commode. Early in his life it would have been inconceivable!

The question now arose: Where to take the loudly gleeful Mrs. Robinson to dinner? The New Pickax Hotel was the usual choice for business dinners and social obligations; no one went there for fun. On this evening Polly would be dining there with the library board, a group of genteel older women whose voices never rose higher than a murmur. The dining room was small, furthermore, and other tables would be occupied by lone business travelers intent on their tough steak. Celia's shrieks of laughter would reverberate like a tropical bird in a mortuary.

Qwilleran's own favorite restaurant was the Old Stone Mill, but he was too well known there, and the entire staff kept tabs on his dining companions. The safest choice was a steakhouse in North Kennebeck named Tipsy's. It occupied a large log cabin; the atmosphere was informal; the patrons were noisy; and the restaurant had the distinction of being named after the owner's cat. That would please Celia.

When he called for her, she was obviously wearing her best dress, her best jewelry, and full makeup. She looked nice, although she would be conspicuous at Tipsy's.

"Where are we going?" she asked with excitement. "I saw ads in the paper for Otto's Tasty Eats and the Nasty Pasty. Such funny names! And *Moose County Something* is a crazy name for a newspaper! I also read about a town called Brrr; was that a misprint?"

"Brrr happens to be the coldest spot in the county," he informed her.

"That's a good one!" she exclaimed with hearty laughter. "Wait till I tell my grandson! I write to Clayton once a week, sometimes twice."

"You can plan on plenty of two-letter weeks while you're here," Qwilleran said. "People who live 400 miles north of everywhere tend to be *different*. It's called frontier individualism."

On the way to North Kennebeck Celia continued to be convulsed with merriment at sign-posts pointing to Chipmunk, West Middle Hummock, and Sawdust City. "I don't believe it!" she cried when Ittibittiwassee Road crossed the Ittibittiwassee River. "Are they for real?"

"Sawdust City is not only real but recently it's been the scene of a major financial scandal."

"I like scandals!" she cried happily.

"Virginia Alstock will fill in the details to-morrow, but briefly: The president of a finan-cial institution has disappeared along with his secretary and millions of dollars belonging to depositors. Mrs. Alstock will also take you to meet Lisa Compton at the Senior Care Facility. Would you care for part-time work as a com-panion for elderly shut-ins?"

"Oh, yes! I'm good with old people and in-valids. I cheer them up."

"I believe it!" he said sincerely.

Celia became serious. "Do you think I laugh too much, Chief?"

"How much is too much?"

"Well, my daughter-in-law says I do. My hus-band was just the opposite. He always expected the worst. I've always been an optimist, and I began laughing to make up for his bad humor, but the more I laughed, the worse he got, and the worse he got, the more I laughed. It was funny when you think about it. I noticed you never laugh, Chief, although you've got a ter-rific sense of humor."

"I'm a chuckler," he said. "My laughter is internal. I wrote a column once about the many kinds of laughter. People giggle, titter, guffaw, snicker, cackle, or roar. My friend Polly Duncan, whom you'll meet, has a musical laugh that's very pleasant. Laughter is an expression of mirth involving the facial muscles, throat, lungs, mouth, and eyes. It's usually involuntary, but one can control the volume and tone to suit the time and place. It's called fine-tuning. . . . My next lecture will be at 9 a.m. tomorrow."

"I never thought of that," she said. "I'm going to try fine-tuning."

"There's a hostess at the restaurant where we're going who greets customers with loud, cackling laughter. I always think, There goes another egg."

Celia tried to smother her screams of delight. "What's the name of the restaurant?"

"The Chicken Coop."

She exploded again but cut it short.

"No, it's really called Tipsy's." Then he explained how it was founded in the 1930s and named after a white-and-black cat whose markings made her look inebriated, and whose deformed foot made her stagger. "Her portrait in the main dining room was the subject of county-wide controversy recently," he said, "resolved only when art fakery was revealed."

When they arrived at the restaurant and were greeted by the hostess with a cackling laugh, Celia struggled to keep a straight face as she mumbled to Qwilleran, "Another egg!"

The menu was limited. Qwilleran always ordered the steak. Celia asked if the fish had bones, because she wanted to take some home to Wrigley. During the meal she had many questions to ask.

"Who is your friend with the nice laugh?"

"The administrator of the public library. It's her assistant who will chauffeur you around town tomorrow."

"Where do you live?"

"No doubt you've noticed the evergreen forest behind the theatre parking lot. Beyond that is an old orchard with a hundred-year-old apple barn. That's where I live."

"You live in a *barn*?"

"I've fixed it up a little. You'll see it one of these days. After you're settled, we'll have a talk. I think . . . I may have another assignment for you, Celia."

After dropping his dinner guest at her apartment, Qwilleran hurried to the barn to make a phone call. Just inside the kitchen door he picked up a black felt-tip pen from the floor. "Drat that cat!" he muttered as he dropped it into the pewter mug on the desk. A pen lying on a desktop was fair game to Koko, but he never filched one from the mug. He suspected Yum Yum.

It was the Compton residence that he called, and Lisa answered. "Do you want to speak to my grouchy husband?"

"No, I want to speak with his charming wife. It's about Pals for Patients."

"Sure. What can I do for you?"

"Does the Trevelyan family in West Middle Hummock ever call you for help?"

"All the time! The Pals we send out there never keep the job very long. It's a long drive for only a few hours' work, and it's an unhappy family. No one's assigned to them at the moment—not since the credit union closed. Their daughter worked there, but now she's at home, taking care of her mother herself. Why do you ask?"

"I've met the son. He's building Polly's house. It was his dog who was shot. Did you read about it?"

"Nasty business!" Lisa said.

"I agree. I have no sympathy for Floyd, but I feel sorry for his family, especially his wife, and I have a suggestion. The Celia Robinson I mentioned to you has a cheerful disposition that would do wonders for Mrs. Trevelyan, I'm sure. Mrs. Robinson will call at your office tomorrow, and I wish you'd see what you can do."

"You don't think she'd mind the drive?"

"She's just driven for three days with a cat in the backseat, and there were no complaints— from either of them. She's an inspiration, I tell you! She could even make Lyle smile."

"Hands off my husband!" Lisa said. "He may be an old curmudgeon, but he's mine! . . . Okay, I'll see what I can do."

Qwilleran hung up slowly with a satisfied

feeling of accomplishment. Already his logical mind was telling him how to brief Celia for her assignment. As he sat at the desk, making notes with a black felt-tip, he realized that neither cat had greeted him at the door. He glanced around casually, then with mounting concern. That's when he saw the blood-red splotch on a light-colored sofa.

Logic gave way to panic! He jumped up, knocking over the desk chair, and rushed toward the lounge area. "Koko! Yum Yum!" he shouted. There was no answer.

EIGHT

Words can hardly express Qwilleran's panic when he glimpsed the blood-red splotch in the lounge area, nor his relief upon finding that it was the swatch of fabric in the Mackintosh tartan. The Siamese had stolen it! The envelope containing the application for membership in the clan was on the floor nearby. And where were the culprits? On top of the fireplace cube, observing Qwilleran's brief frenzy with wonder, as if thinking, *What fools these mortals be!*

"You devils!" he said, shaking his fist in their direction. Then he had second thoughts. It was not necessarily a two-cat caper. Which one of them was guilty? They both looked annoyingly innocent. Most likely Koko had heisted the envelope for some obscure reason of his own. Did he smell the red dye in the cloth? At one time in his brief but stellar career he had chewed red neckties.

Then Qwilleran had a quirky thought. "If you're trying to get me into a kilt," he shouted at Koko, *"no dice!"*

Nevertheless, he read the application blank once more. By nature he was not a joiner of clubs, societies, or associations (apart from the press club). Yet, as Big Mac had said, it would be a tribute to his mother if he joined the clan; she had been so proud of her Scottish heritage. Having reached middle age, he now found himself thinking about her with appreciation and admiration. He remembered her precepts: Give more than you get. . . . Be yourself; don't imitate your peers. . . . Always serve beverages on a tray.

She had died when he was in college. If she had lived longer, she would have gloried in his success as a journalist, wept over the crisis that almost ruined his life, and finally delighted in his new prosperity, especially since it was her Klingenschoen connection that sowed the seed.

Qwilleran filled out the membership application. Polly would be happy. "But no kilt!" he muttered to himself.

"YOW!" came a comment from the top of the fireplace cube.

The day after his visit with Eddie Trevelyan, Qwilleran drove to the mailbox with another cooler of soft drinks in the trunk. This was Phase One in his plan to get into the Trevelyan household by the back door. For Phase Two he would need Celia's help and the cooperation of Lisa Compton.

There were five trucks at the building site; electrician and plumber were "roughing in," according to Eddie. Qwilleran dropped off the cooler and returned to the barn to read his mail. One letter piqued his curiosity. The stationery had character, and the envelope was hand written in a distinctive script. He read:

Dear Mr. Q,

Just a note to say I'm sending you a memento from my father's personal collection. Whenever you sit in it, your creativity will scintillate. I want you to have this souvenir because I shall never forget that you saved my life on the island and encouraged me to improve my life-style.

My brother will bring it over on his boat, and Derek will pick it up at the pier in Mooseville and deliver it in his truck.

Gratefully,
Liz

*   *   *

Qwilleran's first thought was: No! Not a pyramid! What will I do with it? Where can I put it? How large is it? Can I donate it to a school or museum without hurting Elizabeth's feelings? She had wanted him to call her Liz, a diminutive that only her father had used, but Qwilleran had no desire to be a surrogate parent.

He read the rest of his mail, throwing most of it into the wastebasket or red-inking it for handling by the secretarial service. A few letters he would answer himself, by postal card or phone call. Cards required fewer words than letters and were cheaper to mail. Despite his new wealth, there was an old frugality in his nature.

After that he went to work in his balcony studio, which was off-limits to the Siamese. The closed-door policy, he liked to explain, kept the cats out of his hair and the cat hairs out of his typewriter. Now he was trying to find something different to say about baseball for the "Qwill Pen" column.

He wrote, "Compared to a nervous, hyped-up, violent, clock-watching game like football, baseball is a spectator sport that encourages relaxation. The leisurely pace—punctuated by well-spaced spurts of running, sliding, and arguing—promotes a feeling of well-being, enhanced by the consumption of a hot dog or beverage of choice. The continual pauses—for bat-swinging, mitt-thumping, cap-tugging, belt-hitching, hand-spitting, and homeplate-dusting—produce a pleasant hypnosis."

Qwilleran's concentration was interrupted by the urgent ringing of the doorbell, as well as banging on the kitchen door. He ran down the ramp and found Derek Cuttlebrink towering on the doorstep. "Special delivery from Breakfast Island!" he announced. "Want me to carry it in?"

"Will it come through the doorway?" Qwilleran asked. A pyramid large enough to sit in, he reasoned, would have awkward dimensions.

"No problem," Derek yelled as he returned to his pickup and unloaded an item of furniture. "Where d'you want me to put it?" he asked as he maneuvered it through the kitchen door.

"Do I have to tell you?" Qwilleran responded tartly. "What is it supposed to be?"

"A rocking chair! Handmade! Antique! One size fits all! It belonged to Elizabeth's old man." Derek set the rocker down and sat in it. "Comfortable, too! Try it; you'll like it!"

It was made entirely of bent twigs, except for the rockers—and the bowl-shaped seat that appeared to be varnished treebark. Qwilleran thought, It's the ugliest chair I've ever seen! He slid into the seat cautiously and was immediately tilted back as if ready for dental surgery. It was, however, a remarkably comfortable sling.

"There's something I'm supposed to give

you." Derek dashed out to his truck and returned with a snapshot. "This is her old man, posing with his chair. She thought you'd like to see what he looked like. Now I've gotta get to work. I'm on for the dinner hour, five to eight."

"What about your rehearsal?" Qwilleran called after him.

"The rude mechanicals aren't scheduled tonight."

After Derek had driven away, raising more dust than other visitors had done, Qwilleran grabbed the phone and called Amanda's Studio of Design, hoping Fran Brodie would be in-house. She answered.

"Stay there! I'll be right over!" he shouted. He hung up while she was still sputtering, "What . . . What . . . ?"

He usually chose to walk downtown, but this time he drove. At the design studio he barged through the front door and threw a snapshot on Fran's desk. "Know anything about this? The chair, not the man."

The designer's eyes grew wide. "Where did you get this picture? Who is he? Is he selling the chair?"

"The man's dead. The chair is in my barn. It's supposed to be a thank-you from Elizabeth for saving her life on the island. If I'd known I was getting this, I'd have thrown her back in the swamp."

"Very funny," Fran said, "but you don't know what you're talking about. This is a twistletwig rocker, a hundred years old, at least. It was the poor man's bentwood, made of willow."

"Well, the poor man can have it! Even Whistler's Mother would think it was ugly. Koko sniffed it and made a face. Yum Yum won't go anywhere near it; that should tell you something!"

"I don't consider Yum Yum an arbiter of taste!" The two females had feuded briefly at one time, and Yum Yum won. "As a matter of fact, it's a beautiful piece of folk art, and a dealer on the East Coast recently advertised one for $2,000."

"You're pulling my leg!"

"I'm not! This is a choice collectible! Do you want to sell? Amanda will give you a thousand without blinking. Is it comfortable?"

"Very, but I still think it's a nightmare masquerading as furniture."

"Go back! You're not ready!" Fran said impatiently. "The chair is linear sculpture! It'll be a dynamic accent for your light, contemporary furniture. Live with it for a while, and you'll be writing a treatise for the "Qwill Pen" on the charms of twistletwig. I'll help you do some research."

She had said the magic word; whenever anyone mentioned material for his column, Qwilleran went on red alert. To save face he pointed to a wooden box on her desk. "What's that? Is that another high-priced collectible?" It was slightly crude, in the size and shape of a two-pound loaf of bread.

"That's an English pencil box," Fran said. "A country piece, rather old. I believe it's walnut. It came from the Witherspoon estate in Lockmaster."

The wood was a mellow brown enhanced by the distress marks of age. The lid was rimmed with a fine line of brass, and there was a small brass key in the lock. Qwilleran lifted the lid and found a shallow compartment.

"You could use it for cufflinks," she suggested.

"I don't use cufflinks. No one in Pickax uses cufflinks! What I need is a place to lock up my pens. One of our resident cat burglars has been swiping them, and I suspect Koko."

"This would be perfect, and you could use the drawer at the bottom for paper clips."

"Yum Yum opens drawers and collects paper clips." He tugged at the drawer. "It's jammed."

"No, it isn't. There's a secret latch."

"I'll take it," he said. "Also my snapshot."

Carrying the pencil box under his arm, Qwilleran walked to his car two blocks away; parking was a major problem in downtown Pickax. He could never set foot in the center of town without meeting a dozen acquaintances, and today he threw greetings to his barber, an off-duty patrolman, the cashier from Toodles' Market, and the proprietor of Scottie's Men's Store, who said, "Aye, there's the Laird hi'self!

When will you be comin' in to be measured for a kilt?"

"Not until you hear from my undertaker," Qwilleran retorted.

Then Larry Lanspeak, on the way to the bank, stopped him to ask, "What's that you're carrying? Your lunch bucket?"

"No, a pistol case. I'm on my way to a duel. . . . How's the play coming, Larry?"

"We've had problems. Fran and the new girl from Chicago wanted to incorporate a pyramid in the forest scenes. Imagine cluttering the stage, complicating the blocking, and confusing the audience with such a senseless gimmick! Carol, Junior, and I had to threaten to drop out before Fran would listen to reason. That girl is a good client of hers and also made a sizable donation to the club's operating budget. Politics! Politics!"

Arriving home with his English pencil box, Qwilleran filled the top compartment with felt-tip pens. One of the black ones was missing again, and he found it in the foyer. The drawer he filled with jumbo paper clips. The Siamese watched, their inquisitive tails curved like scimitars.

"Foiled, you villains!" he said as he locked the lid. He left the key in the lock, since neither cat had learned how to turn keys. It would be only a matter of time, he surmised.

He and Polly dined early at the Old Stone

Mill, as she was attending a dessert-and-coffee wedding shower for one of the library clerks. "Would you care to join us?" she asked teasingly. "Men often attend showers now, you know."

"This man doesn't," he said, putting a brusque end to the subject. "The electrician and plumber were working on your house this morning. It's beginning to look less like a lumberyard and more like a habitation."

"What am I going to do with all those mounds of soil they excavated for the foundation?" she asked with a worried frown.

"I suppose they'll use some of it for fill and then grade the lot. They'll move the dirt anywhere you say, with two swipes of the bulldozer."

"I'd love to have a berm between the house and the highway. With plantings it would give a sense of privacy, but I don't want it to look landscaped. I want it to look completely natural. How does one do that?"

Rather too sharply Qwilleran said, "One calls Kevin Doone. He attended horticultural college for four years to learn how to do that."

"Do I bore you with my concerns about the house, dear?" Polly asked with a frank gaze.

"You never bore me! You know that. But—for your own sake—I wish you'd delegate your problems to the professionals instead of trying to make all the decisions yourself."

"It'll be the only house I'll ever build, and I

want it to express *me*," she said meekly. "I've always lived in places where I've had to compromise and make do."

"I understand, and I apologize for being flip. What else is preying on your mind? I want to hear."

"Well . . . the interior. I'd love to have white plastered walls and Williamsburg blue woodwork. I saw it in a magazine—with country antiques—but one needs good furniture with such a stark background. My things aren't good, but they're family heirlooms, and I couldn't part with them. I know wallpaper backgrounds are more flattering to a hodgepodge of furniture, but . . . I'm absolutely smitten with the idea of white walls and blue woodwork. Last night I couldn't sleep for thinking about it."

The solution would be so easy, he thought, if she would let him bankroll a houseful of pedigreed country antiques. She could have the twistletwig rocker for starters. But Polly would never approve of such largess. He said, "Suppose one of your clerks came to you with such a problem. How would you advise her?"

After a pause, she said with an abashed half-smile, "I'd tell her to keep the things she loves and use wallpaper."

"And I believe you'd be right."

Polly breathed a large sigh. "I've been doing all the talking. How thoughtless of me! What have you been doing?"

"Well, I had a chat with your builder, and

he's not a bad fellow, in spite of his raggle-taggle appearance and double negatives. I've come to the conclusion that Moose County is bilingual. Half of us speak standard English, and the other half speak Moose."

"What did you talk about?"

"Soccer, and the fact that one of his ancestors built the barn. Neither of us mentioned his father, of course, but I inquired about his mother's health. He seems to think that a Swiss doctor has a cure for her rare disease. One wonders how true it is, and how effective, and how safe."

"It's not to be dismissed out-of-hand," Polly asserted. "Alternative medicine has always been practiced in other countries, and now by maverick physicians here."

Then it was time for her to leave for the wedding shower. Qwilleran drove her back to the library, where her car was parked, and then went home to phone Celia.

She was waiting eagerly for his call. "I had a ball!" she cried. "Virginia is a lot of fun. She's contralto soloist at the Little Stone Church. She told me I could sing in the choir. And do you want to hear something funny? There's a cat that attends services every Sunday! They leave the front door ajar, and she walks in, picks out a lap, and sleeps all through the sermon. . . . Besides working at the library, Virginia has three teenagers, a dog, two cats, a hutch of rabbits, and some chickens."

"Where did you have lunch?"

"Lois's Luncheonette, and Lois sent two free desserts to our table—bread pudding. It wasn't as good as mine. I use egg whites to make it fluffy and whole wheat flour to make it chewy, plus nuts and raisins, and vanilla sauce."

"How do I place an order?" Qwilleran asked. "Do you accept credit cards?" There was laughter on the line before he could ask, "Did you meet Lisa Compton?"

"Yes, I did, and she's very nice. She told me about a sad case in West Middle Hummock where she can send me to—"

"Celia," he interrupted, "why don't you jump into your little red car and drive down here? You can see the apple barn, meet the cats, and tell me about the sad case."

Moments later she stepped out of her car in the barnyard and gasped at the sight. "I grew up on a farm and never saw anything like this!" She was equally enthralled by the interior but shocked at the condition of the orchard.

"According to legend," Qwilleran explained, "a curse was placed on the orchard a hundred years ago. I thought the curse had exceeded the statute of limitations, but lately the property's been under surveillance by the FBI."

"Really?"

"Yes, we have our own Feline Bureau of Investigation."

Celia laughed at his quip, but it was controlled laughter. She was fine-tuning.

The Siamese were listening to the conversation from a safe distance, sitting alertly and ready for flight if the visitor's laughter should hit the wrong note. Meanwhile they were sensing that she came from a poultry farm, lived with a black-and-white cat named Wrigley, and manufactured Kabibbles in her kitchen.

"Seriously," he said, "I'm glad you've enlisted in the Pals for Patients program. You're perfect for the job. What do you know about your first assignment?"

"Only that the patient is the wife of the man who disappeared with a lot of money that doesn't belong to him. It must be terrible for the poor woman, to be ill and have that happen. A practical nurse comes in five mornings a week, and I work afternoons. The rest of the time her daughter is there."

Qwilleran said, "I've heard that they're two lonely and unhappy women. With your cheerful personality you'll be very good for them. And you can do more than that! There's an element of mystery surrounding the scandal. I believe there's more to the story than people think." Then he added with heavy implication, "The police investigators may be on the wrong track."

Excitedly she asked, "Are you investigating it yourself, Chief?"

"I have no authority to do so, and the Trevelyans' lawyer has instructed them not to talk to the media."

"But you're not really media," she protested. "You just write a column, don't you?"

Qwilleran took a moment to enjoy an internal chuckle. "Be that as it may, it would be inadvisable for me to involve myself personally in the case."

Celia was sitting on the edge of her chair. "Could I help you, Chief?"

"I'm sure you could. When do you start?"

"Tomorrow afternoon."

"Suppose you get the lay of the land, and we'll talk again tomorrow evening. By that time I'll have planned our strategy."

"Is there anything special I should do tomorrow?"

"Just be friendly and sympathetic. They may welcome the chance to talk to someone. Don't ask too many questions; keep it conversational. And never . . . *never* let them know you're associated with me!"

"I'll write it down," she said. "I always write everything down." Her large handbag was on the floor near her chair, and she fumbled in it for a notepad, whereupon two quiet slinky Siamese approached in slow motion to explore its contents.

"No!" Qwilleran said firmly, and they withdrew backward at the same slow pace. "It's never a good idea to leave your handbag open while they're around," he explained. "Koko is an investigator, and Yum Yum is a kleptomaniac."

NINE

With unusual anticipation Qwilleran awaited
Celia Robinson's report on her first day in West
Middle Hummock. He patted his moustache
frequently as he assured himself he was finally
on-line with the investigation.

Copy was due for his Friday column, but his
profound treatise on baseball was not quite finished, so he dashed off a thousand words on
"the sweet corn of August," one of Moose
County's much-vaunted crops. Like vintners
with certain wines that don't travel well, farm-
ers produced only enough sweet corn for local

consumption—a rare delicacy that had never been exported.

He delivered the copy by bicycle, then took a long ride, hoping the monotony of pedaling would crystallize his thoughts about the Trevelyan case. It was an inspiration, he believed, to use Celia as a secret agent. In Florida she had proved herself to be entirely trustworthy: she used common sense; she followed instructions; she read spy novels. They would call this investigation Operation Whistle.

As Qwilleran approached the Park Circle, he was wondering whether to make an illegal left turn into the theatre driveway, or cut through the park where biking was prohibited, or circle the park and make an illegal U-turn. Before he could make up his mind, a police car pulled him to the curb, and Andrew Brodie stepped out.

"See your license?" the chief barked. "Attempting to elude an officer. Biking without a helmet. Exceeding the speed limit. Failure to provide a reflector on the rear fender."

"Write me a ticket," Qwilleran shot back, "and I'll see you in court on your day off."

Brodie was an imposing figure on the Pickax landscape, always growling and scowling and snapping commands—except when he was playing the bagpipe at weddings and funerals. He did both very well. Qwilleran considered him one of his best friends, and the two friends rarely missed an opportunity to exchange gibes.

After the usual banter, the chief dropped his official brusqueness and said in a voice brimming with innuendo, "I've noticed some activity behind the theatre."

The eagle-eyed cop had apparently seen the red car, but Qwilleran ignored the oblique reference and launched a long explanation that had nothing to do with the question. One of his many skills was his seemingly innocent failure "to get it."

"Yes, the parking lot's busy these days," he began. "They're in the throes of producing a new play, and you know what that means: actors rehearsing every night, set builders and costume makers on the job every day. It's quite an ambitious project: *A Midsummer Night's Dream* with a cast of hundreds. Your daughter's directing it. Shakespeare wrote it. Junior Goodwinter is playing Puck. Carol and Larry are doubling as—"

"Knock it off!" Brodie interrupted. "You've rented your carriage house to somebody—older woman—drives a red car—Florida plates."

Qwilleran's aimless babbling about the play had given him time to formulate a defense. "The real estate division of the K Foundation handles rentals. I don't get involved with that."

"But you know who she is," the chief said accusingly.

"Of course! Everyone knows who she is: a friend of Euphonia Gage in Florida."

"What's she doing up here?"

"I'm not entirely clear about this, but I believe it had to do with doctor's orders. She was in a deep depression following the death of her favorite grandson—or something like that—and Euphonia had praised Moose County as a good place to start a new life."

Brodie was unconvinced. "What kind of new life does she expect to start at her age?"

"Again: Don't quote me! But I've heard that she's a good cook, and the rumors are that she intends to start a small catering business. And you have to admit this town could stand some improved food service. The catering department at the hotel is an abomination. In fact, I wouldn't be surprised if the economic development division of the K Foundation had been instrumental in bringing this woman up from Down Below."

"So what was she doing in West Middle Hummock today? She was seen driving into Floyd Trevelyan's property."

"What time was it?"

"Around noon."

Qwilleran had to think fast. "She was probably delivering a hot lunch to a shut-in. Mrs. Trevelyan is said to be—"

"So why didn't she come out until after five o'clock?"

"Andy, how many spies do the state police have stationed in Floyd's trees? And why haven't they found the guy yet? Maybe they're looking in the wrong place."

"Go home! You're wasting my time." Brodie jerked his thumb over his shoulder and headed back to his official vehicle.

"It was your idea to stop and chat," Qwilleran called after him.

"Go home and get that two-wheeled suicide contraption off the street."

"Okay, tell me how to get out of this traffic without breaking the law!"

"Follow me!" The police car led the way to the head of the circle with light flashing and stopped the flow of traffic in both directions while the richest man in the northeast central United States made his illegal U-turn.

Arriving at the barn he said to Yum Yum, "I had a touch-and-go session with your boyfriend a minute ago." She was in love with Brodie's badge.

Polly was dining with the Hasselriches that evening, an obligation she usually dreaded, so he thawed a frozen dinner for himself and opened a can of crabmeat for the Siamese. Then, at a suitable hour, he telephoned Celia and invited her to the barn "for a cold drink on this warm evening."

She arrived with a joyful, toothy smile and, while Qwilleran reconstituted limeade concentrate, wandered about the barn in search of the Siamese. They were nested together in the bowl-shaped seat of the twistletwig rocking chair.

"We used to have a rocker like yours at the farm," she said when they were seated with their cold drinks. "It was handed down in my husband's family. He burnt it when we got television."

"What was the connection?" Qwilleran asked with genuine curiosity.

"Well, for TV he had to have a recliner, and we didn't have room for both. You've got lots of room here. Where are your TV sets?"

"We have only one. It's in the cats' loft apartment. They enjoy nature programs or commercials without the audio."

Celia laughed with delight. "I wish my husband was alive, so I could tell him that! We had barn cats, and they weren't allowed in the house. They certainly didn't have TV in the hayloft!"

After a few minutes of polite small talk, Qwilleran broached the subject. "How did you fare at West Middle Hummock today?"

"Well! It was very interesting! It's a nice drive out there, and I didn't mind it at all. They have a cute mailbox like an old railroad engine, and they call the house The Roundhouse on the sign, but it isn't round at all!"

He explained that railroad yards used to have round buildings for servicing locomotives in the days of steam, and there was a turntable in the center to shunt the engines into different stalls.

"Learn something every day!" she said with an airy wave of the hand.

"How well were you received?"

"Well, first I met the nurse, who was in a hurry to go off duty. She impressed me as being kind of a cool cucumber. I'll bet she lives in Brrr." Celia stopped to enjoy a laugh at her own humor. "She showed me the medicines and told me not to get off schedule or the patient might wind up in the hospital. Then she left, and I met the patient's daughter. She could be quite pretty if she was happy, but I'm afraid she's a very bitter young lady—in her early twenties."

"What's her name?"

"When I asked, she didn't answer right away, but then she said it was Tish. Later, though, her mother called her Lettie. She hates Lettie. I know how she feels. I always hated Celia."

As his informer rambled on, Qwilleran was doing some quick arithmetic: Lettie plus Tish equals the young woman he met in the bank; she claimed her last name was Penn, although the teller called her Trevelyan. He said, "Her name is probably Letitia—a bad choice, any way you look at it. Letitia Trevelyan sounds like 'thank you' in a foreign language."

Celia giggled. "I must remember to tell that one to my grandson." She dug in her large handbag for her notebook and wrote it down, then went on: "Tish was polite but not what you'd call friendly. That's all right; I didn't expect an afternoon social. She said she was going out and would be back at five o'clock—my quitting time—but first she took me into her mother's room. Oh, my! That poor woman! She can't be more than fifty, but her body is so frail, and her face is so white! The way her eyes looked, they were searching for something. I don't think she gets enough *attention,* although she's never left alone."

"That could be true," Qwilleran said. "Attendance is not attention."

"She told me to call her Florrie. I fixed her a nice little lunch but had to coax her to eat. She wanted to talk. Her voice is thin and whiney."

"What did she talk about?"

"Well, she skipped around a lot. She doesn't like vegetables. Someone killed their dog. The nurse is mean to her. No one comes to see her. She hates what's on TV. Lettie goes out and never says where she's going." Celia stopped for breath. "I listened and sympathized with her until she got tired and wanted to lie down. I asked if she'd like me to sing to her."

"Don't tell me you sang *Mrs. Robinson*!" Qwilleran said teasingly.

"Oh, you remembered!" That was cause for more laughter. "No, I sang hymns, and she fell asleep and had a peaceful nap. That gave me time to poke around the house. It's big and has an elevator, but it doesn't look as if anybody loves it, if you know what I mean. And those electric trains in the basement! Never saw anything like it! Do you suppose they let schoolkids come and see them at Christmas-time?"

"Probably not."

"There was a family album in Florrie's sitting room, and when she woke up I asked if we could look at it together. I took her down on the elevator and wheeled her out on the stone patio, and we had a good time looking at snapshots."

"Did you learn anything?"

"Oh, I learned a lot! She grew up in a railroad family. Her father was a famous engineer. They lived in Sawdust City near the tracks. Railroad people liked to live near the tracks, Florrie said. Watching the trains was big entertainment, I guess. They knew everybody. Everybody waved."

Qwilleran said, "You have a good ear for detail and apparently an excellent memory."

Celia waved her small notebook. "I wrote everything down. Her grandfather, uncles, and brothers all worked on the railroad. They were firemen, brakemen, engineers, flagmen, crossing guards, and hostlers, whatever they are."

"Did Florrie wonder why you were writing things down?" he asked with a note of concern.

"I know what you're thinking, Chief, but I was careful to explain that I wrote long letters to my grandson twice a week and jotted down things to tell him."

"Smart thinking! Perhaps we should put Clayton on the payroll."

She laughed, of course, before continuing. "Let me tell you about Florrie's wedding pictures! She married a carpenter who was crazy about trains, and he married her because her father was an engineer. That's what she said! And here's where it gets good: The marriage ceremony was in the cab of a steam locomotive, with everyone wearing coveralls and railroad caps—even the bride and the preacher! Her flowers were tied on a shiny brass oilcan, and when the couple was pronounced man and wife, the preacher pulled the handle that blows the whistle. That meant the best man had to fire the boiler, too, and it got very hot in the cab, and there was coal dust on her flowers." In recounting it, Celia rocked back and forth with mirth.

"Did Florrie think this was funny?"

"No, she didn't laugh or smile or anything. It was just something she thought Clayton would be interested to hear about. They had the reception in the depot. Her mother-in-law made the wedding cake like a train of cars coming around a curve. It was all done with loaf cakes and chocolate icing. For music they had a man with a guitar singing songs about train wrecks."

"No wonder her husband turned out the way he did," Qwilleran said. "He was a nut even then."

"Now comes the sad part. After a few pictures of the young couple and their two young children, the pages of the photo album were blank. I wanted to know why no more snapshots, and Florrie said, 'My husband got too rich. I never wanted to be the wife of a rich man. I liked it when he'd come home tired and dirty from digging a basement or shingling a roof, and we'd sit at the kitchen table and drink a beer and talk before we ate supper. . . .' Isn't that sad, Chief?"

"It is indeed. Did she say anything else about her husband?"

"Not a word, and I didn't think I should ask."

"You're right. The questions will come later."

"When Tish came home, I said good-bye to Florrie, and she held out her arms for a hug." Celia blinked her eyes at the recollection. "On the way out I had a few words with Tish. She'd brought home an armful of library books, and we talked a bit about our favorite authors. She said she'd like to be a writer herself. I asked if she'd studied it in college, and she said, 'My father didn't think college was necessary, because I could go right into the family business.' "

"How did she say it? Regretfully? Apologetically? Matter-of-factly? Bitterly?"

"Kind of stiffly, I thought. So then I looked innocent and said, `What business is your family in?' She looked surprised, so I explained that I'd just moved to town a couple of days ago and didn't know anything about anything. She said they were in the financial business, but she was on vacation."

"I'm proud of you, Celia," Qwilleran said. "You've done very well for starters."

"Thank you. I really enjoyed every minute. And before I left, I told Tish I was sorry to hear their dog had been shot. Tish felt sick about it. He was a beautiful chow. And that gave me an idea! Pets are supposed to be good for elderly patients—for their morale, you know—so I suggested bringing Wrigley to visit her mother. He's a lovable cat, very clean, very quiet. Tish thought it would be wonderful, so that's what I'm going to do. Do you have any other suggestions, Chief?"

"Yes. Continue to do your Pals for Patients job. Take Wrigley, by all means. Both of those lonely women need your cheery presence, and Tish may prove to be your best source of information. Continue to play the uninformed newcomer. At the same time, acquaint yourself with all the published facts on the scandal to date. I have a file of clippings for you to take home and read. Good luck! I'll call you tomorrow night."

"Oh, I'm so excited!" she exclaimed. She reached for a long wooden object on the coffee table. "Is this what I think it is?" She blew one end and produced the high-pitched whistle of a steam locomotive. Yum Yum vanished; Koko stood his ground and swiveled his ears wildly.

Qwilleran could do his best thinking with his feet elevated, a legal pad in his left hand and a black felt-tip in his right, and this is how he settled down in the library area after Celia had driven away. Yum Yum immediately came trotting down the ramp. Whenever he sat down, her built-in antenna signaled his whereabouts and flashed green. There she was, ready to curl up on his lap, and who could deny that appealing little creature? He had known her when she was a trembling, mistreated kitten. Now she was a self-assured young lady who wanted her own plate at dinnertime and who had once tried to steal the police chief's badge off his chest. Qwilleran propped his writing pad against the furry body on his lap and started an off-the-cuff list of questions that needed to be explored. The writing surface rose and fell as she inhaled and exhaled:

Does Tish have any life of her own, apart from job and family responsibilities? Did she, or does she, resent her father's interference in her career possibilities?

When he was gallivanting around the country in pursuit of his personal pleasures, how did Tish feel about being a live-in Cinderella? How did she react to his all-night absences and travels with his secretary, while Florrie wasted away at The Roundhouse?

How much, if anything, does Tish know about the embezzlement? Was she a collaborator in juggling the books? Was that Floyd's reason for wanting her in his office instead of in college? Did she collaborate willingly, or was Floyd a tyrant who gave orders and insisted on being obeyed?

Does she know where he is? Does she have any guesses where he is?

It was about eleven o'clock when headlights came bobbing through the Black Forest. Koko announced the fact, having seen them first. Qwilleran switched on the exterior lights and went out to investigate. There were two sets of headlights. He stood with his fists on his hips and listened to the owl hooting until the vehicles came into full view.

The first was a pickup truck, and Derek Cuttlebrink unfolded his long frame from the driver's seat. "Brought you a load of wood," he announced flippantly.

Two women from the second vehicle walked forward. "Hi, Qwill," said Fran Brodie. "We're delivering a surprise!"

Elizabeth was with her. "You can sit in it, Mr. Q, and wonderful things will happen! I have it on good authority."

"Not another rocking chair!" he said, trying not to sound ungrateful, yet leaving himself leeway to refuse it.

What Derek was unloading from the truck was an armload of five-foot poles. "Where shall I set 'em up?" he asked, pausing on the threshold.

Fran, who had led the way into the barn, pointed toward the lounge area. "Over there, Derek. There's plenty of space between the fireplace and the sofa." Having been the interior designer for the barn, she retained a proprietary interest in it. Whenever she visited, she went about straightening pictures, moving furniture, and giving unsolicited advice. Her sincere, good-natured aggressiveness usually amused Qwilleran, but he drew the line at five-foot poles.

"What the devil are those things supposed to be?" he demanded in a cranky voice.

"It's a portable pyramid," Elizabeth announced with the air of a generous benefactor. "Wally Toddwhistle designed it; Derek will put it together for you."

"Only takes a jiffy," Derek said. "All you need is a screwdriver. Got a screwdriver?"

"There's a toolkit in the broom closet." Qwilleran threw himself on the sofa and watched with a dour expression as five-foot poles were joined to become ten-foot poles, which fitted together to make a ten-foot square; then four other ten-foot poles were attached to the corners and joined at the apex.

"Voilà! A pyramid!" cried Elizabeth.

Derek crawled into the cagelike structure and

sat cross-legged. "Wow! I'm getting vibrations! I'm getting ideas! How about selling Elizabeth the barn, Mr. Q, and I'll open a restaurant?"

"How about telling me what this damm fool thing is all about?" Qwilleran retorted.

Fran spoke up. "Larry and Junior ganged up on us and wouldn't let us use it in our stage set. I thought you'd enjoy experimenting with it. Then you could write a column about pyramid power. It has something to do with the electromagnetic field."

"Hmmm," he murmured, mellowing a trifle.

Derek, still in the pyramid, said, "Somebody get my guitar!"

Elizabeth ran out to his truck, returning with the instrument, and he sang a ballad titled "The Blizzard of 1912." Everyone said he'd never done it better. Derek said he'd felt inspired. Qwilleran suggested some refreshments.

With their drinks and bowls of Kabibbles, they sat around the big coffee table, facing the pyramid. Fran and Derek were in the usual rehearsal clothes, straight from the ragbag, but Elizabeth was striking in a baggy red jumpsuit tied about the middle with a long sash of many colors. The Siamese sat a safe distance from both guests and pyramid.

"How are the rehearsals progressing?" Qwilleran asked.

"Situation normal," said the director. "Larry is allergic to green makeup . . . The prop girl has eloped, and we can't find any of the props . . . The stage manager broke his thumb. And the donkey head hasn't arrived from Down Below."

"Hee-haw! Hee-haw!" Derek put in for dramatic effect.

Yum Yum scooted up the ramp and looked down from the second balcony, but Koko merely wiggled his ears.

"When is the first dress rehearsal?"

"Monday. The tickets are selling very well. We may not have a show, but we'll have an audience."

"How many intermissions?"

"One. We're cutting after Bottom and Titania are bewitched. It sends the audience out smiling and brings them back ready for more."

"Hey! What are those ducks up there?" Derek asked, pointing to the top of the fireplace cube.

Qwilleran said, "From left to right: Quack, Whistle, and Squawk. They're hand-carved decoys that Polly brought from Oregon. Actually, left to right, they're a merganser, a pintail, and a lesser scaup."

Derek tried quacking, whistling, and squawking like a duck before the conversation returned to community theatre: its problems, calamities, and embarrassments.

"Like the time we were doing a romantic costume play," Fran recalled. "Hoop skirts, powdered wigs, and satin breeches! The female lead was in a car crash on opening night, and Larry had to do her whole part, reading from the book, wearing a beard and tattered jeans. Talk about embarrassing! To the audience it was high comedy. They loved it!"

Then Qwilleran remembered, "In my first stage experience, I played the butler and dropped a silver tray with a whole tea service—*crash!* I felt like cutting my throat with the butter knife."

"The worst thing," Derek said, "is when somebody forgets his lines—freezes—goes blank! For some reason the audience stares at *you!* And you're standing there with egg on your face."

At that moment, Qwilleran, who was keeping an eye on Koko and the cheese, saw the cat approach the pyramid and cautiously step into the so-called electromagnetic field. When he reached the exact center, the hair on his back stood on end! His tail puffed up like a porcupine! Then the lights went out.

"Don't move," Qwilleran warned his guests. "Stay where you are till I find the flashlights." He groped his way to the kitchen, while the others said, "What happened? . . . There's no storm . . . Transformer blew, somewhere in the neighborhood, maybe . . ."

Qwilleran announced that everything was out: refrigerator, electric clock, everything. He distributed flashlights and asked Derek to go to the top balcony and check for lights on Main

Street. "If we're the only ones affected, I'll call the power company."

Soon Derek shouted down to the main floor, "The whole county's without power! It's blacked out in every direction."

"We'd better go home," Fran said.

Qwilleran accompanied them to their vehicles and collected the flashlights after they had turned on their headlights. On the way to the parking area, Fran grabbed his arm and said in a low voice, "They found the girl."

"What girl?"

"Trevelyan's secretary, but not him."

"How do you know?"

"My mother got it from Dad when he came off his shift. The girl was in Texas, but not hiding out—just driving around to the mall and the hair-dresser as if nothing had happened."

"Did they pick her up?"

"Not yet. They're checking out her story— that she was fired two weeks before the surprise audit, which she claims to know nothing about."

Qwilleran said, "That sounds like a well-rehearsed explanation. She was on the Party Train with her boss on the day of the audit."

"Well, according to her story, the management had fired her with two weeks' notice. The train ride was her farewell party. After that, she drove to her home state, alone. One thing she volunteered: Her boss always talked about Alaska and might have gone there."

Or Switzerland, Qwilleran thought. Floyd must have known an audit would be inevitable, but how would he know the timing? And then he thought, The person who tipped him off to leave town may have been the one who blew the whistle. It was improbable, but not impossible.

When Qwilleran returned to the barn, he made a cursory search for the Siamese, flashing his battery-operated lantern to left and right. To his surprise, Koko was still in the pyramid, sitting in dead center, looking as large as a raccoon.

"Koko! Get out of that thing!"

There was no response.

He likes it, Qwilleran decided. He's getting a treatment.

Then he yelled the word that always got results: "Treat!"

Yum Yum's paws could be heard pelting down the ramp. As for Koko, he stepped calmly out of the pyramid and shook himself until he returned to his normal size and shape. One thing disturbed Qwilleran: the instant that Koko left the center of the pyramid, the lights came on, and the refrigerator started humming. There was a glow above the trees to the west: the lights of Main Street.

Whether his suspicions were right or wrong, Qwilleran immediately went to work with the screwdriver, disassembling the pyramid. He carried the poles gingerly from the barn and pitched them into the jungly remains of the orchard.

"Whoo-hoo-hoo . . . hoo-hoo," flashed a message from Marconi.

"Same to you!" Qwilleran shouted.

TEN

The morning after the blackout, Qwilleran regretted his impulsive dumping of the pyramid poles. Was the power failure a coincidence or not? With some experimentation he might be able to write a column about it, if Koko would cooperate. The cat never liked to do anything unless it was his own idea, and any attempt to deposit him bodily in the cagelike contraption would be thwarted by a whirlwind of squirming, kicking, spitting, and snarling. Then . . . the morning newscast on WPKX affected Qwilleran's decision:

"Police are investigating last night's homicide at the Trackside Tavern in Sawdust City. James Henry Ducker, twenty-four, of Chipmunk Township, was the victim of a knifing during a power failure, while soccer fans held a post-game celebration. The Moose County Electric Cooperative is unable to explain the power outage that blacked out the entire county between eleven-thirty and eleven forty-five. There was no equipment failure, according to a spokesman for the co-op. No storm conditions or high winds were recorded by the WPKX meteorology department. An inquiry is continuing."

The murder changed Qwilleran's thinking entirely. If he even hinted at his conjecture in print, the national media—always hungry for bizarre news from the boondocks—would pounce on it. TV crews and news teams from Down Below would descend on Moose County, and the family of James Henry Ducker would sue Koko for three billion. Forget it! he told himself.

As for the victim, residents of Chipmunk were subject to mayhem, and post-game soccer celebrations were notoriously violent, especially in Mudville, which was known for its roister-doister taverns. Qwilleran could imagine the yelling, table banging, brawling, and bottle smashing prompted by the total darkness. In the resulting bedlam someone could empty a semiautomatic without being heard.

Bedlam was the order of the day as he prepared breakfast for the Siamese. "Feeding time at the zoo!" he shouted above the cacophany of yowls and shrieks. "Let's hear it for Alaska smoked salmon!" he exhorted in his Carnegie Hall voice. "Smoked over alderwood fires! Age-old process!" He was reading from the can, and the louder he projected, the louder they howled. All three of them enjoyed exercising their lungs. On such a day, when the atmosphere was clear and the windows were open, the din could be heard as far as the theatre parking lot.

For his own breakfast Qwilleran walked downtown to Lois's Luncheonette and stopped at the library on the way back, to visit with Polly in her fishbowl of an office on the mezzanine.

"Where were you and Bootsie when the lights went out?" he inquired.

"We both retired early and missed it completely," she said with a weariness unusual so early in the morning. "I felt some discomfort after dining with the Hasselriches. It was rather stressful, and my digestion is below par these days."

"I've reiterated, Polly, that you're worrying too much about your house."

"I suppose so, but it's such a tremendous responsibility. I'm working on my color schemes now. One has to bear in mind the exposure of each room, the choice of advancing or receding hues, tints that are flattering to complexions, and so forth."

"Fran Brodie could do that for you, one-two-three."

"But I want to do it myself, Qwill! I've told you that!" she said curtly. "If I make mistakes, I'm prepared to live with them." Then, with a slight inquiring lift of eyebrows, she asked, "How did Mrs. Robinson enjoy dinner at Tipsy's?"

Ah! The women have been talking, Qwilleran thought: Robinson to Alstock to Duncan. He replied, "She seemed favorably impressed. It would have been more enjoyable if you were there. What did your literary ladies have for dinner? Was it chicken pot pie again?"

"Turkey chow mein," Polly said stiffly.

The mention of food was his cue to invite her to dinner. Instead, he asked where he would find dog books. He said he planned to write a column on chows. Dinner dates with Polly were becoming more of an obligation than a pleasure.

On the way out, Qwilleran stopped to check on Homer Tibbitt's current project.

"Railroads!" the old man said. "The SC&L Line was the lifeblood of the county in mining and lumbering days, and it was all done with steam. I grew up on a farm outside Little Hope and knew the language of the whistles before I knew the alphabet. When I was five years old, my brothers and I would go into town on Sat-

urdays to watch the trains go by. I remember
the station platform: wood boards put together
with nailheads as big as dimes. Little Hope was
only a flagstop, and most trains went straight
through. I could hear them coming, getting
louder and louder, until the big wheels went
roaring past. It was frightening, I tell you!
Seventy-five tons of iron, breathing fire!"

"Were there many wrecks?"

"Yes, a lot of blood was spilled, most of it
for the sake of being on time. Being on time
made money for the SC&L and meant a bonus
for the engineer, so he'd go too fast, trying to
get his lading to a cargo ship that was ready to
sail. . . . One of these days I'll write a book."

When Qwilleran picked up his mail and daily
paper, he usually walked down the trail, but
now he drove in order to deliver a cooler of
beverages. The morning after the blackout, Eddie's only helper was one of the Herculean
young blond men indigenous to Moose County.

"Where's Benno?" Qwilleran asked.

Eddie walked over to him and started sharpening a pencil. "I dunno. Prob'ly hung over."

"Where were you when the lights went out
last night?"

"Over at a friend's place. It di'n't last long."

Eddie looked red-eyed and minus pep, and
Qwilleran was in no mood to linger. He wanted
to go home and read what the *Something* had
to say about the murder.

The headline read: BLACKOUT SPAWNS KILLING IN BAR.

When the lights went on again at the Trackside Tavern in Sawdust City, following last night's brief power outage, one customer was found dead, the victim of a knifing. The body of James Henry Ducker, 24, of Chipmunk Township, was slumped in a booth, bleeding profusely from wounds apparently inflicted by a hunting knife or similar weapon. He was pronounced dead at the scene.

The table in the booth had been swept clean of beer bottles and shot glasses in the scuffle that preceded the assault, according to barkeeper Stan Western.

"We always have a noisy demonstration when the lights go out," he said, "but last night was a blinger! Never heard such rowdy carrying-on. Soccer fans, mostly."

The rowdy outburst followed an Intercounty League game between Sawdust City and Lockmaster, which the visiting team won by the close score of 5 to 3.

Police questioned patrons, but no one in the dimly lighted bar had noticed the deceased or his drinking partner in the corner booth.

Western said Ducker was not a regular
customer. Barmaid Shirley Dublay had
noticed a ponytail on the man who
was later killed, but she was unable to
describe the second individual in the
booth where the crime was committed. "I was too busy," she said. "The
other barmaid called in sick, and I was
working the floor all alone."

No arrests have been made. Sawdust
City police and state troopers are investigating.

The reason for the 15-minute blackout
remains a mystery, according to a
spokesperson for the Moose County
Electric Cooperative.

Also on page one was a sidebar with Roger
MacGillivray's by-line, describing the scene of
the crime:

On a normal night the Trackside Tavern on East Main Street in Sawdust
City is a quiet neighborhood bar,
where folks drop in for a nip, a
friendly chat, and maybe a game of
pool. When the TV set isn't covering
sports, the radio is tuned to country
western and the new rock station, but
there are no video games.

Factory workers, downtown business-
men, truckers, railroad personnel, and

retirees mingle at the long bar, or in the handful of booths, or at the small scarred tables. It's strictly a male hangout, following an incident ten years ago that made it unpopular with women.

Otherwise, its hundred-year-old history includes some swashbuckling fights when it was Sully's Saloon before Prohibition, a period as a blind pig, and a series of different owners as the Trackside Tavern.

The typical old north-country atmosphere of the tavern has remained unchanged, however: Knotty pine walls hung with mounted deer heads, wide pine floorboards rippled with a century of workboots and scraping chairs, and a wood-burning stove that heats the barnlike interior in winter. On the rare summer occasions when air conditioning is needed, the front and back doors are opened to funnel lake breezes through the barroom.

The mood is easygoing, relaxing— except on Thursday nights if the local soccer team is playing a home game. "Strangers come in and whoop it up," said barkeeper Stan Western. "They're always welcome. Good crowd, mostly. Never had anything like this happen before. I think that fights between fans that started on the field after the game carried over into the bar."

Roger was honing his craft as a newswriter, Qwilleran thought, but he should have explained the incident that kept women away from the Trackside.

As for the soccer-brawl theory as a motive for murder, Qwilleran had a different idea, and he wanted to run it past his friend at the police station. He phoned first, to be sure Brodie was there, then drove downtown in a hurry. The sergeant waved him into the inner office.

"Too late for coffee, if you came for a hand-out," the chief said.

"That's all right," Qwilleran said lightly. "Your constabulary brew leaves something to be desired. Nothing personal, of course."

Brodie grunted a constabulary reply.

"What did you think of the mysterious black-out, Andy?"

"Hard to figure. A woman called the station this morning and wanted us to investigate. She thought it was done purposely by UFOs. We told her it was only a large fish going over the dam near the hydro plant."

"Did she buy that?"

"I don't know. The sergeant hung up."

"Whatever the cause," Qwilleran said, "it was a convenient cover-up for murder. Did you like the coverage in the paper?"

"Not bad. Most of it was accurate. It wasn't

a hunting knife, though. That was a reporter's guesswork. It was some other kind, but that's classified. It could affect the investigation."

"Are you in on the case, Andy?"

"We cooperate with the Sawdust PD and the state troopers."

"Do you find it strange that none of the customers noticed the person who was with Ducker?"

Brodie gave him a sharp glance. "Don't believe everything you read in the paper."

"Are you implying that you have a description of the suspect?"

"Are you just here to ask questions?" the chief growled.

"No, as a matter of fact, I have a theory to bounce off your official skull. As you know, Polly is building a house at the corner of the orchard trail and Trevelyan Road."

"How's she comin' with it?"

"That's a long story, but my point is that one of the carpenters is a young Chipmunk fellow with a ponytail—"

"A lot of guys have 'em if they jog or do sweaty work outdoors," Brodie interrupted.

"Hear me out, Andy. This guy failed to show up for work today. His peers call him Benno. I have a wild hunch—" Qwilleran stroked his moustache. "I have a hunch that Benno is James Henry Ducker, and that the murder was not soccer-related but drug-related. I know you don't have a big drug problem up here . . ."

"But it's starting, and Chipmunk is where it's at."

"That being the case, he could have been dealing in bennies."

"Who does he work for?"

"Polly's contractor is Eddie Trevelyan, Floyd's son."

"Sure, I knew him when he was in high school and I was with the sheriff's department. Eddie got into trouble and would have had a juvenile record, only his father pulled strings to get it off the books. He was good at that! Even so, Eddie was expelled from Pickax High, and—wouldn't you know?—Floyd-boy sued the school board."

Qwilleran said, "Eddie seems to be doing all right now. He works hard and does a good job, as far as I can see. Drinks heavily, I suspect, but not during work hours. Smokes a lot—only the legal stuff. Keeps a sharp pencil, so he can't be all bad."

"Yeah, all he needs is a shave and a haircut."

"Eddie told me that Benno had been his buddy since high school."

"Then your hunch is right. Benno is James Henry Ducker, and Eddie has lost a carpenter as well as a father who can pull strings."

"Any news on the manhunt, Andy?"

"Nothing for publication."

"I wonder what happened to the Lumbertown Party Train."

"It's on a siding in Mudville."

"One more question, and then I'm leaving," Qwilleran said. "What happened at the Track-side Tavern ten years ago that scared women away?"

"Who knows? That's not my beat. Look it up in your newspaper files."

"The *Something* wasn't publishing ten years ago, and the *Pickax Picayune* was never more than a chicken dinner newspaper. But there's some hushed-up reason why women don't patronize that bar."

Brodie waved the subject away, saying impatiently, "Maybe they didn't like the cigars and four-letter words. Maybe the bartender wouldn't mix pink drinks. Who cares? It was ten years ago. Why don't you ask your smart cat? Lieutenant Hames was asking about him the other day. He was up here for a few days."

"What was he doing here?" Qwilleran asked. He had known the detective Down Below while working for the *Daily Fluxion,* and now he wondered why a metropolitan lawman would be involved in an investigation 400 miles north of everywhere, unless—

"He was up here with his family, doing some camping and fishing. They caught some big ones. I met him at a drug seminar Down Below a while back and gave him a big selling on Moose County. His kids were crazy about it."

As Qwilleran was leaving the police station, he saw Dwight Somers coming out of city hall.

"Dwight, you old buzzard! Where've you been?"

"Buzzin' around the county, picking up clients," the publicity man said. "How about an early dinner at the Mill?"

"Suits me. I'll meet you there after I go home and feed the cats."

Dinner at the Old Stone Mill was brief. Dwight had another appointment, and Qwilleran was anticipating another report from Celia.

The younger man was elated. He had lined up the Moose County Community College as a client and was working on a great project with the K Foundation. "That's the good news," he said. "On the down side, I'm being hounded by Floyd-boy's creditors. Just because I promoted his party train, they think I'm going to pay his outstanding bills. It's strange they haven't found him, isn't it?"

"Are you in touch with the family?" Qwilleran asked.

"Only with their attorney. He doesn't allow them to talk to anybody, including me."

"Didn't you tell me that Floyd's secretary had an apartment in your building in Indian Village?"

"Yeah, but I never got an invitation to drop in for a neighborly visit. Perhaps I'm too neat and clean. I've seen some scruffy types knocking on her door, and Floyd himself was a little on the wild side, sartorially."

It was a one-drink, small-steak, no-dessert dinner, and the publicity man apologized for having to rush away. As they walked to the parking lot, Qwilleran asked, "Do you happen to remember the name of the engineer who drove the locomotive when we took our historic ride?"

"Historic in more ways than one," Dwight said bitingly. "There'll never be another. The government will be sure to get their hands on Floyd's rolling stock. . . . But to answer your question: Sure, his name is Ozzie Penn. He's Floyd's father-in-law."

"If he could tell me some good railroad stories, I'd interview him—not for the 'Qwill Pen.' I want to write a book on the Steam Age of railroading."

"Well, he's in his eighties, but in good shape and mentally sharp. We got a doctor's okay before letting him drive No. 9. He lives at the Railroad Retirement Center in Mudville," Dwight said as he stepped into his car. There was a packet on the seat, which he handed to Qwilleran. "Here's the video of our train ride. Run it and see if you think we could sell copies to benefit the college."

"Thanks. I'll do that," Qwilleran said, "and . . . uh . . . keep it under your hat, Dwight, about the railroad book. I'll be using a pseudonym, and I haven't told anyone but you."

The two men went their separate ways.

*   *   *

At home Qwilleran looked up the phone number of the Railroad Retirement Center; the address was on Main Street. Then he checked the Trackside Tavern. First, out of curiosity, he called the bar.

"*Not open!*" the man's harried voice shouted into the phone before slamming the receiver.

At the Retirement Center the male switchboard operator paged Ozzie Penn and tracked him down in the TV room.

"Hello? Who is it?" said a reedy voice with the surprise and apprehension of one who never receives a phone call.

"Good evening, Mr. Penn," Qwilleran said slowly and distinctly. "I was one of the passengers on the Party Train when you drove old No. 9. We all had a good time. That engine's a wonderful piece of machinery."

"Yep, she be a beaut!"

"My name is James Mackintosh, and I'm writing a book on the old days of railroading. Would you be willing to talk to me? You've had a long and honorable career, and I'm sure you know plenty of stories."

"That I do," said the old man. "Plenty!"

"May I visit you at the Center? Is there a quiet place where we can talk? You'll receive payment for your time, of course. I'd like to drive out there tomorrow."

"Tomorrow?"

"Saturday."

"What be yer name again?"

"Mackintosh. James Mackintosh. How about one o'clock?"

"I ain't goin' no place."

As Qwilleran replaced the receiver, he thought, This old man speaks a fascinating kind of substandard English that will fade out in another generation. Eddie Trevelyan's speech was simply the bad grammar common in Moose County. Ozzie Penn spoke Old Moose.

"May I use your TV?" Qwilleran asked the Siamese, who had been watching him talk into the inanimate instrument. The telephone was something even Koko had never understood.

The three of them trooped to the highest balcony, furnished to feline taste with soft carpet, cushioned baskets, empty boxes, a ladder, scratching pads and posts, and a small TV with VCR. There was one chair which the cats commandeered, while Qwilleran sat on the floor to watch the video.

It was a festive collage of important people arriving at the depot and milling about on the platform, with the camera lingering on certain subjects: woman with large hat, man with oversized moustache, woman in expensive-looking pantsuit, man in Scottish tartan. (Koko yowled at certain images for no apparent reason.) The car valets jumped around like red devils. The brass band tootled. Then the great No. 9 came puffing around a curve, blowing its whistle. The elderly engineer leaned from his cab; two firemen posed in the gangway with their shovels. Then the conductor bawled the destinations, and feet mounted the yellow step-stool. When the diners drank a toast in ice water, Qwilleran thought, It was symbolic!

Although the camera occasionally panned picturesque stretches of countryside, the emphasis was on the passengers, who might be induced to buy the video to benefit the college. Qwilleran rewound the tape, thanked the Siamese for the use of their facilities, and went down the ramp to greet Celia Robinson.

Her face was lively with smiles, and her large handbag produced a box of chocolate chip cookies. "We can have a party. They're good with milk. Do you have any milk, Chief?"

"No, only a milk substitute called black coffee," he apologized, "but I'm a master at its preparation." With a grand flourish he pressed a button on the computerized coffeemaker, which started the grinding, gurgling, and dripping. The brew that resulted was good, Celia said, but awfully strong.

As they sat down with their coffee and cookies, Qwilleran said to her in an ominous tone of voice, "Celia, you're being tailed by the police."

"What!" she cried. "What have I done?"

"Only kidding; don't be alarmed. The police chief has seen your red car in the parking lot and knows you're living in the carriage house, and the detectives staking out the Trevelyan property know you've visited The Roundhouse.

Next, they'll see you driving through the Black Forest for these meetings."

"Should I get my car painted?"

"That won't be necessary, but it emphasizes the need to keep Operation Whistle under wraps. Here's what I suggest for your cover: You're planning to start a specialized catering service: hot meals for shut-ins . . . refreshments for kids' birthday parties . . . gourmet delicacies for cats and dogs. We might run an ad in the paper to that effect."

"Do you mean it?" she asked in astonishment.

"Only to fool the cops. You might take a casserole to Florrie, just in case you're stopped. . . . And now, what happened today? Did you take Wrigley?"

"Oh, he was a big hit! He sat on Florrie's lap, and she stroked him and looked so happy! Tish didn't want to miss the fun, so she fixed lunch for us and gave Wrigley a bit of tuna. After a while I asked the name of the bank that they own, so I could open an account. Tish said it was a credit union especially for railroad workers, and she began to get very fidgety. Pretty soon she said she had to go and buy groceries. Then I thought of a sneaky question to ask Florrie . . . It would be nice if I could tape these conversations, Chief."

"It would arouse suspicion," he said.

"I mean, with a hidden tape recorder. My grandson had one that he used in Florida. I could phone him, and he'd send it by overnight mail."

"It's illegal, Celia, to tape someone's conversation without permission. Thousands of persons do it and get away with it, but if it came to light in this case, you'd be in trouble, and Operation Whistle would be involved. It's a bright idea, but please forget it. You're doing very well with your little notebook. Did you do your homework?"

"Yes, I read all the clippings about the scandal and figured out some ways to get the women to talk. After Tish left, I asked Florrie what time her husband usually came home to supper. She looked at me funny—all bright-eyed and excited—and said, 'If he comes home, they'll put him in jail, and they'll take all his trains away. He stole a lot of money.' She finished with a wild laugh that frightened Wrigley. I tried to calm her down, but she wanted to go down on the elevator and show me the trains. Have you ever seen them, Chief?"

"I have indeed—a fantastic display! I wrote a column about Floyd's model railroad a couple of months ago, before he absconded."

"Well! Wait till you hear this! Florrie told me to press the button and start the trains running, but I was afraid of pressing the wrong one and wrecking the whole shebang. So Florrie wheeled herself to the switchboard and started pushing buttons and turning knobs. All the trains started to move at the same time—faster

and faster until they crashed into each other
and into bridges and buildings! I screamed for
her to turn it off, but she was enjoying it and
laughing like crazy. Then a fuse blew, I guess,
because all the lights went out, but it was too
late. The whole thing was wrecked! I was a
wreck myself, believe me! When Tish came
back from the store, I was still as limp as a rag,
and I couldn't find Wrigley."

"How did she react to the disaster?"

"Quite cool. She disconnected something and
said it was all right—no danger. But after we
tucked Florrie in for her afternoon nap, Tish
put her face in her hands and started to bawl.
She really sobbed and wailed! I said, 'I'm terribly sorry about the trains, but there was nothing I could do.' She shook her head from side to
side and said it wasn't the trains she cared
about; it was other things. I put my arm around
her and said, 'Have a good cry, dear. It'll do
you good. Don't be afraid to tell me your troubles. I'm your friend.' That started another
gush of tears."   .

Qwilleran said, "You tell this story very well,
Celia."

"Do you think so? I used to tell stories to
Clayton when he was little . . . So after a while
Tish dabbed her eyes and sniffled and suddenly
said in a bitter voice, '*I despise my . . . mother's
husband!*' I tried to get her to talk about it and
unburden herself."

Qwilleran nodded, but his thoughts were

elsewhere. If Tish despised her father—for whatever reason—could she have been the one who blew the whistle? Or could her show of hostility be camouflage for her own involvement in the fraud?

"Yow!" came a warning from Koko, who was looking out the kitchen window.

"Someone's coming!" Qwilleran jumped to his feet. "He heard a car coming through the woods!"

"Police? Where shall I go?" Celia asked in alarm, grabbing her handbag.

"Stay where you are."

It was only Mr. O'Dell, the maintenance man, wanting to pick up his check for services rendered.

"So . . . go on, Celia. Did Tish talk?"

"Yes, she told me about F.T. That's what she calls her father. He terrorized her and her brother Eddie when they were growing up. Today she resents the fact that he made her take business courses in high school and go to work in his office instead of going to college. But mostly she hates the way he ruined Florrie's life—with his neglect, and his stingy way with money, and his girlfriends."

Qwilleran checked the notes he had been taking. "It's not true, you know, that the Lumbertown Credit Union is only for railroad employees. Tish was trying to steer you away from the subject."

"I believe it. She's very cagey about certain

things. Just before I left, I said to her, 'Florrie told me something I didn't understand. She said her husband stole some money and might go to jail. Was she out of her head?' When I said that, Tish got terribly flustered, saying there are some complications at his office, and no one knows for sure what it's all about. Then she froze up, so I didn't ask any more questions. We searched for Wrigley and found him crouched in his sandbox, as if it was the only safe place in the house. They want me to take him again on Monday, but . . . Oh! Look at the parade!" she squealed, pointing to the top of the fireplace cube.

Soberly Qwilleran said, "Left to right, their names are Quack, Whistle, Squawk, Yum Yum, and Koko."

The two cats were in perfect alignment with the decoys, folded into compact bundles that made them look like sitting ducks.

"You can't tell me," he said, "that cats don't have a sense of humor!"

Celia's explosive laughter disturbed the masquerade, and the two "live" ducks jumped to the floor. "I'm sorry, kitties," she apologized. "I've always heard that cats don't like to be laughed at. . . . Well, that's all I have to report. I'd better go home and see if Wrigley is recovering from his scare."

As Qwilleran escorted her to the parking area, he said, "I may devise a new strategy this weekend. Shall we get together for a briefing Sunday evening?"

"Okay with me, Chief," she said blithely.

Back at the barn, another pantomime was in progress. Koko was on the telephone desk, pushing the English pencil box with his nose, pushing it toward the edge of the desk.

"NO!" Qwilleran thundered. Rushing to the spot, he caught the antique treasure before it landed on the clay tile floor. "Bad cat!"

Koko flew up the ramp in a blur of fur.

ELEVEN

For his interview with Ozzie Penn, Qwilleran went equipped with his usual tape recorder plus some snapshots of No. 9 making her comeback on Audit Sunday, as the newspaper called it. Before leaving, he trimmed his moustache somewhat and hoped he would look more like James Mackintosh, author, than Jim Qwilleran, columnist.

The Railroad Retirement Center was directly across Main Street from the Trackside Tavern, still closed. Two police vehicles were parked at the curb, one obviously from the forensic lab.

The Center, formerly a railroad hotel, was a three-story brick building without such unnecessary details as porches, shutters, or ornamental roof brackets.

When Qwilleran walked into the lobby, it was vacant except for a young male telephone operator at the switchboard. Behind him was a bank of pigeonholes for mail and messages, with a room number on each; all were empty. The lobby was clean, one could say that for it. Brown walls, brown floors, and brown wood furniture gleamed with high-gloss varnish, reminding Qwilleran of a press club Down Below that occupied a former jail. Through double glass doors he could see a television screen, lively with colorful commercials. Several elderly men sat around it, staring or dozing. A few others were playing cards.

"Are you Mr. Mackintosh?" the operator asked. "Ozzie's waiting for you. Room 203. Elevator down the hall; stairs at the back."

Qwilleran trusted his knees more than he trusted the grim-looking elevator with folding metal gate. He chose to walk up the brown varnished stairwell to a brown hallway, where he knocked on the brown door of 203. It opened immediately, and there stood the old engineer he remembered from Audit Sunday—a big, husky man, though slightly stooped. He had changed, however, since the debut of No. 9. The ruddy face that had beamed with pride in the window of the engineer's cab was now gray and weary.

"Good afternoon, Mr. Penn. I'm the one who's writing a book on railroading in the Age of Steam. Mackintosh is the name."

"Come in. I been waitin'. Where ye from?"

"Chicago."

"Set ye down. Call me Ozzie." His welcome was cordial, although he seemed too tired to smile. He slapped his denim chest and said, "Wore my over-halls for the pitcher."

"Sorry I didn't bring a camera, Ozzie, but I have some good photos of you in the cab of No. 9, and they're yours to keep."

The old man accepted the snapshots gratefully. "By Crikey, she be a purty hog, no mistake."

They sat with a small lamp table between them, and Qwilleran set up his tape recorder. "Mind if I record this? Did you drive No. 9 in the old days?"

"Yep. I were a young-un then. Them diesels, they be okay, but ain't nothin' like steam!" The man spoke pure Old Moose.

Qwilleran's practiced eye roved over the shabby furnishings without staring or criticizing. "That's a beautiful oil can," he said, nodding toward a shiny brass receptacle with a thin, elongated spout. "How was it used?"

"That were for oilin' piston rods and drivers. Kep' the wheels on the rails for nigh onto fifty year, it did. They give it me when I retired. Better'n the gold watch, it were."

"I believe it! You were a master of your craft, I'm told. What does it take to make a good engineer?"

Ozzie had to think before answering. "L'arnin' to start up slow and stop smooth ... L'arnin' to keep yer head when it be hell on the rails ... Prayin' to God fer a good fireman ... And abidin' by Rule G," he finished with a weak chuckle.

"What's the fireman's job on a steam locomotive?"

"He be the one stokes the firebox an' keeps the boiler steamin'. Takes a good crew to make a good run and come in on time. Spent my whole life comin' in on time. Eleventh commandment, it were called. Now, here I be, an' time don't mean nothin'."

Qwilleran asked, "Why was it so important to be on time?"

"Made money for the comp'ny. Made wrecks, too ... takin' chances, takin' shortcuts."

"Were you in many wrecks?"

"Yep, an' on'y jumped once. I were a youngun, deadheadin' to meet a crew in Flapjack. Highballin' round a curve, we run into a rockslide. Engineer yelled 'Jump!' an' I jumped. Fireman jumped, too. Engineer were killed."

"What do you know about the famous wreck at Wildcat, Ozzie?"

"That were afore my time, but I heerd plenty o' tales in the SC&L switchyard. In them days the yard had eighteen tracks and a roundhouse for twenty hogs." His voice faded away and his eyes glazed as his mind drifted into the past.

Qwilleran persisted with his question.

"It weren't called Wildcat in them days. It were South Fork. Trains from up north slowed down to twenty at South Fork afore goin' down a steep grade to a mighty bad curve and a wood trestle bridge. The rails, they be a hun'erd feet over the water. One day a train come roarin' through South Fork, full steam, whistle screechin'. It were a wildcat—a runaway train—headed for the gorge. At the bottom— crash!—bang! Then hissin' steam. Then dead quiet. Then the screamin' started. Fergit how many killed, but it were the worst ever!"

Both men were silent for a moment. Qwilleran could hear the gold watch ticking. Finally he asked, "Did they ever find out what caused the wreck?"

"Musta been the brakes went blooey, but the railroad, they laid it on the engineer—said he were drinkin'. Saved the comp'ny money, it did, to lay it on the engineer. Poor feller! Steam boiler exploded, an' he were scalded to death."

"Horrible!" Qwilleran murmured.

'Yep. It were bad, 'cause he weren't a drinkin' man."

"So that's why they changed the name of the town to Wildcat! You're a very lucky man,

Ozzie, to have survived so many dangers! If you had your life to live over again, would you be a hoghead?"

"Yep." After the excitement of telling the story, the old man was running out of steam.

Qwilleran said, "Too bad the Trackside is closed. We could get some food and drink."

"There be another place down the street," said Ozzie, reviving somewhat. "Better'n the Trackside."

As the two men walked down Main Street, slowly, Qwilleran asked if any women lived in the Retirement Center.

"Nope."

"I hear women never go into the Trackside. Do you know why?"

"Nope."

"Railroads are hiring women as engineers now," Qwilleran said.

"Not up here! Not the SC&L!"

The old man was breathing hard when they arrived at the bar and grill called The Jump-Off. A middle-aged woman with a bouncer's build and a rollicking personality greeted them heartily. Four young women in baseball jerseys were talking loudly about their recent win. A few elderly men were scattered about the room. The hearty greeter took their order: rye whiskey straight for Ozzie, ginger ale for Qwilleran.

When Ozzie had downed his drink, Qwilleran asked, "How did you feel about driving old No. 9 and hauling the Party Train?"

"Purty good" was the answer.

"It hasn't made any more runs since then."

"Nope."

"Too bad the credit union had to close. Saw-dusters must be feeling the pinch. Were you affected?"

"Nope. Had m'money in a bank."

Hmm, Qwilleran mused; why not in his son-in-law's corporation? "Can you stand another rye, Ozzie? And a burger?"

"Doc says one won't do no harm, so I figger two'll do some good."

Qwilleran signaled for refills. "Did someone tell me Floyd Trevelyan is your son-in-law?"

"Yep."

"How do you like the model trains at his house?"

"Never see'd 'em," Ozzie said, staring into space.

There was an awkward silence, which Qwilleran filled with questions about the quality of the burgers, the degree of doneness, the availability of condiments, and the kind of fries. The bar served railroad fries: thick, with skins on. Finally he said, "I met your daughter once. Do you have other children?"

Ozzie's reply was bluntly factual: "One son killed on the rails. One killed in Vietnam. One somewheres out west."

"Sorry to hear that. Do you see your daughter often?"

"Nope. Don't get around much."

Qwilleran coughed and took a bold step. "Did you know she's seriously ill? You ought to make an effort to visit her. She may not have long to live."

Ozzie blinked his eyes. Was it emotion or the rheuminess of old age? Suddenly he said angrily, "Ain't see'd 'er since she married that feller! Way back then I said he weren't no good. They wasn't even married in church! Guess she l'arned a lesson."

In a voice oozing with sympathy, Qwilleran said, "She tells people she's very proud of you, Ozzie—proud to have a father who's a famous engineer. No matter what happened, you were always her hero."

"Then why di'n't she listen to me? She were a good girl till she met that crook. I knowed he'd turn out bad."

"Yet you agreed to drive No. 9 for him."

"That publicity feller wanted me to do it. Paid good money. It were an honor. All those people cheerin' and the band playin'! Nobody knowed No. 9 were owned by a crook!"

"Have you never seen your grandchildren?"

"Nope."

"The boy is a house builder, and the girl is an accountant, I believe. Is your wife living?"

"Nope. Been gone nine year."

"How did she feel about being estranged from your daughter?"

"Never talked about it. Wouldn't let her say Florrie's name in the house. . . . You say the boy's buildin' houses? Like father, like son. Prob'ly turn out to be another crook!"

Qwilleran thought of their physical resemblance; Eddie had the black Trevelyan hairiness. He said, "Ozzie, a reunion with your daughter might prolong her life. It would mean so much to her. You might find it painful, but it could be the finest thing you've ever done. How long since you've seen her?"

"Twenty-five year. She were on'y nineteen when they had that sham weddin' in an engine cab. In over-halls! Not even a white dress! I di'n't go. Wouldn't let m'wife go neither."

Ozzie hung his head and said no more, and Qwilleran thought, He'd be shocked if he saw her!

After a silence during which they munched their burgers, Qwilleran said, "The woman who takes care of Florrie could pick you up some afternoon and bring you back. Her name is Mrs. Robinson."

There was no response from Ozzie.

"Mrs. Robinson has a video of you driving No. 9 for the Party Train. She'd be glad to show it to you."

"Like t'see that! Fred and Billy, they'd like t'see it, too."

"Who are they?"

"Fred Ooterhans, fireman, and Billy Poole, brakeman. We worked together since I-don't-know-when. We was the best crew on the

SC&L. Still together at the Center, playin' cards, shootin' the breeze."

Qwilleran paid the tab and said, "It's been a pleasure meeting you, Ozzie. Thank you for the interview."

"Gonna print it in the book?"

"That's my intention. And don't be surprised if you get a call from Mrs. Robinson."

Shared weekends had always been important to Qwilleran and Polly, ever since he lost his way in a blizzard and stumbled into her country cottage looking like a snowman with a moustache. And yet, weekends were losing their savor, and he blamed it on Polly's house. In an effort to restore some of the magic, however, he proposed Saturday night dinner at the Palomino Paddock in Lockmaster, a five-star, five-thousand-calorie restaurant.

Polly was surprised and pleased. "What is the occasion?"

"You don't know it, but we're exchanging our vows tonight," he said. "You're vowing to stop worrying about your house, and I'm vowing to end the Cold War with Bootsie."

"I'll wear my opals," she said, entering into the spirit of the occasion.

The Paddock was a mix of sophistication and hayseed informality, decorated with bales of straw and photographs of Thoroughbreds. The servers were young equestrians, fresh from a day of riding, eventing, jumping, or hunting.

The chef-owner lived on a two-hundred-acre horsefarm.

Seated in a stall, Polly and Qwilleran drank to their new resolve—she with a glass of sherry and he with a glass of Squunk water.

He said, "Don't forget, the play opens Thursday evening, and I have four tickets. We can have dinner with the Rikers."

"Who's playing my namesake?" Polly had been named Hippolyta by a parent who was a Shakespeare scholar.

"Carol Lanspeak. Who else?"

"She's not very Amazonian."

"She doesn't look like a fairy queen, either, but she's doubling as Titania." He pronounced Titania to rhyme with Britannia.

"According to my father, Qwill, Shakespeare took Titania from Ovid and undoubtedly used the Elizabethan pronunciation of the Latin, which would be Tie-tain-ia."

"Try that on Moose County for size," Qwilleran quipped. "Did your father ever explain *Hold, or cut bowstrings*?"

"He said that etymologists have been debating its source for two centuries. I could look it up for you."

"No thanks. Sometimes it's more fun not to know. . . . By the way, I've uncovered another Hermia case: a father who forbade his daughter to marry the man of her choice, disowning her when she disobeyed, and forbidding his wife ever to mention their daughter's name."

"Shakespeare at least had a happy ending. Is there more to your story?"

"There may be. Meanwhile, I've been reading the play aloud, and Koko gets excited whenever I mention Hermia. He also knocked *Androcles and the Lion* off the shelf—not one of Shaw's best, but I enjoyed reading it again. I played the lion when I was in college. It was a good role; no lines to learn."

"What else have you been reading?"

"A mind-boggling book on the engineering of the Panama Canal. Do you realize the Big Ditch took ten years to complete? It's forty miles long, and they dug out 240 million cubic yards of earth!"

She listened in a daze, and Qwilleran knew she was wondering how many cubic yards of earth would be necessary to build a berm on her property.

He rattled on, doubting that she was really listening. "The book was written by Colonel Goethals, the engineer in charge. It was published in 1916. The flyleaf of my copy was inscribed by Euphonia Gage to her father-in-law. It was a Christmas present. He would be Junior Goodwinter's great-grandfather. I'll give the book to Junior when I've finished reading it."

"That will be nice," Polly mused.

When it was time to order from the menu, Qwilleran had no problem in making a choice: she-crab soup, an appetizer of mushrooms stuffed with spinach and goat cheese, a Caesar salad, and sea scallops with sun-dried tomatoes, basil, and saffron cream on angel hair pasta. Polly ordered grouper with no soup, no appetizer, and no salad.

"Are you feeling all right?" he asked anxiously. She tended to keep her ailments a secret.

"Well, I've been plagued with indigestion lately," she confessed, as if it were a character flaw. "I have an appointment with Dr. Diane this week."

He thought, She's getting ulcers over that damned house!

Polly seemed to enjoy her spartan dinner and seemed to be having a good time. And yet, Qwilleran sensed a curtain between them. She was really thinking about her house, and he, to tell the truth, was really thinking about the briefing of his secret agent.

Celia arrived at the barn Sunday evening in a flurry of smiles and youthful exuberance. "I had a wonderful weekend!" she cried. "I attended service at the Little Stone Church and met the pastor during the coffee hour in the basement. The choirleader said she could use another voice, and everyone was so friendly! Then Virginia took me to Black Creek to meet her folks, and we had a lovely brunch. I know I'm going to like it here, Chief."

"Good!" he said. "Make yourself comfortable while I concoct an exotic drink."

While he opened cans of pineapple juice and

grapefruit juice, Celia found the wooden whistle on the coffee table and blew a few toots. "This takes me back!" she said. "When I was little and living on a farm, I could hear train whistles blowing all the time. That was to warn people to get off the tracks. Anybody who didn't have a car or a truck used to walk the rails to get to the next town." She sipped her drink. "My! This is good! What did you put in it?"

"I never reveal my culinary secrets," Qwilleran replied pompously.

"In the newspaper the police say they're investigating the scandal. Aren't they getting anywhere?"

"They do things their way, Celia, and we do things our way. We're searching for answers to questions, not hard evidence, which is what they have to have. That's why any scraps of information you pick up at The Roundhouse will help solve the puzzle."

"Something's bothering me, Chief. I feel guilty because I'm sort of . . . *spying* on Tish and Florrie."

"No need to feel that way. You're giving them something they desperately need: friendship, warmth, and sympathy, and at the same time helping to bring a criminal to justice. Just remember not to sound like an interrogator; keep the conversation chatty. Talk about your grandson, and ask Tish about her grandparents. Talk about your brothers, and inquire about hers."

Celia laughed at this. "I'll never go to

heaven, Chief, after telling so many lies for you.
I only had sisters."

"St. Peter will understand this ignoble means
to a noble end. You must also bear in mind,
Celia, that Tish may be lying to you; she may
be part of the scam."

"Oh, my! That's hard to believe!"

"Nevertheless, keep your wits about you. It
would be interesting to know what they're
doing for money. Tish is laid off; all credit
union deposits are frozen; her father has disappeared; that house must be costly to maintain,
to say nothing of the cost of nursing care and
medication. Did Floyd provide for the family
before decamping? Did he keep a safe in the
house? Is that where he kept his ill-gotten
gains? Or did he have millions stashed in a suitcase under the bed?"

Celia laughed uproariously. "Now you're really kidding, Chief. How could I find out stuff
like that?"

"They're merely questions to keep in the
back of your head. How did Tish feel about the
secretary who absconded with Floyd? The attorney has instructed them not to talk about the
case, but if you can get her to break down, find
out what kind of work she did at the Lumbertown office. Did she suspect tampering with the
books? If so, did fear of her father prevent her
from reporting it? Perhaps . . . Tish was the one
who blew the whistle. This is all long-range
probing, of course."

"It's going to be so much fun!" Celia said in great glee.

"Then let's confer again tomorrow evening."

"Do you mind if it's later than usual? Choir practice is Monday nights at seven."

"Not at all. Call me at your convenience," Qwilleran said as he escorted her to the parking area. "How's your little car running?"

"Just fine! It gets good mileage, and I love the color!"

After the red car had driven away, Qwilleran walked the floor to collect his thoughts—through the much-used library area, the seldom-used dining area, the spacious foyer, the comfortable lounge, and back to the library. Twenty-eight laps equalled one mile, Derek Cuttlebrink had computed in one of his goofy moments. Whenever Qwilleran traversed this inside track, both cats would fall into line behind him, marching with tails at twelve o'clock.

Around and around the fireplace cube the three of them traipsed, the man feeling like a Pied Piper without pipes. On the sixth lap he noticed the twistletwig rocker in front of the fireplace cube, its intricately bent willow twigs silhouetted against the white wall. According to Elizabeth Hart, one could sit in the grotesque piece of furniture and expect to think profound thoughts. What Qwilleran needed at the moment was a little profundity, and he undertook to test her theory.

He slid into the rocker's inviting contours gingerly, not quite trusting it to bear his weight. When there was no sign of collapse, he relaxed and began to rock, slowly at first, and then more vigorously. The action attracted Koko, who circled him three times and then leaped lightly into his lap. This was surprising; Koko was not a lap-sitter.

"Well, young man, what's this all about?" Qwilleran asked.

"Yow!" Koko replied as he started to dig in the crook of Qwilleran's elbow. Yum Yum sometimes gave a few casual digs before settling down, but Koko was excavating with zeal. His claws were retracted, but his paws were powerful. Could this be blamed on the twistletwig mystique?

"Who do you think you are?" Qwilleran demanded. "Digger O'Dell? Colonel Goethals? This is not the Panama Canal!"

The cat stopped for a few moments, then resumed his chore with increased energy. The game was not only ridiculous; it verged on the painful.

"Ouch! *Enough*!" Qwilleran protested. *"Hold or cut bowstrings!"*

TWELVE

Qwilleran started the week by grinding out a thousand pseudo-serious words on the history of sunburn. It was inspired by an oil painting in Polly's apartment depicting a beach scene at the turn of the century; the women wore bathing suits with sleeves, knee-length skirts, matching hats, and long stockings. The ninety miles of beaches bordering Moose County were now frequented by summer vacationers without stockings, hats, sleeves, or skirts—and sometimes without tops. He titled his column "From Parasols and Gloves . . . to Sunscreen with SPF-

30." For his readers who had never seen a parasol, he described it as a light, portable sunshade carried like an umbrella, its name derived from French, Italian, and Latin words meaning "to ward off the sun."

He had to work hard to stretch the subject into a thousand words, and he was not particularly proud of the result when he delivered the copy to Junior Goodwinter. "Consider it a summer space filler," he said as he threw it on the editor's desk.

After scanning the pages, Junior said, "It's topical, but I've seen better from the Qwill Pen. Want us to run it without a by-line and say you're on vacation?"

"It's not *that* bad," Qwilleran protested. "Any more news from Mudville?"

"There's a rumor they've located Floyd-boy's secretary in Texas, but nobody will confirm it."

"How about the murder in the tavern?"

"The police are being cagey, which means (a) they're onto something big or (b) they're not onto anything at all and hate to admit it. What's really odd is that the power company can't explain the outage. Being countywide, it couldn't be part of a local murder plot—or could it? I'm beginning to agree with the UFO buffs. Do you have a theory, Qwill? You usually come up with a wild one."

Qwilleran smoothed his moustache. "If I told you my theory, you'd have me committed."

Leaving the managing editor's office, he

stopped in the city room and put a note in Roger MacGillivray's mailbox: "While you're scratching for stories in Mudville, find out what happened at the Trackside Tavern ten years ago. Your reference to it was provocative. Perhaps you know what happened. Perhaps it's too horrendous to mention in a family newspaper. Whisper in your uncle Qwill's ear."

On the way out of the building, Qwilleran passed Hixie Rice's office. The vice president in charge of advertising and promotion hailed him. "Qwill, I loved your column about the sweet corn of August—and about this being the corniest county in the state! I sent Wilfred out to buy several dozen ears. We're sending them to advertisers as a promo."

He grunted a lukewarm acknowledgment of the compliment. "Not to change the subject," he said, "but was Floyd Trevelyan a customer of yours?"

"Yes and no. He was tight-fisted with advertising dollars."

"His son lives in Indian Village. Do you know him?"

"I see him in the parking lot. I thought Gary Pratt looked like a black bear, but Floyd's son is *too much*!"

"Is he in your building?"

"No, I think he's in Dwight's building. Why? Is it important?"

"No, I'm just addressing my Christmas cards early," Qwilleran said with a nonchalant shrug.

Hixie looked at him with suspicion. "You've got something up your sleeve, Qwill! What is it?"

"Are you still chummy with the manager at Indian Village?"

"Not exactly chummy, but she's on my Christmas list in a big way, and she's extremely cooperative. What can I do for you?"

"Floyd Trevelyan's secretary had an apartment in G building. Tell the manager you have a friend Down Below who's being transferred to Pickax and wants to rent an upscale apartment. Ask if Nella Hooper's is vacant—or will it be vacant soon."

"Would you like to tell me what this is all about?"

"Only my journalistic curiosity," he said. "If the apartment is not available, someone must be paying the rent, and it would be interesting to know who—or why."

"I smell intrigue," Hixie said. "Anything else?"

"Find out when Eddie Trevelyan moved in. That's all. Get back to work! Sell ads! Make money for the paper!"

"How's Polly? I haven't seen her lately."

"She's fine—excited about her new house, of course. By the way, she's due for a physical and wants to switch doctors. She doesn't care for the man who bought Melinda's practice. Have you heard any good reports about the Lanspeaks' daughter?"

Hixie waggled an accusing finger at him. "Qwill, you old rogue! Is that your under-handed way of finding out what happened to my late lamented romance? Well, I'll tell you. He was a wonderful, sincere, thoughtful, attentive *bore*! But I still see his mother once a week for French lessons."

"Pardonnez-moi," he said with a stiff bow.

Qwilleran next stopped at Amanda's Studio of Design to see Fran Brodie. She was in-house three days a week, sketching floor plans, working on color schemes, and greeting customers.

"Cup of coffee? Cold drink?" she asked.

He chose coffee. "Have you started dress rehearsals?"

"Tonight's the first. We test our system for handling extras. A busload of lords and ladies will come from the high school in time for the first act—complete with sweeping robes and elaborate headdresses. After the first scene they're not needed until the end of the play. What do we do with them in the meantime? There's no room backstage. Do we put them on the school bus to wait? Do we send them back to school for an hour? You know how giddy kids can get if they're having to wait."

Qwilleran thought for a moment. "Would the Old Stone Church let you use one of their social rooms? Bus the kids across the park, give them a horror video, and pick them up an hour later."

"Super!" Fran exclaimed. "Why didn't we think of that? The Lanspeaks are pillars of the church; they can swing it for us. . . . More coffee?"

While she poured, he asked, "What's the latest from your confidential source? The last thing you told me, the police were checking the secretary's story."

"It turned out to be true, Qwill. Nella Hooper was really fired two weeks before Audit Sunday. She collected severance pay and filed for unemployment benefits."

"How long ago did you do her apartment in Indian Village?"

"More than a year."

"I suppose Floyd paid for the furnishings."

"No, the credit union paid the bill; they could take it as a business expense. Did I tell you the FBI went in with a search warrant? Nella hadn't left anything but the furniture and a tube of toothpaste."

"What brand?"

Fran smirked at his humor. "How do you like my flowers?" A magnificent bouquet of white roses stood on her desk.

"You must have acquired a well-heeled admirer," Qwilleran said. "How come I can't smell them? How come I'm not sneezing?"

"They're silk! Aren't they fabulous? Amanda found this new source in Chicago. My grandmother used to make crepe paper flowers during the Depression and sell them for a dollar a dozen. These are twenty-five dollars *each!* Why don't you buy a big bunch for Polly?"

"She'd rather have fresh daisies," he said truthfully.

"Qwill, why doesn't Polly let me help her with her house?" Fran said earnestly. "I don't mean to belittle your beloved, but she's a color-fusser. I showed her some fabrics, and she fussed over the colors, trying to get a perfect match. I could teach her something if she'd listen."

"I don't know the answer, Fran. I'm even more concerned than you are." He started to leave.

"Wait a minute! I have something for you to read." She handed him the working script of a play. "See if you think we should do this for our winter production. The action takes place at Christmastime. I'd love to play Eleanor of Aquitaine. . . . You could grow a beard and play Henry," she added slyly.

"No thanks, but I'll give it a read."

On the way home Qwilleran took a detour into the public library to see Polly, but she was out of the building, the clerks informed him. They always considered it appropriate to tell their boss's friend where she had gone and why: to Dr. Zoller's office to have her teeth cleaned, or to Gippel's Garage to have her brakes adjusted. Today she had an appointment with the vet; Bootsie had been vomiting, and there was blood in his urine.

"If she returns, ask her to call me," he said in a businesslike tone, but he was thinking, That's all she needs to push her over the edge! A sick cat!

At the barn he loaded a cooler of soft drinks into his car and drove down the trail for his mail. Eddie was bending over a whining table saw, lopping off boards as if slicing bread, while two new helpers climbed about the framed building, hammering nails with syncopated blows.

"Comin' right along!" he called out encouragingly.

"Yeah," said Eddie, walking in his direction and sharpening a pencil. "If it don't rain tonight, I'll do some gradin'. I'll do all that fill and start on that hill she wants next to the road."

"That'll make a long day for you," Qwilleran said.

"Yeah . . . well . . . a guy in Kennebeck'll rent me a skim-loader cheaper at night."

"How do you transport it all that distance?"

"Flatbed trailer."

Qwilleran asked, "Do you live in Kennebeck? That's where they have that good steakhouse."

"Nah, I live in . . . uh . . . out in the country."

"Where's Benno? Still hung over?"

"Di'n't you hear? He got his!"

"You mean, he was killed? In an accident?"

"Nah. A fight in a bar."

"That's too bad," Qwilleran said. "You'd known him a long time, hadn't you?"

"Yeah . . . well . . . gotta get back to work."

Driving back to the barn, Qwilleran wondered why Eddie considered it necessary to conceal his Indian Village address. The development on the Ittibittiwassee River was swanky by Moose County standards, catering to young professionals with briefcases and styled hair: Fran Brodie, Dwight Somers, Hixie Rice, and Elizabeth Hart had apartments there. Eddie hardly fitted the picture, with his rough appearance and rusty pickup.

Qwilleran arrived at the barn in time to hear the phone ringing and see Koko hopping up and down as if on springs. It was Polly, calling in a state of anxiety. Bootsie was in the hospital. He had feline urological syndrome. They were giving him tests. He might need surgery.

Listening to her anguished report, his reaction was: I told you so! Many times he had warned Polly that she was overfeeding Bootsie; he was gorging on food to compensate for loneliness; what he needed was a cat friend.

Now Qwilleran tried to comfort her by mumbling words of encouragement: She had caught it in time; Bootsie was in good hands; the vet was highly skilled; Bootsie was still a young cat and would bounce back; would she like to talk about it over dinner at the Old Stone Mill?

No, she said. Unfortunately the library was open until nine o'clock, and it was her turn to work.

It was raining slightly when Celia arrived for her briefing—not really raining, just misting. "Good for the complexion," they liked to say in Moose County.

She was wearing a plastic hat tied under her chin. "Did anyone expect this rain?" she asked.

"In Moose County we always expect the unexpected. Come in and tell me about the day's excitement at The Roundhouse. Did Wrigley steal the show? Did Tish break down and tell all? Did Florrie plant a bomb in the elevator? This is better than a soap opera."

"I decided not to take him," she said. "That train wreck really scared him! So I told them his little tummy was upset from eating a rubber band. I'm getting good at inventing stories, Chief."

"I'm proud of you, Celia."

"Well, wait till you hear! When I arrived, they both hugged me—Tish and Florrie—and said they'd been lonely over the weekend, and they wanted to know if I'd come and live with them! I and Wrigley! I almost fell over! I had to think quick, and I said my grandson was coming up from Illinois to live with me so he could go to school in Pickax, starting in September. They said Clayton could move in, too! I told them I was really touched by the kind invitation and would have to think about it. Whew!"

"Nice going," Qwilleran commented.

"So we had lunch and talked about this and that. Tish reads your column, Chief, and she raved about the one on sweet corn. I was dying to tell her I know you, but I didn't. They asked about Clayton, and I asked if they had many relatives. Tish has one brother—no sisters—grandmother dead, aunts and uncles moved away, grandfather a retired railroad engineer in Sawdust City. And here's the sad part: He lives twenty miles away and has never been to visit them! Her grandmother never even sent a birthday card! Tish hasn't met either of them. This family is very strange, Chief."

"Was anything more said about the dog?"

"I asked if they were going to get another watchdog. I said my son had a German shepherd. Tish got all teary-eyed and talked about Zak and how sweet and cuddly he was. She said he might have been killed by her brother's best friend; they'd been having some violent arguments. Isn't that terrible!"

Qwilleran agreed but was not surprised. The pieces of the puzzle were beginning to fit together. "Could you get her to talk about the credit union?"

"Not yet, but I'm getting there! After Florrie went to have her nap, I told Tish she was a wonderful person to give up college and stay home to take care of her mother. I said office work must be boring for someone with her talent. Then she showed me a clipping of a book review she wrote for your paper, and they paid her for it! She was so thrilled to see her name in print! She signed it Letitia Penn. That's Florrie's maiden name. . . . I asked what kind of work she did at the office, and she said a little bit of everything. She seems afraid to talk about it."

"You're doing very well, Celia. Now I think it's time for that strange family to have a reunion. The grandfather has reached an age when many persons look back on their lives with remorse and a desire to make amends for past mistakes. I mentioned it to Mr. Penn when I interviewed him, and you might sound out the women tomorrow."

"I know they'll love it!"

"Do you mind picking up the old gentleman in Sawdust City?"

"Be glad to."

"When the family is together, you can show a video of the Party Train, with Mr. Penn in the engineer's cab," he said, and then thought, Unfortunately, it includes shots of F.T. in the engineer's cab and F.T. with his secretary.

"Oh, we'll have a ball!" Celia squealed. "I'll make some cookies." She stood up. "I should drive home now. When the sky's overcast, it gets dark early, and the woods are kind of scary at night."

Qwilleran accompanied her to her car and asked if she had noticed a lot of cars in the theatre parking lot. "It's a dress rehearsal for *Midsummer Night's Dream,* and I have a pair of tickets for you for opening night, if you'd like to see the show."

"I'd love it! Thank you so much! I'll take Virginia; she's been so good to me . . . What's that rumbling noise?"

"Only a bulldozer working overtime at the end of the orchard." He opened the car door for her. "Fasten your seatbelt. Observe the speed limit. And don't pick up any hitchhikers."

The irrepressible Mrs. Robinson was laughing merrily as she started through the block-long patch of woods at a bumpy ten miles per hour.

To Qwilleran the rumbling of the tractor was a welcome sound. It meant that Polly could cross off one item on her worry list. The manmade hill between house and highway would give her a sense of privacy, though there was little traffic on Trevelyan Road. Paving it had been a political boondoggle; no one used it except locals living on scattered farms.

So Qwilleran listened to the comforting grunting and groaning of Eddie's skim-loader. Lounging in his big chair, he asked himself: What have we learned to date? Benno *may* have killed Zak. Yet, even if he were a vengeful victim of the embezzlement, he would have known that the dog was not Floyd's. Tish had said the two young men had been arguing violently.

Over what? A soccer bet? A woman? Drugs? Eddie *may* have killed his friend in a fit of drunken passion. The tension between boss and helper had been evident on the job—ever since Audit Sunday. When Eddie visited the barn, Koko hissed at him.

"Yow!" said Koko, sitting on the telephone desk, perilously close to the English pencil box. His comment gave Qwilleran another lead: The police were being evasive about the murder weapon at the Trackside Tavern. "Not a hunting knife" was all Andy Brodie would say. Could it have been a well-sharpened pencil?

With a growl and an abrupt change of mood, Koko sprang from the desk and launched a mad rush around the main floor—across the coffee table, up over the fireplace cube, around the kitchen. Objects not nailed down were scattered: books, magazines, the wooden train whistle, one of the carved decoys, the brass paperweight. Qwilleran grabbed the wooden pencil box from the path of the crazed animal.

"Koko!" he yelled. "Stop! Stop!"

Another decoy went flying. There was the sound of breaking glass in the kitchen. Then the cat flung himself at the front door. He bounced off, picked himself up, gave his left shoulder two brief licks, and stormed the door again like a battering ram.

"Stop! You'll kill yourself!" Qwilleran had never interfered in a catfit; it usually stopped as suddenly as it had started. But he honestly feared for Koko's safety. He rushed to the foyer and threw a scatter rug over the writhing body and pinned him down. After a few seconds the lump under the rug was surprisingly quiet. Cautiously he lifted one corner, then another. Koko was lying there, stretched out, exhausted.

It was then that the growl of the bulldozer floated up the trail on the damp night air. So that was it! The constant stop-and-go noise was driving Koko crazy. Or was that the only reason for the demonstration? Qwilleran felt an urgent tingling on his upper lip. He pounded his moustache, put on his yellow cap, and started out with a flashlight.

THIRTEEN

Following Koko's significant catfit, Qwilleran jogged to the building site, where the skimloader was making its nervous racket—starting and stopping, advancing and retreating, climbing and plunging. He could see bouncing flashes of light as the vehicle's headlights turned this way and that. While he was still a hundred yards away from the earth-moving operation, the noise stopped and the headlight was turned off. Time for a cigarette, Qwilleran thought; he'd better not leave any butts around.

At that moment there was a gut-wrenching

scream—a man's scream—and then an earth-shaking thud—and then silence.

"Hey! Hey, down there!" Qwilleran shouted, running forward and ducking as something large and black flew over his head.

His flashlight showed the tractor lying on its side, half in the ditch. The operator was not in sight. Thrown clear, Qwilleran thought as he combed the area with a beam of light. Then he heard a tortured groan from the ditch. The operator was pinned underneath.

Futilely he threw his shoulder against the machine. Desperately he looked up and down the lonely highway. A single pair of headlights was approaching from the north, and he waved his flashlight in frantic arcs until it stopped.

"Gotta CB? Gotta phone?" he yelled at the driver. "Call 911! Tractor rollover! Man trapped underneath! Trevelyan Road, quarter mile north of Base Line!" Before he could finish, the motorist was talking on his car phone. He was Scott Gippel, the car dealer, who lived nearby.

Almost immediately, police sirens pierced the silence of the night. Seconds later, red and blue revolving lights converged from north and south, accompanied by the wailing and honking of emergency vehicles.

While Gippel turned his car to beam its headlights on the scene, Qwilleran climbed down into the ditch, searching with his flashlight. First he saw an arm, grotesquely twisted . . .

next a mop of black hair . . . and then a bearded face raked with bleeding clawmarks.

A police car was first to arrive, followed by the ambulance from the hospital and the volunteer rescue squad from the firehall. Seven men and a woman responded. They had rescue equipment and knew what to do. They jacked the tractor and extricated the unconscious body from the mud.

Qwilleran identified him for the police officer: Edward Trevelyan of Indian Village; next of kin, Letitia Trevelyan in West Middle Hummock. The door closed on the stretcher, and the ambulance sped away.

The others stood around, somewhat stunned, despite their composure during the rescue.

"I heard the tractor," Qwilleran said, "and was on my way here to watch the action, when I heard a scream and the machine toppling over and a huge bird flying away. I think it was a great horned owl. There's one living in the woods."

"When they're after prey at night, they can mistake anything for an animal," the officer said. "You're smart to wear that yellow cap."

Gippel said, "That guy'll never make it. His bones are crushed. Do you realize how much that tractor weighs?"

"The soil is wet, though," Qwilleran pointed out. "He was partially cushioned by the mud."

"Don't bet on it!" Gippel was notorious for

his pessimism, being the only businessman in town who refused to join the Pickax Boosters Club.

As Qwilleran walked back to the barn, he dreaded the task of notifying Polly. The thought of a serious accident on her property would blight her attitude toward the house and add to her worries.

By the time he arrived, his phone was ringing. It was Celia. "Bad news!" she said breathlessly. "Tish just called. Her brother's been in a terrible accident. He's in Pickax Hospital, and she asked me to go there, because she can't leave Florrie."

"Call me if there's anything I can do, no matter how late," he said. "Call and tell me his condition."

He turned on all the lights in the barn in an effort to dispel the gloom that hung over him. The Siamese felt it, too. They forgot to ask for their bedtime treat and were in no mood for sleep. They followed him when he circled the main floor. After several laps, he considered the twistletwig rocker, wondering if its efficacy included the therapeutic. When he gave it a try, both cats piled into his lap, Koko digging industriously in the crook of his elbow. Qwilleran endured the discomfort, remembering that it was Koko's catfit that had sent him down to the building site—before the accident happened!

Eventually Celia called back. "He's unconscious, and only a relative is allowed to see him. I said I was his grandmother. He looks more dead than alive. The nurse wouldn't tell me anything, except that he's critical . . . *What's that*?" she cried, hearing a crash.

"Koko knocked something down," he said calmly.

"The hospital will call me if there's a turn for the worse. Tomorrow morning, after Florrie's nurse reports, Tish will drive to town, and we'll go to the hospital together."

"That's good. She'll need moral support. Keep me informed, but right now you'd better get some rest. Tomorrow could be a hectic day for you." Qwilleran spoke softly and considerately; he returned the receiver to its cradle gently. Then he turned around and yelled, "Bad cat! Look what you've done!"

Koko gave him a defiant stare, while Yum Yum scampered away guiltily. The epithet could refer to either male or female, but it was Koko who had been nosing the pencil box for several days. Now it lay on the clay tile floor in two pieces. The tiny hinges had pulled out of the old wood, and the box had burst open. The drawer with the secret latch held firm, and the paper clips were secure, but pens, pencils, a letter-opener, and whatnot were scattered all over the floor. As Qwilleran gathered them up, he saw Koko walking away, impudently carrying a black-barreled felt-tip in his mouth.

"Bad cat!" he bellowed again. *"Bad cat!"* It

may have vented his anger, but it did nothing to dent the cat's equanimity.

Qwilleran set his alarm clock for six forty-five, an unprecedented hour for a late-riser of his distinction. He wanted to break the news to Polly before she heard it on the radio.

At seven a.m. the WPKX announcer said, "A bulldozer rolled over late last night on the outskirts of Pickax, injuring Edward P. Trevelyan, twenty-four, of Indian Village. He was grading a building site in a secluded area when he was attacked by a large bird, thought to be an owl. He lost control of the tractor, which rolled into a ditch, pinning him underneath. The accident victim was taken to Pickax Hospital by the emergency medical service, after being freed by the volunteer rescue squad. His condition is critical."

Qwilleran called Polly shortly after her wake-up hour of seven-thirty and heard her say sleepily, "So early, Qwill! Is something wrong?"

"I have an early appointment and want to inquire about Bootsie before leaving."

"I phoned the hospital last night," Polly said, "and Bootsie was resting comfortably after the initial treatment. It was nice of you to call."

"One other thing . . . I'm sorry to report that Eddie Trevelyan is in the hospital."

"How do you know?" she asked anxiously.

"It was on the air this morning. He was in an accident last night."

"Oh, dear! I hope it wasn't drunk driving."

"They called it a tractor rollover. It looks as if he won't be able to supervise his crew for a while."

In the pause that followed, Qwilleran could imagine the questions racing through Polly's mind: How bad is it? How long will he be incapacitated? Can his helpers proceed without him? Will it delay my construction?

"Oh, no!" she cried. "Was he working on my property?"

"I'm afraid so. He was doing a little midnight grading while he had the use of a rented skimloader."

"I feel terribly guilty about this, Qwill. I've been nagging him about the grading," Polly said in anguish. "It's so discouraging. Everything seems to be happening at once. First Bootsie, and now this!"

"One thing I can assure you, Polly. You have no reason to worry about the house. If any problem arises, it'll be solved. Just leave everything to me."

Qwilleran hung up with a sense of defeat, knowing his advice would be ignored; she would worry more than ever. It was nearly eight o'clock, and he walked briskly down the trail in the hope of finding workmen on the job. The site was deserted. The tractor lay on its side in the ditch; across the highway its flatbed trailer was parked on the shoulder; the pavement was a maze of muddy tracks. Soon a pickup pulled onto the property, and one of Eddie's workmen jumped out.

Qwilleran went to meet him. "Do you know your boss is in the hospital?"

"Yeah. He's hurt bad."

"Can you continue to work on the house?"

The man shrugged. "No boss, no pay. I come to pick up my tools."

"Do you know where Eddie rented this machine?"

"Truck-n-Track in Kennebeck."

At that moment a late-model car stopped on the shoulder, driven by Scott Gippel on his way to work.

"Did you hear the newscast, Scott?" Qwilleran asked.

"Sure did! That guy's gonna cash it in, take it from me. It's the Trevelyan curse, all over again. Same place. Same family. Look! You can see the foundation where their farmhouse burned down."

"Well, don't be too worried about Eddie. He's young, and he's strong—"

"And he drinks like a sponge," the car dealer said. "He's probably got alcohol instead of blood in his veins."

Qwilleran let that comment pass. There had been a time when he fitted the same description, more or less. He said, "Could your tow truck get this thing out of the ditch and deliver it to Kennebeck?"

"Who pays?"

"I do, but I want it done fast . . . immediately
. . . now!"

Without answering, Gippel picked up his car
phone and gave orders.

Qwilleran waited until the carpenter had
picked up his tools—and nothing belonging to
Eddie. He waited until the tractor had been
towed away. Only then did he go home and
feed the cats. They were unusually quiet; they
knew when he was involved in serious business.

He himself breakfasted on coffee and a two-
day-old doughnut while pondering Koko's
bizarre behavior in recent weeks: the inter-
minable vigils at the front window . . . his
perching on the fireplace cube with the decoys
. . . his vociferous and absurd reaction to the
name Hermia . . . his digging in the crook of
Qwilleran's elbow, ad nauseam.

As the man ruminated, the cat was investigating the bookshelf devoted to nineteenth-century
fiction.

"You'd better shape up, young man,"
Qwilleran scolded him, "or we'll send you to
live with Amanda Goodwinter."

"Ik ik ik!" said Koko irritably as he shoved a
book off the shelf. It was a fine book with a
leather binding, gold tooling, India paper, and
gilt edges. With resignation and the realization
that one can never win an argument with a
Siamese, Qwilleran picked up the book and
read the title. It was Dostoyevsky's *The Idiot*.

"Thanks a lot," he said crossly.

*   *   *

Qwilleran's telephone was in constant use that morning. He called Kennebeck and instructed Truck-n-Track to send him Eddie's rental bill, not forgetting to credit the deposit. He instructed Mr. O'Dell to pick up Eddie's table saw and other tools and store them in a stall of the carriage house.

At one point he telephoned the Lanspeaks, who called their daughter at the medical clinic, who spoke to the chief of staff at the hospital, who revealed that the patient was in and out of consciousness, having sustained massive internal injuries and multiple fractures. The next twenty-four hours would be decisive.

Soon after, Celia called again. She had been to the hospital with Tish. Eddie was conscious but didn't recognize his sister. "I think they had him all doped up," she said. "We were wondering how to break the news to Florrie and how she'd take it, and we decided that the reunion with Grandpa Penn might soften the blow. What do you think, Chief?"

Qwilleran thought, It'll either soften the blow or deliver the coup de grace. He said, however, "Good idea!"

"So I'll phone him and ask if I can pick him up this afternoon. I hope it isn't too short notice."

"It won't be. The social schedule at the Retirement Center seems to be flexible."

"Also, I have something to report right now,

Chief, if you can see me for a few minutes before I leave for The Roundhouse."

When she arrived, she was flushed with excitement.

"Coffee?" he asked.

"I haven't time." Sinking into the cushions of the sofa, she rummaged in her handbag for her notebook and then dropped the roomy carryall on the floor, where its gaping interior immediately attracted the Siamese. It was used to transport such items as cookies, paperback novels, house slippers, drugstore remedies, and more. "What do you think they're looking for?" she asked, as the two blackish-brown noses sniffed the handbag's mysteries.

"Wrigley," Qwilleran said. "They think you've got Wrigley in there, and they want to let the cat out of the bag."

Celia howled with more glee than the quip warranted, Qwilleran felt, but he realized she was overexcited by the day's happenings. He waited patiently until she calmed down, then asked, "Where's Tish now?"

"Still at the hospital. They have a comfy waiting room for relatives in the intensive care wing, and that's where we had a heart-to-heart talk this morning—Tish and I. I asked if Eddie had friends we should notify, but she doesn't know any of his friends . . . I told you they're a strange family, Chief . . . Then she said Nella Hooper liked Eddie a lot and would be sorry to hear what happened, but she didn't leave a forwarding address. Nella, I found out, is the secretary at the credit union who was fired a couple of weeks before it closed. She and Eddie lived in the same apartment building. She wasn't a secretary, Tish said, but more like an assistant to the president. She had a degree in accounting and knew computers and made a big impression on Tish. They used to go to lunch together."

"First question," Qwilleran said. "What was this highly qualified woman doing in a tank town like Sawdust City? Besides everything you mention, she has smashing good looks! I've seen her."

"She loved trains! That's all. It was a dream job, traveling around the country with the president, looking at trains and—"

She was interrupted by the phone. Hixie was calling to say that Nella Hooper's apartment would not be available until October first—and maybe not then if she decided to come back. The credit union always paid her rent—quarterly—in advance. Eddie Trevelyan had moved to Indian Village four months before Audit Sunday. Hixie concluded, "Is he the one who was in that bad accident last night?"

"He's the one. Floyd's son. Thanks, Hixie. Talk to you later."

As Qwilleran returned to the lounge area, he was thinking, If they were going to fire Nella in July, why would they pay her rent until October? To Celia he said, "Did Tish mention why Nella was fired?"

"She wasn't fired, really. Nella's father in Texas has Alzheimer's disease, and her mother needed her at home, so Nella had to quit her job. But the office made it look like she was fired, so she could collect benefits. She left without saying good-bye, which really hurt Tish's feelings, although she realizes Nella had family troubles on her mind."

"Hmmm, makes one wonder" was Qwiller-an's comment. "As I recall, Tish said she hated her father for cheating on Florrie. How does she react to Nella's relationship with her father?"

"Strictly business, she said. Her father's real girlfriend owns a bar in Sawdust City. Tish told Nella how she felt about F.T. and how he wouldn't spend the money to send Florrie to Switzerland. Nella was very sympathetic and said it would be easy to switch $100,000 into a slush fund for Florrie, and F.T. would be none the wiser. Also, it would be legal because it was all in the family. . . . Do you understand how this works, Chief?"

"I don't even understand why seven-times-nine always equals sixty-three."

"Me too! Glad I'm not the only dumbbell. . . . Well, anyway, the next thing was that Tish introduced Eddie to Nella, because he wanted money to build condos. If he could buy the land, he could borrow against it to start building, but F.T. wouldn't back him. Nella told him not to worry; she could work the same kind of switch because it was all in the family. But before anything happened, Nella had to quit, and the credit union went bust. Tish was lucky to have her savings in a Pickax bank. She didn't trust F.T." Celia had been talking fast. She looked at her watch. "I've gotta dash. If I'm late, the nurse gets snippy."

As Qwilleran walked with Celia to the parking area, she said, "Someone backed a truck up to the carriage house today and started unloading stuff. I went downstairs to see what it was all about, and I met the nicest man! He said he works for you."

"That's Mr. O'Dell. You'll see him around frequently. He's the one who cleaned your windows before you moved in."

"They may need cleaning again soon," she replied with a wink, and she drove away laughing.

Indoors Qwilleran found something on the floor that belonged on the telephone desk: the paperback playscript that Fran wanted him to read. Koko was under the desk, sitting on his brisket and looking pleased with himself. Qwilleran smoothed his moustache with a dawning awareness: There was a leonine theme in Koko's recent antics, starting with the lion in *A Midsummer Night's Dream* . . . then *Andro- cles and the Lion* . . . and now the *Lion in Win-*

ter. Did he identify with the king of beasts? For a ten-pound house cat he had a lion-sized ego.

Or, Qwilleran thought, he's trying to tell me something, and I'm not getting it!

FOURTEEN

When Qwilleran's secret agent reported to Operation Whistle HQ on Tuesday evening, she was in a state of exhaustion. "I'm absolutely whacked!" she said. "First, the hospital this morning . . . then the family reunion . . . and then some flabbergasting news!"

"Sit down before you fall down," Qwilleran said. "Relax. Have a swig of fruit punch. Say hello to Koko and Yum Yum."

The Siamese came forth, looking for her handbag. When plumped on the floor it looked like a treasure-filled wastebasket. "Have you been good kitties?" she asked them.

"No," Qwilleran replied. "Koko is still in the doghouse for malicious destruction of property. . . . Now go on with your story. In the last episode of *The Trials of the Trevelyans*, you were having a heart-to-heart talk with Tish, and Nella had just left without saying good-bye."

"Yes, that was the Sunday they had that train ride at $500 a ticket. After the train ride, Floyd came home, got a mysterious phone call, and said he had to go and see a man about a train. He left, and they never saw him again."

"When did Tish tell you this?"

"This morning at the hospital. I couldn't tell you because I had to rush off to The Roundhouse. . . . So then I called Grandpa Penn and said I'd pick him up at two o'clock. He sounded as if it was the video he was really excited about. I didn't mention Eddie's accident."

"Did Florrie know he was coming?"

"Oh, yes! She was thrilled at the idea of seeing 'Pop' after so many years. She wanted to get all dressed up. At two o'clock, like I promised, I drove out to Sawdust City. That retirement home is a depressing building. Have you seen it?"

"I have, and I think the residents spend most of their waking hours at the Trackside Tavern and the Jump-Off Bar. Who can blame them?"

Celia told how she walked into the lobby and

found three old fellows sitting in a row—all shaved and combed and respectable in white summer shirts. "They all stood up, and I asked which one was the famous engineer. The tallest one said, 'I'm the hoghead.' I told him my car was at the curb, and he said, 'Full steam ahead.' But when I led the way to my car, all three men followed me! Before I knew it, three husky old men were squeezing into my little car. I was worried about my springs, but what could I do? I said, 'I didn't know you were bringing your bodyguards, Mr. Penn.' They all laughed."

"Well put," Qwilleran said.

"It turned out they were his fireman and brakeman, who'd always worked as a crew and still stuck together. Their names were Fred and Billy, and they were all excited about seeing the video. On the way to The Roundhouse they talked a mile a minute!"

"NO!" Qwilleran shouted, and Yum Yum—caught pilfering a pocketpack of tissues from the wonderful hand bag—dropped it and ran. "Sorry, he said. "Go on with your story."

"Well, when we got to the house, Tish ran down the steps and threw her arms around her grandpa. Florrie was in her wheelchair on the porch, wearing a pretty dress. Her old dad stumbled up the steps, crying 'My little Florrie!' And he dropped down on his knees and hugged her, and they both cried. When she asked, 'Where's Mom?' I cried, too."

"A touching scene," Qwilleran said.

"I took Fred and Billy out to the patio, so the others could have a private talk. The men remembered Florrie when she was a pretty young girl, waving at them as the train went by. They also knew about her wedding and didn't like it one bit! Then they started cursing F.T. to high heaven for stealing their life savings. They hoped he'd be caught and get prison for life. When I showed them the trains Florrie had wrecked, they laughed and cheered."

"Did you show the video?"

"Twice! Tish refused to look at it, and Florrie had to go to bed because the excitement had knocked her out, but the three men thought the video was wonderful. After that, I drove them back to Sawdust City."

"I'd say you handled everything nobly, Celia."

"Thanks, Chief, but that's not the end. When I got back to The Roundhouse, I got the shock of my life! Are you ready for it?"

"Fire away."

"It's something the lawyer had just told Tish. He said Floyd had put the Party Train in Florrie's name to protect himself from creditors and lawsuits!"

"Well! That puts a new complexion on the matter, doesn't it?" Qwilleran said. "The train can be sold and the proceeds used to send Florrie to Switzerland."

"But you haven't heard the whole story, Chief. *Grandpa Penn is buying the train!*"

"Wait a minute! Does he have that kind of money?"

"That's what I wondered," Celia said, "but Tish says he's had a good railroad job for fifty years and always believed in saving for a rainy day. What's more, his money is in banks and government bonds, so it's not tied up. He's turning everything over to Florrie. They've called the lawyer already."

"Will the old man have enough left to live on?" Qwilleran inquired.

"She says he has his railroad pension and social security and good medical insurance. He doesn't need much else. . . . What do you think of it, Chief?"

"Sounds like the ending of a B-movie made in the 1930s, but I'm happy for everyone. You didn't say how much he's turning over to Florrie, but he can sell the train for well over a million. More likely, two million. I heard that Floyd had put $600,000 in the locomotive alone. Just imagine! An old engineer's dream! To own the celebrated No. 9!"

Celia looked puzzled. "But if he wants to sell the train, who would buy it? That's an awful lot of money to spend on a thing like that."

"Train collecting is a growing hobby. More people than you think are pursuing it." It also occurred to Qwilleran that the economic development division of the K Foundation, currently promoting tourism, might take over the Party Train and operate it as Floyd intended.

"Well, it's time for me to go home and see what Wrigley's doing," she said.

Qwilleran handed her an envelope. "Here are your tickets for the play Thursday night, plus a little something extra in appreciation of your work."

"Oh, thank you!" she said. "I'm enjoying this assignment so much, I don't expect a reward."

"You deserve one. And the next time you talk to Tish, see if she has any idea who tipped off the auditors to the Lumbertown fraud . . . and why they haven't been able to find Floyd . . . and who made the mysterious phone call on the night of his disappearance. She's a smart young woman. She might be able to make some guesses."

"Yes, but I don't know how much longer she and Florrie will be here. Tish has already phoned the airline. They'll probably leave this weekend."

After Celia had driven away, Qwilleran walked around the barn exterior several times and pondered a few more questions: Does Tish want to leave the country in a hurry for reasons other than those stated? Is there really a doctor in Switzerland who has a miracle cure? Is Florrie actually as ill as she appears to be?

After the shocks, successes, and surprises of the last twenty-four hours, the next forty-eight were consistently disappointing. Operation Whistle came to a sudden standstill; Polly upset the plans for opening night at the theatre; and Qwilleran's imaginings about lurid secrets at the Trackside Tavern were squelched.

Wednesday morning: He ran into Roger MacGillivray at Lois's Luncheonette, and the reporter said, "Hey, Arch told me to check out what happened at the Trackside Tavern ten years ago. Women boycotted it because they weren't allowed to use the pool tables."

"Is that all?"

"That's all. They picketed the bar for a couple of weeks and then got a better idea. They opened the Jump-Off Bar and went into competition with the Trackside. The food's better, and the owner is a buxom, fun-loving gal that everyone likes. Floyd lent her the dough to get started and helped her to get a license."

"I've been to the Jump-Off establishment," Qwilleran said, "and I don't remember seeing any billiard tables."

"Right! I asked the boss lady, and she said the women didn't want to shoot pool when no one told them they couldn't. She considers that a big laugh."

Qwilleran huffed into his moustache. "Well, I suppose I'll see you at the play tomorrow night."

"I'm afraid not. We'd have to hire a babysitter, and that costs more than the tickets. Besides, Sharon's the Shakespeare nut, not me."

Wednesday afternoon: Celia phoned. "I won't have anything to report tonight, Chief.

They didn't need me at The Roundhouse. Tish is there with Florrie. They're getting ready for their trip. I went to the hospital, and they've got Eddie trussed up like a mummy and hooked up to tubes and bottles. He doesn't look like anything human."

Wednesday evening: Qwilleran telephoned Polly to inquire about Bootsie.

"I'm bringing him home tomorrow," she said. "If you don't mind, I'll stay with him instead of going to the theatre. You can go and concentrate on your review. I'll look forward to reading what you think of the production."

With a hint of annoyance he replied, "What I think about it and what I say about it in print aren't necessarily the same. I don't need to remind you this is a small town."

Thursday morning: Celia called again, saying somberly, "Eddie isn't expected to last the morning. The hospital notified Tish to come right away. I'll meet her there and let you know what happens."

Thursday afternoon: "Chief, I have sad news. Eddie passed away at ten thirty-seven. Tish is in Pickax, and I'm looking after Florrie, but I'll be back in time for the play."

A gala crowd attended the opening of *A Midsummer Night's Dream*. There was excitement in the hum of voices in front of the theatre, in the foyer, and in the upstairs lobby. Half of the playgoers were friends, relatives, or classmates of the young extras. The rest were people Qwilleran knew. Among them:

The Comptons. "Where's Polly?" they asked him.

Hixie Rice and Dwight Somers. They too wanted to know why Polly was absent.

Dr. Diane Lanspeak with Dr. Herbert, Hixie's former attachment. As luck would have it, both couples had tickets in the same row.

Celia Robinson with her new friend, Virginia Alstock. Celia and Qwilleran exchanged discreet nods.

Dr. Prelligate of the Moose County Community College with a few faculty members.

Scott Gippel, the worried treasurer of the club. "Looks like we'll end up in the black, but you never know."

Three generations of the Olsen family. Jennifer Olsen was playing Hermia.

Amanda Goodwinter, alone. "I hate this play, but Fran's directing it, and she gave me a ticket."

Qwilleran met his guests in the upstairs lobby: Arch and Mildred Riker and Mildred's daughter, Sharon, who had driven in from Mooseville to use Polly's ticket.

"What's with Polly?" Riker asked.

Qwilleran described the situation.

"Look here, Qwill! We've got to do something about your most favored friend. She's not herself these days. I realize how she feels about Bootsie, but her house is driving her batty. A sister of mine once had a nervous breakdown over the remodeling of her kitchen. What can we do about Polly?"

"I wish I knew. To make matters worse, her builder died this morning."

The lobby lights blinked, and they took their seats in the fifth row.

The play was wildly acclaimed. The audience applauded the students dressed as lords and ladies, as they made their entrance down the central aisle. Derek Cuttlebrink and the crew of rude mechanicals brought down the house, as expected. The greenies with their weird makeup and robotic movements stole the show, however. Meanwhile, the Shakespeare buffs waited for their favorite lines: *I am amazed and know not what to say . . . The course of true love never did run smooth . . . What fools these mortals be!*

As the king of the greenies delivered his line, *I am invisible,* and disappeared in a puff of smoke, Qwilleran heard the wail of a siren passing the theatre. It always alarmed him; he thought of fire. Then it faded away in the distance beyond the city limits. Moments later, he heard the honking of the rescue squad's vehicle. Then, just before intermission, Riker's beeper sounded, and the publisher, sitting on the aisle, made a quick exit to the lobby.

As soon as the first act ended, Qwilleran hurried up the aisle and found Riker in front of the telephone booth.

"Qwill, there's been a bad train wreck—south of Wildcat. The city desk is sending a man, but I think I should go, too. Want to come along? Sharon can take Mildred home."

The two men missed the second act. As they pulled out of the theatre parking lot, Riker said, "I'm taking you away from the play, and you have to write a review for tomorrow's paper."

"That's all right," Qwilleran said. "I know what I'm going to say about the first act, and I'll wing it for the second."

Outside the city limits Riker drove fast, and conversation was terse.

"Roger's baby-sitting. He'll be sorry to miss a hot story."

"Yeah . . . well . . ."

"Who's on tonight?"

"Donald. The new guy."

"He's getting his baptism by train wreck. Wonder what kind of train it is."

"Freight is all they pull on SC&L."

"Northbound or southbound?"

"They didn't say."

Reaching the town of Wildcat, they noticed unusual activity. The hamlet consisted of a general store, bar, gas station, and antique shop, with railroad tracks running parallel to the main street. People were milling around the intersection or standing on the tracks and staring to the south. Riker had to sound the horn to get through. "It's supposed to be a half-mile south of town."

"If you remember the Party Train," Qwilleran said, "the tracks veer away from the highway south of Wildcat. We saw views from the train that we'd never seen before."

It was still daylight but overcast, and a strange glow lighted up the gloom ahead of them. As they rounded a curve, they found the highway blocked with police vehicles, ambulances, and fire trucks. A few private cars were parked on the shoulder, their occupants gawking at the emergency equipment. Riker found a space, and they walked toward the center of activity. As soon as an ambulance was loaded, it took off for Lockmaster or Black Creek, and another took its place. All surrounding towns had responded. Medics running into the woods and stretcher bearers come back from the wreck had to push through underbrush, although rescue personnel with axes and chain saws were frantically trying to clear a path.

Riker showed his press card to a state trooper. "Can we reach the scene of the accident?"

"Follow those guys, but stay out of their way," the officer said. "Take flashlights. It'll be dark soon."

The newsmen plunged into the woods, Riker grumbling that it was going to ruin his new shoes.

Voices could be heard shouting orders that bounced off the cliffs on both sides of the creek. The whining of chain saws and hacking of axes added to the feeling of urgency. When they emerged from the brush, they were on a railroad right-of-way with a single track and a string of old telegraph poles. A team of paramedics, carrying a victim strapped to a stretcher, came running up the track, hopping awkwardly from tie to tie.

As the newsmen hobbled toward the wreck, they could see a flatcar with a huge floodlight that illuminated the trestle bridge. On the opposite bank of the creek was another flatcar with a railroad wrecking crane. Then a surreal scene came into view: a row of dazed victims sitting or lying on the embankment, while white-coated doctors moved among them. No train was in sight.

"There's our guy!" Riker said. "Hey, Donald! Getting anything?" They ran to meet him.

"Not much," said the young reporter. "Only pictures. Nobody knows anything for sure."

"Keep on shooting," said the boss. "We'll hang around and try for quotes."

"They think the train was stolen from a siding in Mudville."

"My God!" Qwilleran shouted as he ran toward the gulch. "It's No. 9!"

Three jack-knifed cars were piled on top of a locomotive lying on its side in the mud—a grotesque monster still breathing smoke and steam.

FIFTEEN

The Friday edition of the *Moose County Something* came off the presses two hours early, following the episode at Wildcat. The banner headline read:

TRAIN WRECKED IN BLACK CREEK
No. 9 and Party Train Crash
After Whittling Joyride

The fabled engine No. 9 roared at top speed through the village of Wildcat Thursday night before plunging down a steep grade and around a treacherous curve. It derailed and crashed into the muddy water of Black Creek. One person was killed. Forty were injured, some seriously.

The ill-fated run, unscheduled and allegedly unauthorized, left the switchyard at Sawdust City about 9:15, according to witnesses. It raced south with whistle blowing through Kennebeck, Pickax, and Little Hope, narrowly missing a consist of 20 freight cars being shunted at Black Creek Junction.

Residents of Wildcat heard the continuous screaming whistle that signified a runaway train and rushed to the crossroads in time to see the last car hurtling down the grade. Signals to slow down are clearly posted on the approach to Wildcat. An investigation is under way to determine whether the accident was due to mechanical failure or human error.

In either case the SC&L disclaims responsibility, a spokesman for the railroad said, since the Party Train was privately owned and berthed on a private siding.

At presstime, the reason for the unexpected run had not been ascertained. A spokesman for the Lockmaster

County sheriff's department called the ill-fated run "a joyride for railroad nuts who knew how to shovel coal."

The Party Train is known to be the property of Floyd Trevelyan, who is wanted on charges of fraud in connection with the Lumbertown Credit Union. The crew and passengers were all residents of the Railroad Retirement Center in Sawdust City. The only fatality was the engineer, Oswald Penn, 84, retired after 50 years with SC&L. He had an outstanding safety record. He was Trevelyan's father-in-law.

Passengers and other crew members jumped to save their lives before the crash. Eighteen sustained injuries requiring hospitalization; 22 were treated and released. They were being questioned by investigators. Conspiracy has not been ruled out.

A paramedic on the scene said, "All these old fellows are long past retirement age. Looks like they wanted to make one last jump. They didn't know their bones are getting brittle. We've got a lot of fracture cases here."

Emergency medical teams, volunteer rescue squads, and volunteer firefighters from Lockmaster, Black Creek Junction, Flapjack, and Little Hope responded. The sheriffs of two counties were assisted by state police. SC&L wrecking equipment was brought from Flapjack to clear the right-of-way for northbound and southbound freight consists.

The Black Creek trestle bridge itself was not damaged, but tracks and ties are being replaced. A repair foreman on the scene said, "The train was traveling so fast, it tore off the curved tracks and made them straight as a telephone pole. Man, that's real whittlin'."

Twelve hours before the headlines hit the street, Riker and Qwilleran drove away from the wreckage with divided reactions. One was exhilarated; the other was troubled.

Riker conjectured that the train was stolen by depositors defrauded by Trevelyan, who were indulging in a senseless act of revenge. It was ironic, he said, that the embezzler's father-in-law lost his life, trapped in the cab and scalded to death by the steam. Why didn't he jump, like the others? The alleged thieves knew what they were doing; the engine was fueled with plenty of coal and water for a short high-speed run.

Qwilleran, on the other hand, had privileged information that he could not divulge without exposing Operation Whistle. His professional instincts required him to tell Riker what he knew, but it would all be revealed in the end. Meanwhile, he had to protect his private mission—and Celia's part in it, for that matter. He had no doubt that Ozzie had intended to "go out whittlin' " and never intended to jump. He wondered if the old man had consciously wanted to re-enact the famous 1908 wreck at Wildcat, hoping to go down in railroad history.

While Riker had been flashing his press credentials on the embankment, Qwilleran had been talking quietly with the survivors. They balked at talking to the press, but Qwilleran introduced himself as a friend of Ozzie's. There were no secrets at the Retirement Center. They had heard all about this "Mackintosh feller from Chicago," who had interviewed Ozzie for a book he was writing and who had bought him two shots and a burger at the Jump-Off Bar. Now they all related the same story: The idea had come up suddenly, the day before, during a huddle at the bar. Ozzie Penn had said it would be a helluva joke to steal the train and wreck it. He would drive the hog, and he'd need a crew of three to keep up a good head of steam for a fast run. Anyone else could go along for the ride, unless he was too old to jump. Everyone would be expected to jump before the hog hit the curve north of the bridge. They all knew how to jump. Now—waiting on the embankment, fortified by a good dose of painkiller—they had no regrets. It was the most excitement they'd had in years!

They had known instinctively that Ozzie would not jump. He'd keep his hand on the throttle no matter what, and to hell with the reverse bar. He was a brave man. He'd proved it in countless emergencies. He always said he didn't want to die in bed; he wanted to go out whittlin'.

It gave Qwilleran a queasy feeling to realize that his own suggestion of a Penn family reunion had resulted in Ozzie's purchase of the train, Florrie's possible cure in Switzerland, the train's destruction, and Ozzie's death. Call it heroic or not, being scalded to death by steam was blood-chilling. Could it have been an old man's penance for abandoning his daughter so cruelly?

The next morning Qwilleran wrote his review of the play in time for the noon deadline and also dashed off the lyrics for a folksong, titled *The Wreck of Old No. 9*. These he took to the Old Stone Mill when he went there for lunch. He asked to be seated in Derek's station.

"Good show last night," he told the tall waiter. "Best role you've ever done."

"Yeah, I was really up," the actor acknowledged.

"Did you hear about the train wreck on the radio this morning?"

"Nah. I slept in, but they're talking about it in the kitchen."

Qwilleran handed him an envelope. "Here's a new folksong to add to your collection. You can sing it to the tune of the *Blizzard* ballad."

"Gee, thanks! Who wrote it?"

"Author unknown," said Qwilleran. He had done his bit to launch Ozzie Penn into the annals of local folk history. He knew Derek would sing it all over the county.

Another news item—one that would never be memorialized in song—appeared in the paper that day:

> Edward Penn Trevelyan, 24, son of Floyd and Florence Trevelyan, died yesterday as a result of injuries suffered in a tractor accident. He had been on the critical list in Pickax Hospital since Monday.
>
> Trevelyan was a resident of Indian Village and had recently started his own construction firm. He attended Pickax High School, where he played on the soccer team. He is survived by his parents and a sister, Letitia, at home. Funeral arrangements have not been announced

It was Polly's day off, and Qwilleran phoned her at home. He assumed she would have read the obituary and the account of the train wreck. She had read both, yet she seemed unperturbed by either.

"How's Bootsie?" he asked.

"He's glad to be home."

"You missed a good play last night."

"Perhaps I can go next weekend."

Something's wrong with her, Qwilleran thought; she's in another world. "Would you like to drive up to Mooseville and have dinner on the porch at the Northern Lights?" he asked.

"Thank you, Qwill, but I'm really not hungry."

"But you have to eat something, Polly."

"I'll just warm a bowl of soup."

"Want me to bring you a take-out from Lois's? Her chicken soup is the real thing!"

"I know, but I have plenty of soup in my freezer."

"Polly, aren't you feeling well? You sound rather down. Is it indigestion again? Did you tell Dr. Diane about your condition?"

"Yes, and she gave me a digestant, but she wants me to take some tests, and I dread that!"

"I think I should drive over there to cheer you up. You need some fresh daisies and a friendly shoulder."

"No, I just want to go to bed early. I'll be all right by morning; we have a big day at the library tomorrow. But thanks, dear."

Following that disturbing conversation, Qwilleran stayed in his desk chair, staring into space and wondering what to do, whom to call. Koko was on the desk, rubbing his jaw against Cerberus, the three-headed dog, and he said to him quietly, "That's a paperweight, friend—not a fang scraper."

Koko went on rubbing industriously. One

never knew when he was trying to communicate and when he was just being a cat. There was the matter of the felt-tip pens he had been stealing recently—not red ones, not yellow, only black. Was it a coincidence that Polly had hired the black-haired, black-bearded Edward Penn Trevelyan? Penn was Florrie's maiden name. Tish's pen name was Letitia Penn. Koko's attempts to convey information—if that's what they were—failed to get through to Qwilleran. He went for a long bike ride to clear his head. It was good exercise, and he filled his lungs with fresh air, but no questions were answered.

When Celia arrived that evening, she flopped on the sofa, dropped her shapeless handbag on the floor, and said, "Could you put a little something in the lemonade tonight, Chief? I need it!"

"I mix a tolerable Tom Collins," he said. "I take it you've had a hectic day."

"We've had two deaths in the family on the same day! Both funerals are on Saturday. The women leave for Switzerland on Sunday. Tish is upset! Florrie is hysterical!"

"Drink this and relax awhile," he said, presenting the tray. "Tell me what you thought of the play."

"I liked it! We both did. I had to read it in high school, but I'd never seen it on the stage. The greenies were fun—better than fairies. And

I loved that young man who's so tall. Derek Cuttlebrink was the name in the program."

Qwilleran assured her that there was a whole village full of Cuttlebrinks. "They're all characters!" he said.

"That nice Mr. O'Dell was there with his daughter. He talked to us in the lobby. Charming Irish accent!" She looked around the barn. "This would make a good theatre—with people on the balconies and the stage on the main floor."

Qwilleran said, "Everyone wants to convert it into a theatre or a restaurant or a poor man's Guggenheim. You've never seen the view from up above. Let's take a walk. Bring your drink."

They climbed the ramps, and he showed her his studio, the guestroom, the cats' loft apartment, and the exposed beams where the Siamese did their acrobatics.

When they returned to ground level, Celia dug into her handbag for her notebook. "Well! Are you ready for this, Chief? Tish told me some terrible things after Eddie died. Do you think a dying man comes back to life just before his last breath?"

"Sometimes there's a moment of lucidity before death," he said. "Great men utter memorable last words, according to their biographers, and others reveal lifelong secrets."

"Well, here's what happened yesterday morning. It's lucky the nurse was at the house when the hospital called. Tish drove into town in a hurry. Eddie was slipping away, but she talked to him, and all of a sudden his eyes moved, and he struggled to speak—just snatches of this and that."

"Were you there?" Qwilleran asked.

"I was waiting outside the room. Tish told me about it after. We came back to my apartment for a cup of tea, and she began to cry. Eddie had been mixed up in more dreadful things than anyone guessed."

At that moment the telephone rang. "Excuse me," he said and took the call in the library.

A shaking voice said, "Qwill, take me to the hospital. I don't feel well."

"I'll be right there!" he said firmly. "Hang up! Hang up!" As soon as he heard the dial tone, he punched 911. Then he dashed to the back door, calling to Celia, "Emergency! Gotta leave! Let yourself out!"

He drove recklessly to Goodwinter Boulevard and arrived just ahead of the ambulance. Using his own key, he let the EMS team into the apartment and ran up the stairs ahead of them.

Polly was sitting in a straight chair, looking pale and frightened. "Chest pains," she said weakly. "My arms feel heavy."

While the paramedics put a pill under her tongue and attached the oxygen tube with nose clips, Qwilleran made a brief phone call.

She was being strapped onto the stretcher when she turned a pathetic face to him and said, "Bootsie—"

"Don't worry. I've called your sister-in-law. She'll take care of him. I'll follow the ambulance." He squeezed her hand. "Everything will be all right . . . sweetheart."

She gave him a grateful glance.

He was there at the hospital when Polly was admitted and when Lynette Duncan arrived shortly afterward. The two of them sat in a special waiting room and talked about Polly's recent worries.

"You know," Lynette confided, "before she visited that friend in Oregon and got hooked on the idea of building a house, I wanted her to come and share the old Duncan homestead. I just inherited it from my brother. He'd had it ever since our parents died. Polly was married to my younger brother. He was a volunteer firefighter and lost his life in a barn fire. Tragic! They were newlyweds. Maybe she told you. Anyway, now I own this big house, over a hundred years old, with large rooms and high ceilings. Really nice! But too big for me. I think Polly would love it, and Bootsie could run up and down stairs."

It was the kind of nervous, rambling chatter heard in hospital waiting rooms when relatives wait for the doctor's verdict.

Finally a young woman in a white coat appeared. Qwilleran held his breath.

"Mrs. Duncan is doing very well. Would you like to see her? I'm Diane Lanspeak; I happened to be a few blocks away when they brought her in."

Qwilleran said, "I know your parents. We're all glad to have you back in Pickax."

"Thank you. I've heard a lot about you. One question: the cardiologist may recommend a catheterization. It's good to take pictures and determine exactly what the situation is. A mild heart attack is a warning. If Mrs. Duncan needs help in making a decision, who will—?"

"I'm her nearest relative," Lynette said, "but Mr. Qwilleran is—" She turned to look at him. No more needed to be said.

In the hospital room they found Polly looking peaceful for the first time in weeks, despite the clinical atmosphere and the tubes. They exchanged a few words, Polly speaking only about the capable paramedics, the kind nurses, the wonderful Dr. Diane.

When Qwilleran returned to the barn, Celia had gone, leaving a note: "Hope everything is okay. Call me if I can help."

The Siamese, unnaturally quiet, walked about in bewilderment; they knew when Qwilleran was deeply concerned, but not why. As soon as Qwilleran sat in the twistletwig rocker to calm his anxiety, Yum Yum hopped into his lap and comforted him with small, catly gestures: an extended paw, a sympathetic purr. Koko looked on with fellow-feeling, and when Qwilleran spoke to him, he squeezed his eyes.

The gentle rocking produced some constructive ideas: Polly would recover, move into the Duncan homestead, and forget about building a house. The K Foundation would reimburse Polly for her investment and complete the building as an art center. The Pickax Arts Council had been campaigning to get the carriage house for that purpose before Celia arrived.

As Qwilleran rocked and gazed idly about the lounge area, he caught sight of a small dark object on the light tile floor. His first thought: a dead mouse! Yet it was too geometric for that, more nearly resembling a large domino. Unwilling to leave the comforting embrace of the bent willow twigs, he tried to guess what the foreign object might be, but eventually he succumbed to curiosity.

"You'll have to excuse me for a minute, sweetheart," he said to Yum Yum as he hoisted himself out of the underslung rocker.

The unidentified object was the smallest of tape recorders, and the truth struck Qwilleran with suddenness: Celia's grandson had mailed it from Illinois; the cats had stolen it from her handbag; she had been secretly recording her meetings with Tish, in spite of his admonition. That explained her graphic reports and remarkable memory for details. She had transcribed the taped dialogue into her notebook, which she then consulted so innocently at their briefings. While admiring her initiative, he frowned at her noncompliance.

Nevertheless, he lost no time in playing the tape.

SIXTEEN

Before playing Celia's secret tape, Qwilleran asked himself, Shall I embarrass her by returning it . . . or let her think she lost it? He set it up on the telephone desk and prepared to take notes. The first sounds were nothing but sobs and whimpers, with sympathetic murmurs and questions from Celia. Then he heard a wracked voice say:

"I can't believe it, Celia! I thought she was my friend—my best friend! But she used me! She used all of us!"

"What do you mean, Tish?"

"She was going to divert funds for Mother's treatment in Switzerland! She was going to divert money for Eddie's condos, too. We believed her, because she was so knowledgeable and so *nice!* (Burst of sobs.) I even cheated so it would look as if she'd been fired. She's the one who suggested it. . . . Oh-h-h! She was so clever! Why didn't I see through her scheme?"

"What was her scheme, Tish? What did she do that was so bad?"

"It's what Eddie tried to tell me before he died. She wanted someone to do a special job for her, and he took Benno to see her."

"What kind of job? Didn't Eddie ask questions?"

"I guess not. My poor brother wasn't smart. He only went to tenth grade. And he drank too much. He ended up being an accomplice in a terrible crime." (Choking sobs.)

"Oh, dear! What kind of crime?"

(Long pause.) "Murder! When F.T. disappeared, they said he'd skipped with millions of dollars that didn't belong to him, but it was Nella who skipped. Floyd was dead!"

"Was Eddie able to tell you all this?"

"In snatches. He was gasping for breath. I had to put my ear close to his lips to hear him."

"Are you sure it's true?"

"People don't lie when they're dying, do they?"

"Maybe you're right, Tish. But how was Eddie an accomplice?"

"He helped Benno bury the body. But Nella was gone, and Benno didn't get his blood money. He wanted Eddie to pay off."

"How much? Do you know?"

"No, but it must have been a lot. Eddie's money was tied up. They argued. Benno shot his dog for spite. Then, one night in a bar, the lights went out. Benno pulled a knife. Eddie tried to get it away from him. He didn't mean to kill him—"

"Oh, Tish, I feel so sorry for you! I wish I could do something to help. What can I do?"

"Nothing. It just helps to have someone to talk to. You've been so good to us, Celia."

"Are you going to do anything about Eddie's confession?"

"I don't know. I can't think straight."

"But Nella should be arrested, if she plotted the murder and stole the money. Where did they bury the body?"

"Eddie tried to tell me, but he couldn't get it out. His eyes rolled up in his head, and he was gone." (Convulsive crying.)

"There must be something I can do to help you, dear."

"I don't know. I just want to get on that plane and never come back."

"Could I handle the funeral arrangements for you?"

"Would you? I'd be so thankful."

"Do you need me at the house this afternoon?"

"No, I'll be there, getting Mother ready for the trip. She's never been on a plane. I haven't either. Wouldn't it be ironic if it crashed in the Atlantic?"

"Oh, Tish! Don't say that!"

"The Trevelyan curse!" (Wild laughter.)

As the tape ended, Qwilleran realized the meaning of Koko's eccentric behavior in recent weeks. The first hint of something wrong was the cat's unusual vigil at the front window; he sensed impending evil!

The day after Audit Sunday, Qwilleran recalled, Koko performed his ominous death dance on the coffee table—specifically circling the scandal headline on the front page of the paper. After that, he became a cat possessed. While Yum Yum pursued wads of crumpled paper and collected paper clips, Koko was infatuated with black pens, duck decoys, the wooden whistle, the brass paperweight, and other significant items. The three-headed dog may have been symbolic of the three felons involved in the Lumbertown fraud and its bloody aftermath. (On the other hand, Koko may have found the sharp edges of the paperweight useful, Qwilleran had to admit.)

Then the question arose: Were Eddie's deathbed accusations only hallucinations? Did Nella really mastermind the plot? Dwight Somers had seen "scruffy characters" knocking on her door; both Eddie and Benno fitted that description. Did Nella urge Eddie to move to Indian Village and into her own building for devious reasons? She was nothing less than gorgeous, everyone agreed, and the unkempt high school dropout from Sawdust City could easily have fallen under her spell.

Qwilleran's eye fell on the wooden whistle that someone had knocked off the coffee table for the twentieth time. Perhaps Nella herself tipped off the auditors; that would account for the neat timing of the scheme. She juggled the books; she plotted the murder; she blew the whistle and collaborated with the auditors; she made the phone call that lured Floyd to the fork in the road, where he parked his car and met a pickup truck with two carpenters, one with a hammer and one with a shovel. His disappearance was intended to confirm his guilt, and it fooled everyone—except Koko.

Qwilleran looked at his watch. It was late, but not too late to call the police chief at home. "What are you doing tomorrow morning, Andy?" he asked, after some teasing about late-night X-rated TV movies.

"Taking the wife shopping" was the gruff reply.

"How about driving over to the apple barn first, for half an hour?"

"Business or social?"

"Business, but I'll have coffee waiting for you."

"Oh, no, you won't! I'm not ready to have my hair fall out. I'll bring a nontoxic take-out from Lois's."

"What time?"

"Nine o'clock."

On Saturday morning Koko knew something was afoot. While eating his breakfast, he kept looking over his shoulder and listening. When Brodie arrived, he was not in uniform, and Yum Yum kept staring at him.

"What's the matter with her?" Brodie asked.

"She's looking for your badge."

Qwilleran had been wondering how to report his information to the police chief without naming his collaborators: a pleasant gray-haired grandmother and an intuitive cat. He began by enlisting Andy's sympathy. "Polly's in the hospital," he said morosely. "Heart attack."

"How bad?"

"I phoned this morning, and she's out of danger. It was a shock, although I should have seen it coming. Too much stress and not enough exercise."

"You've gotta look after that lady, Qwill.

She's an asset to the community. Why don't you and Polly—"

"Never mind," Qwilleran said. "You can go and play your bagpipe at someone else's wedding."

The two men sat at the breakfast bar with their coffee and some doughnuts from Lois's.

"How's the Lumbertown investigation coming along?" Qwilleran asked.

"To tell the truth, I think they've run out of places to look for that guy."

"It's my opinion that he's right here in Moose County—underground."

"You mean—hiding out?"

"No. Buried."

Brodie swallowed a gulp of coffee too fast and coughed. "What makes you think so? Have you been conversing with your psychic cat?"

"I have an informant."

"Who?"

"I'd be crazy to reveal my source."

"Why did he come to you? Why not the police?"

"Well, it's like this, Andy. A lot of people out there don't like the media, but they like the media better than they like the cops. Tipsters, you know, are whispering in our ears all the time."

Brodie grunted. "D'you pay for the information?"

"Why would we pay for it? We didn't ask for it; we didn't want it; we can't use it."

"So what did you find out?"

"Floyd was no financial wizard, but he hired someone who was. That person juggled the books to defraud the depositors, and Floyd wasn't savvy enough to realize it, or he was too involved with his trains to care. Then the true embezzler threw suspicion on Floyd by having him disappear, when actually she had plotted his murder."

"She?" Brodie said with unprofessional astonishment. "You mean—his secretary?"

"She posed as his secretary, although she was second in command, hired to introduce new accounting methods—and she sure did! Not only did she abscond with the loot, but she didn't even pay off her hitman. The investigators questioned her in Texas but let her slip through their fingers."

"She told them she was fired for accusing the Lumbertown president of sexual harassment," Brodie explained.

"Okay, now I want to show you a video of the Lumbertown Party Train on Audit Sunday, if the cats will allow us to use their TV. The suspect appears in several frames."

"Why don't you get a TV of your own?" the chief grumbled as they climbed the ramp to the highest balcony. The Siamese followed them, then bounded ahead to claim the only available chair.

"Sorry, we have standing room only," Qwilleran apologized. "Now watch the crowd scenes for a gorgeous woman in trousers—also in the dining car with Floyd."

The video played. Brodie watched. Koko yowled at intervals.

"So where's the body?" he asked when the tape was rewinding.

"No one knows; that's for you guys to find out. The hitman himself was killed in that fracas at the Trackside Tavern, and his accomplice has since died in an accident. If you ever find the body, I believe your forensic experts will say he was killed by a blow, or blows, to the head, inflicted by a carpenter's hammer."

"You expect me to believe all this? Well . . . thanks for the entertainment. It was better than the play I saw Thursday night." They started down the ramp, and in passing one of the large windows Brodie said, "You should clear out that jungle and build a motel."

"The far end of the jungle," Qwilleran told him, "is where Floyd's son, Eddie, was fatally injured in the tractor rollover."

"Must be true what they say about the Trevelyan curse."

After walking with his guest to the parking area, Qwilleran made a few turns around the barn before letting himself in the front door. As he opened it, something slammed into his legs, throwing him off balance. It was Koko, shooting out of the door like a cannonball!

"Koko! Come back here!" Qwilleran yelled, but the cat was headed lickety-split down the orchard trail. The man charged after him, shouting. Koko kept on going. It was a hundred yards to Trevelyan Road, and he was covering it with the speed of a gazelle. There was the danger that he might dash across the highway in front of a car.

"Koko! Stop!" Qwilleran yelled with all the breath he could muster during the chase.

The cat stopped, but not until he had reached the building site. He ignored the framework of the new building. He went directly to the concrete slab of the garage and started his digging act. His hindquarters were elevated, and his brisket was close to the slab as he scraped the rough surface. Then he flopped on his side and rolled luxuriously on the concrete, twisting this way and that in apparent ecstasy.

The demonstration chilled Qwilleran's blood. He remembered that Eddie had poured the slab early in the morning after Audit Sunday, although the cement work had been scheduled for later in the week. It was on that Monday, also, that Koko had commenced his vigil at the foyer window. Had he witnessed something unusual during the night? From his window on the top balcony he had a view of the orchard trail. With his feline nightsight he might have seen a truck without headlights pulling onto the property. Perhaps he heard the clink of shovels in the rocky soil. Later came Koko's resolute digging in the crook of Qwilleran's elbow, not to mention his interest in the Panama Canal.

Qwilleran grabbed Koko and carried him back to the barn. Now what? he asked himself. If he confided his suspicions to Brodie, the jack-hammers would move in, digging up Polly's garage floor, and she'd have another heart attack.

Carrying a bunch of fresh daisies, Qwilleran went to the hospital and found Polly sitting in a chair, looking remarkably serene. She was feeling fine, she said. She was looking forward to the catheterization; it might be an adventure. The hospital food was better than she expected. Dr. Diane was a dear young woman. The cardiologist from Lockmaster was most encouraging.

There was a sparkle in Polly's eyes that Qwilleran had not seen for several weeks, and finally she said, "I have a subject to broach to you, dear. I hope you won't be offended."

"You know I'm offense-proof where you're concerned, Polly."

"Well, I believe that this little setback of mine is a message from the fates that I should not build a house; Bootsie and I should move into the Duncan homestead with Lynette. That is, if you think I can dispose of my two acres and a half-finished house."

"No problem," he said with a sigh of relief.

SEVENTEEN

It was mid-September, and in Moose County the vicissitudes of summer were simmering down. Most vacationers had left; children were back in school; and the new college reported excellent enrollment for its first semester.

Polly Duncan, who had been flown to Minneapolis for coronary bypass surgery, was convalescing at the Duncan homestead. She claimed to feel better than she had in years! Bootsie was enjoying his new diet, running up and down stairs, and losing weight.

The Pickax Arts Council hoped to move into

its new gallery and studios by Thanksgiving. Thanks to the generosity of the Klingenschoen Foundation, they had taken over the unfinished house on Trevelyan Road. References to the legendary curse were avoided.

Celia Robinson received a postcard from Switzerland: Florrie was improving, and Tish had met an interesting ski instructor.

Word was circulating on the Pickax grapevine that Mr. Q had been seen in Scottie's Men's Store, being measured for a kilt.

As for the Lumbertown scandal, the body of Floyd Trevelyan, buried under concrete, had been disinterred, and Nella Hooper replaced him on the wanted list. It seemed odd to Qwilleran that the law enforcement agencies, with all their technology and expertise, had failed to find this spectacularly good-looking woman. Earlier they had found her and let her go after questioning. Now they had the video of the Party Train, in which she appeared several times. And yet . . . It was Arch Riker's theory that the lawmen weren't trying hard enough, and he wrote an editorial to that effect. Anything that happens 400 miles north of everywhere, he argued, is of lesser importance to the establishment Down Below.

Then, quite by accident, Qwilleran uncovered a new clue. Following the final matinee of *A Midsummer Night's Dream,* theatre club members were invited to an afterglow at the apple barn. Among those present were Fran Brodie, the Lanspeaks, Junior Goodwinter, Derek Cuttlebrink, Elizabeth Hart, and Jennifer Olsen, who was becoming the club's leading ingenue. The Lanspeaks inquired about Polly's health. Derek demonstrated his exuberance by climbing the loft ladder straight up to the third balcony. Fran reminded Qwilleran that he had promised to read her playscript and give an opinion. He apologized for overlooking it.

Derek, having brought his guitar, also volunteered to sing a new folksong, titled *The Wreck of Old No. 9*:

> *There was once a famous hoghead*
> *On the old SC&L.*
> *His name was Ozzie Penn,*
> *And he could drive a hog through hell!*
> *But he had to give up drivin'*
> *'Cause they said he was too old.*
> *They retired him with a dinner*
> *And a watch of solid gold.*
> *"You've survived your share of train wrecks*
> *"In fifty years," they said.*
> *"Now go home and join the lucky ones*
> *"That get to die in bed."*
>
> Chorus:
> *"No, I want to go out whittlin',"*
> *Said good old Ozzie Penn.*

But they said his dreams were over,
And he'd never drive again.

He hung around the switchyard
And told hair-raisin' tales:
How he made the fastest runs
And kept the hog upon the rails.
Then one day he saw a vision
That made his old eyes shine.
On a siding east of Mudville
Sat old Engine No. 9!
The great steam locomotive,
A mighty 4-6-2,
Had a tender full o' coal
And—by Crikey!—looked like new.

Chorus:
"I want to go out whittlin',"
Said the famous engineer.
There was nobody to see him
Wipe away an old man's tear.

He rounded up his buddies
And said, "Let's have some fun!
"Let's take the whole dang consist
"For one last whittlin' run!
"You fellas gotta jump
"Before we hit the final curve.
"So don't sign on with Ozzie
"If you haven't got the nerve."
With a crew of three old-timers
And fifty deadheads, too,

They left the yard at Mudville
To make Ozzie's dream come true.

Chorus:
"I want to go out whittlin',"
They'd often heard him say,
And he'd earned his chance to do it
Now that he was old and gray.

With the whistle screamin' "wildcat!"
They whittled down the line,
All knowin' what would happen
To engine No. 9.
As the fiery, sweatin' monster
Plunged down the steepest grade,
The final order came to jump
And every man obeyed.
But Ozzie at the throttle
Said he'd go down with the hog
As it sank with hissin', scaldin' steam
In the muck o' Black Creek bog.

Chorus:
"I want to go out whittlin',"
Said good old Ozzie Penn,
And the hoghead got his wish
Because he'll never drive again.

Derek's listeners applauded and wanted to know if he'd written it himself. He glanced at Qwilleran, who nodded.

"Yep," said the folksinger in an offhand way.

Elizabeth said, with her eyes shining, "He's so talented!"

Meanwhile, Yum Yum watched the festivities from the balcony, tantalized by the aroma of pizza drifting up from the main floor. Koko, always more adventurous, mingled with the guests, accepting compliments and slices of pepperoni. He was within earshot when Qwilleran commended Jennifer for her portrayal of Hermia.

"Yow!" he said.

"See? Koko agrees with me. I believe his favorite character in all of Shakespeare is Hermia."

"Yow!" Koko repeated with added emphasis.

Qwilleran pondered the incident when the guests had left. The Siamese were enjoying a private afterglow-of-the-afterglow under the kitchen table, nibbling sausage and cheese and fastidiously avoiding the bits of mushroom and green pepper. Qwilleran, watching them, suddenly said, "Hermia!"

Koko looked up from his plate and made the usual comment.

Qwilleran thought, There's more to Hermia than meets the ear! During the summer the cat had exhibited many quirks, which were now abandoned. As soon as the mystery of Floyd's disappearance was solved, Koko stopped staring out the foyer window in the direction of the two-car garage slab. At the same time he stopped his everlasting digging in Qwilleran's elbow and lost interest in the Panama Canal. After the crimes of Edward Penn Trevelyan and James Henry Ducker were exposed, he no longer stole black pens or sat on the fireplace cube with the decoys.

Was it coincidence that he had pursued these activities so assiduously? Was it ordinary feline fickleness when he stopped? Qwilleran knew otherwise. Koko had a gift of intuition and pre-science that was not given to mere humans—or even to the average cat—and he had an unconventional way of communicating. It amused Qwilleran to paraphrase Shakespeare: *There are more things in Koko's head, Horatio, than are dreamt of in your philosophy.*

When the Siamese had finished their gourmet treat and washed up, the three of them ambled into the library for a read.

"What'll it be?" Qwilleran asked. He had asked that question several weeks before, and Koko's choice was *Swiss Family Robinson*. And what happened? Celia Robinson moved to Pickax, and the Trevelyan women flew to Switzerland. Coincidence? "Sure," Qwilleran said with derision.

Now Koko sniffed the bookshelf devoted to drama and nudged the copy of *Androcles and the Lion.*

"We had that book a few weeks ago," Qwilleran reminded him. "Try again."

This time the cat's choice was a slender paperback, Fran Brodie's playscript of the *Lion in Winter.*

In a flash of revelation Qwilleran remembered the young woman in the Pickax People's Bank: Letitia Penn, who turned out to be Letitia Trevelyan . . . and who had a friend named Lionella. Later it developed that the one name was shortened to Tish and the other to Nella.

That was the answer! That remarkable cat knew from the beginning that the Lumbertown fraud was masterminded by Nella a.k.a. Lionella! Now Qwilleran understood Koko and the lions, but what about Hermia? There was something about this H word that triggered Koko's brain cells and was supposed to trigger Qwilleran's. Yet, he was stymied—until he thought about the dictionary. His unabridged dictionary always stimulated the associative process.

As he climbed the ramp to consult its erudite pages, the Siamese followed with vertical tails. On this occasion he had a reason for allowing them into his sanctum. One of them immediately inspected the typewriter and left a few cat hairs among the typebars; the other lost no time in knocking a gold pen off the desk.

Looking up the definition of Hermia, Qwilleran found what he already knew: Hermia was a lady in love with Lysander in *A Midsummer Night's Dream.* There were other proper nouns, however, that might have a similar sound to a cat's ear, and he read them aloud:

"Hermo . . . Hermione . . . Hermitage . . . Hermes." Nothing attracted Koko's attention until he reached "Hermaphrodite."

The sound of the word brought an alarming response that started as an ear-splitting falsetto and ended in a menacing growl.

Qwilleran checked the definitions of hermaphrodite. It referred to a two-masted vessel, square-rigged forward, and schooner-rigged aft. It also referred to a vertebrate or invertebrate having male and female organs.

He read no further. He grabbed the telephone and called the police chief at home. "Andy! I've got a far-out idea!"

"Let's hear it—fast. My favorite program's just beginning."

"It's only a hunch, but it might help your colleagues in their womanhunt. First, it's a fact that Nella Hooper's name was shortened from Lionella. It's my guess that this person's name was really Lionel. The bloodhounds are hunting for a suspect of the wrong sex! Impersonating a woman was part of the scam. Now that Nella Hooper is on the wanted list, Lionel Hooper is probably growing a beard. . . . Now hang up and go back to the tube."

Qwilleran returned to the lounge area and sprawled on the sofa. The Siamese took up positions on the coffee table, where the day's last shaft of sunlight slanted in from a high window to warm their fur and make each guard-hair look like spun gold. It turned their whiskers into platinum. Yum Yum sat comfortably on her brisket like a regular cat. Koko sat tall like an ancient Egyptian deity.

"You've done it again, young man!" Qwilleran said with admiration. "You blew the whistle on the whole crew!"

Koko gazed at the man with a superior cast in his blue eyes, as if he were thinking, *What fools these mortals be!*

*And now, a special excerpt from
the purr-fect mystery starring
Qwilleran, Koko, and Yum Yum . . .*

THE CAT WHO SAID CHEESE

Autumn, in that year of surprises, was particularly delicious in Moose County, 400 miles north of everywhere. Not only had most of the summer vacationers gone home, but civic-awareness groups and enthusiastic *foodies* were cooking up a savory kettle of stew called the Great Food Explo. Then, to add spice to the season, a mystery woman registered at the hotel in Pickax City, the county seat. She was not beautiful. She was not exactly young. She avoided people. And she always wore black.

The townfolk of Pickax (population 3,000) were fascinated by her enigmatic presence. "Have you seen her?" they asked each other. "She's been here over a week. Who do you think she is?"

The hotel desk clerk refused to divulge her name even to his best friends, saying it was prohibited by law. That convinced everyone that the mystery woman had bribed him for nefarious reasons of her own, since Lenny Inchpot was not the town's most law-abiding citizen.

So they went on commenting about her olive complexion, sultry brown eyes, and lush mop of dark hair that half covered the left side of her face. Yet, the burning question remained: "Why is she staying at that firetrap of a flophouse?" That attitude was unfair. The New Pickax Hotel, though gloomy, was respectable and painfully clean, and there was a fire escape in the rear. There was even a presidential suite, although no president had ever stayed there—not even a candidate for the state legislature on an unpopular ticket. Nevertheless, no one had been known to lodge there for more that a single night, or two at the most, and travel agents around the country were influenced by an entry in their directory of lodgings:

NEW PICKAX HOTEL, 18 miles from Moose County Airport; 20 rooms, some with private bath; presidential suite with telephone and TV; bridal suite with round bed. Three-story building with one elevator, frequently out of order. Prisonlike exterior and bleak interior, circa 1935. Public areas unusually quiet, with Depression Era furnishings. Cramped lobby and dining room; no bar; small, unattractive ballroom in basement. Sleeping rooms plain but clean; mattresses fairly new;

lighting dim. Metal fire excape in rear; rooms with windows have coils of rope for emergency use. Dining room offers breakfast buffet, luncheon specials, undistinguished dinner menu, beer and wine. No liquor. No room service. No desk clerk on duty after 11 P.M. Rates: low to moderate. Hospital nearby.

Business travelers checked into the New Pickax Hotel for a single overnight because no other lodgings were available in town. Out-of-towners arriving to attend a funeral might be forced by awkward plane schedules to spend two nights. In the hushed dining room the business travelers sat alone, reading technical manuals while waiting for the chopped sirloin and boiled carrots. Forks could be heard clicking against plates as the out-of-town mourners silently counted the peas in the chicken pot pie. And now, in addition, there was a woman in black who sat in a far corner, toying with a glass of wine and an overcooked vegetable plate.

One Thursday morning in September Qwilleran was closeted in his private suite on the first balcony, the only area in the barn that was totally off-limits to cats. He was trying to write a thousand words for his Friday column "Straight from the Qwill Pen."

Emily Dickinson, we need you!

"I'm nobody. Who are you?" said this prolific American poet.

I say, "God give us nobodies! What this country needs is fewer celebrities and more nobodies who live ordinary lives, cope bravely, do a little good in the world, enjoy a few pleasures, and never, *never* get their names in the newspaper or their faces on TV."

"Yow!" came a baritone complaint outside the door.

It was followed by a soprano shriek. "N-n-now!"

Qwilleran consulted his watch. It was twelve noon and time for their midday treat. In fact, it was three minutes past twelve, and they resented the delay.

He yanked open his studio door to face two determined petitioners.

"I wouldn't say you guys were spoiled," he rebuked them. "You're only tyrannical monomaniacs about food." As they hightailed it down the ramp to the kitchen, he took the shortcut via a spiral metal staircase. Nevertheless, they reached the food station first. He dropped some crunchy morsels on two plates; separate plates had been Yum Yum's latest feline-rights demand, and he always indulged her. He stood with fists on hips to watch their enjoyment.

Today she had changed her mind, however. She helped Koko gobble his plateful; then the two of them worked on her share.

"Cats!" Qwilleran muttered in exasperation. "Is it okay with you two autocrats if I go back to work now?"

Satisfied with their repast, they ignored him completely and busied themselves with washing masks and ears. He went up to his studio and wrote another paragraph:

We crave heroes to admire and emulate,
and what do we get? A parade of errant
politicians, mad exhibitionists, wicked
heiresses, temperamental artists, silly risk-
takers, overpaid athletes, untalented enter-
tainers, non-authors of non-books . . .

The telephone interrupted, and he grabbed it on
the first ring. The caller was Junior Goodwinter,
young managing editor of the *Moose County Something*. "Hey, Qwill, are you handing in your Friday
copy this afternoon?"

"Only if the interruptions permit me to write a
simple declarative sentence in its entirety," he snapped.
"Why?"

"We'd like you to attend a meeting."

Qwilleran avoided editorial meetings whenever
possible. "What's it about?"

"Dwight Somers is going to brief us on the Great
Food Explo. He's spent a few days in Chicago with
the masterminds of the K Fund, and he'll be flying in
on the three-fifteen shuttle."

Qwilleran's petulance mellowed somewhat. The
K Fund was the local nickname for the Klingenschoen Foundation that he had established to dis-
pense his inherited billion. Swight Somers was one
of his friends, a local public relations man with credentials Down Below. "Okay. I'll be there."

Having worked against odds, the writer of the
"Qwill Pen" finished in time for the meeting at the
newspaper office. He said goodbye to the Siamese as
he usually did, telling them where he was going and

when he would return. The more one talks to cats, he believed, the smarter they become. His two Mensa candidates responded, however, by raising groggy heads from their afternoon nap and giving him a brief glassy stare before falling asleep again.

The *Moose County Something* was a broadsheet published five days a week. Originally subsidized by the K Fund, it was now operating in the black. The office building was new. The printing plant was state-of-the-art. The staff always seemed to be having a good time.

The meeting was held in the conference room. Its plain wood-paneled walls were decorated with framed tearsheets of memorable front pages in the history of American journalism: *Titanic Meets a Mightier . . . War in Europe . . . Kennedy Assassinated.* Staffers sat around the large teakwood conference table, drinking coffee from mugs imprinted with newspaper wit: "If you can't eat it, don't print it" . . . "Deadlines are made to be missed" . . . "A little malice aforethought is fun."

"Come on in, Qwill," the managing editor said. "Dwight isn't here yet. Since we hate to waste time, we're inventing rumors about the mystery woman."

There were six staffers around the table:

Arch Riker, the paunchy publisher and editor-in-chief, had been Qwilleran's lifelong friend and fellow journalist Down Below. Now he was realizing his dream of running a small-town newspaper.

Junior Goodwinter's boyish countenance and slight build belied his importance; he was not only the managing editor but a direct descendent of the founders of Pickax City. In a community 400 miles north of everywhere, that mattered a great deal.

Hixie Rice, in charge of advertising and promotion, was another refugee from Down Below, and after several years in the outback she still had a certain urbane verve and chic.

Mildred Hanstable Riker, food writer and wife of the publisher, was a plump, good-hearted native of Moose County, recently retired from teaching fine and domestic arts in the public schools.

Jill Handley, the new feature editor, was pretty and eager but not yet comfortable with her fellow staffers. She came from the *Lockmaster Ledger* in the neighboring county, where the inhabitants of Moose County were considered barbarians.

Wilfred Sugbury, secretary to the publisher, was a thin, wiry, sober-faced young man, intensely serious about his job. He jumped up and filled a coffee mug for Qwilleran. It was inscribed: "First we kill all the editors."

Also present, watching from the top of a file cabinet, was William Allen, a large white cat formerly associated with the *Pickax Picayune*.

Qwilleran nodded pleasantly to each one in turn and took a chair next to the newcomer. Jill Handley turned to him adoringly. "Oh, Mr. Qwilleran, I love your column! You're a fantastic writer!"

Sternly he replied, "You're not allowed to work for the *Something* unless you drink coffee, like cats, and call me Qwill."

"You have Siamese, don't you . . . Qwill?"

"Loosely speaking. It's more accurate to say that they have me. What prompted you to leave civilization for life in the wilderness?"

"Well, my kids wanted to go to Pickax High because you have a larger swimming pool, and my husband found a good business opportunity up here, and I wanted to write for a paper that carries columns like the 'Qwill Pen.' That's the honest truth!"

"Enough!' said the boss at the head of the table. "Any more of this and he'll be asking for a raise . . . Let's hear it for our gold-medal winner!"

Everyone applauded, and Wilfred flushed. He had come in first in the seventy-mile Labor Day Bike Race. Yet, no one at the newspaper knew that he even owned a bike—such was his modesty and concentration on his work.

Qwilleran said, "Congratulations! We're all proud of you. Your pedaling is on a par with your office efficiency."

"Thanks," said Wilfred, "I didn't expect to win. I just signed up for the fun of it, but I decided to give it my best shot, so I trained hard all summer. I was confident I could go the entire route, even if I came in last, but everything turned out right for me, and after the first sixty miles I suddenly thought, Hey, chump, you can win this crazy race! That was between Mudville and Kennebeck, with only a few riders ahead of me, so I gave it an extra push to the finish line. Nine bikers finished, and they all deserve credit for a great try. They were as good as I was, only I had something going for me—luck, I guess. I'm hoping to compete again next year."

This was more that the quiet young man had said in his two years of employment, and all heads turned to listen in astonishment. Only Qwilleran could think of something to say: "We admire your spirit and determination, Wilfred."

Riker cleared his throat. "While we're waiting for the late Mr. Somers, let us resume our deliberations." Then he added in a loud, sharp voice, *"Who is the mystery woman and what is she doing here . . . ?"*

THE CAT WHO WENT INTO THE CLOSET: Qwill's moved into a mansion . . . and it has fifty closets for Koko to investigate! But among the junk, Koko finds a clue—and now Quill's unearthing some surprising skeletons. . . .

THE CAT WHO CAME TO BREAKFAST: Qwill and the cats face a puzzle when peaceful Breakfast Island is turned upside-down by real-estate developers, controversy—and murder . . .

THE CAT WHO BLEW THE WHISTLE: An old steam locomotive has been restored, causing excitement in Moose County. But a mysterious murder brings the fun to a screeching halt—and Qwill and Koko are tracking down the culprit. . . .

THE CAT WHO SAID CHEESE: At the Great Food Explo, scheduled events include a bake-off, a cheese tasting, and a restaurant opening. Unscheduled events include mystery and murder. . . .

THE CAT WHO TAILED A THIEF: A rash of petty thievery—and death of a wealthy young woman—leaves a trail of clues as elusive as a cat burglar. . . .

THE CAT WHO SANG FOR THE BIRDS: Spring comes to Moose County—and a young cat's fancy turns to crime solving . . .

THE CAT WHO SAW STARS: UFOs in Mooseville? When a backpacker disappears, Qwill investigates a rumored "abduction"—with the help of his own little aliens. . . .

THE CAT WHO ROBBED A BANK: As the Highland Games approach, Qwill has a lot of mysteries to sort out—not the least of which is Koko's sudden interest in photographs, pennies, and paper towels. . . .

THE CAT WHO SMELLED A RAT
Available in hardcover from G. P. Putnam's Sons

And turn to the back for a special excerpt from . . .
THE CAT WHO SAID CHEESE

THE CAT WHO KNEW SHAKESPEARE: The local newspaper publisher has perished in an accident—or is it murder? This is the question. . . .

THE CAT WHO SNIFFED GLUE: After a rich banker and his wife are killed, Koko develops an odd appetite for glue. To solve the murder, Qwill has to figure out why. . . .

THE CAT WHO WENT UNDERGROUND: Qwill and the cats head for their Moose County log cabin for a relaxing summer—but when a handyman disappears, Koko must dig up the buried motive for a sinister crime. . . .

THE CAT WHO TALKED TO GHOSTS: Qwill and Koko try to solve a haunting mystery in a historic farmhouse.

THE CAT WHO LIVED HIGH: A glamorous art dealer was killed in Qwill's high-rise apartment—and he and the cats are about to reach new heights in detection as they try to find out whodunit. . . .

THE CAT WHO KNEW A CARDINAL: The director of the local Shakespeare production dies in Qwill's orchard—and the stage is set for a puzzling mystery!

THE CAT WHO MOVED A MOUNTAIN: Qwill moves to a new home in the beautiful Potato Mountains. But when a dispute between local residents and developers boils over into a murder case, he has to keep his eyes open to find the culprit!

THE CAT WHO WASN'T THERE: Qwill's on his way to Scotland—and on his way to solving another purr-plexing mystery!

Read ALL the CAT WHO mysteries!

THE CAT WHO COULD READ BACKWARDS: The world of modern art is a mystery to many—but for Jim Qwilleran and Koko it's a mystery of another sort . . .

THE CAT WHO ATE DANISH MODERN: Qwill isn't thrilled about covering interior design for *The Daily Fluxion.* Little does he know that a murderer has designs on a woman featured in one of his stories . . .

THE CAT WHO TURNED ON AND OFF: Qwill and Koko are joined by Yum Yum as they try to solve a murder in an antique shop . . .

THE CAT WHO SAW RED: Qwill starts his diet—*and* a new gourmet column for the *Fluxion.* It isn't easy—but it's not as hard as solving a murder case!

THE CAT WHO PLAYED BRAHMS: Fishing at a secluded cabin, Qwill hooks on to a mystery—and Koko develops a strange fondness for classical music . . .

THE CAT WHO PLAYED POST OFFICE: Koko and Yum Yum turn into fat cats when Qwill inherits millions. But amid the caviar and champagne, Koko starts sniffing clues to a murder!

THE CAT WHO HAD 14 TALES: A delightful collection of feline mystery fiction from the creator of Koko and Yum Yum!

*TURN THE PAGE FOR MORE
CAT WHODUNITS . . .*